Harry Potter™

KNITTING MAGIC

FROM THE FILMS OF

Harry Potter™

KNITTING MAGIC

 THE OFFICIAL HARRY POTTER
KNITTING PATTERN BOOK

TANIS GRAY

PHOTOGRAPHY BY Laura Flippen

PAVILION

CONTENTS

PROJECT SKILL LEVELS

⚡ BEGINNER

⚡⚡ EASY

⚡⚡⚡ INTERMEDIATE

⚡⚡⚡⚡ ADVANCED

⚡⚡⚡⚡⚡ COMPLEX

07 INTRODUCTION

09 CRAFTY CREATURES

Knitted stuffed animals bring your favourite magical creatures to life, no special effects required!

11 Cornish Pixie ⚡⚡

17 Fluffy the Three-Headed Dog ⚡⚡⚡⚡⚡

23 Hedwig ⚡⚡⚡⚡

31 WIZARDING WARDROBE

True-to-screen replicas of iconic costume pieces straight from the wardrobe department.

33 Mrs Weasley's Home-Knit Christmas Jumpers ⚡⚡⚡

43 Hogwarts House Scarves ⚡⚡

47 Hogwarts House Cardigans ⚡⚡

55 Professor Umbridge's Cat Scarf ⚡⚡⚡

61 INSPIRED APPAREL

Clothes and accessories inspired by characters, artifacts and themes from the films.

63 Harry Potter 'Wizarding World' Jumper ⚡⚡⚡⚡⚡

71 Mirror of Erised Cabled Cowl ⚡⚡

77 Golden Snitch Socks and Mittens ⚡⚡⚡

83 Wizarding Transportation Scarf ⚡⚡⚡⚡

89 Hogwarts Duelling Club Fingerless Mitts ⚡⚡⚡

95 'Show Your House Colours' Quidditch Socks ⚡⚡⚡

99 Owl Post Pullover ⚡⚡⚡

107 *Expecto Patronum*! Mittens ⚡⚡⚡⚡⚡

115 Buckbeak Pullover ⚡⚡⚡⚡

125 Beauxbatons Academy of Magic Capelet ⚡

131 The Chamber of Secrets Beanie ⚡⚡⚡

137 Hermione's Time-Turner Jumper ⚡⚡⚡⚡

145 Dark Mark Illusion Scarf ⚡⚡

155 Nagini Lariat ⚡

159 Luna Lovegood's Spectrespecs Gloves ⚡⚡⚡⚡⚡

165 The Deathly Hallows Lace-Knit Beaded Shawl ⚡⚡⚡⚡

171 DELIGHTFUL DECOR

Dress your home with these film-inspired Harry Potter decorative accents.

173 Hogwarts House Mug Cosies ⚡

177 The Sorting Hat Hanging Display ⚡⚡⚡

185 The Seven Horcruxes Washcloths ⚡

195 Order of the Phoenix Lace-Knit Throw Blanket ⚡⚡⚡

202 GLOSSARY

205 ABBREVIATIONS

206 YARN SUBSTITUTION & YARN RESOURCE GUIDE

207 ACKNOWLEDGEMENTS

INTRODUCTION

The world of the Harry Potter films is filled with magic, mystery and a *lot* of knitting. From Mrs Weasley's homemade jumpers (page 33) to the distinctive Hogwarts House scarves (page 43), knitted apparel and ephemera are embedded in the fabric of the wizarding culture. And for good reason – Hogwarts is located in chilly Scotland, after all.

Real-world knitters have long found inspiration in the films of the Wizarding World. Our imaginations have run wild with thoughts of Molly Weasley's enchanted needles, magical motifs and otherworldly creatures. Now those dreams can take shape with this official book of knitting patterns inspired by the magical movies. Featuring designs for cuddly toys, home decor projects, apparel featuring movie motifs and even authentic costume replicas, this book offers movie lovers a new way to engage with their favourite films and celebrate their fandom through the magic and art of knitting.

The patterns are supplemented with techniques for every skill level, such as cabling, stranded colourwork, lace, illusion knitting, beading and short rows. Each project is rated according to difficulty level and includes all the information you need to re-create it in your own home. Plus, behind-the-scenes facts and insights, concept art and film stills accompany the projects, so you can learn more about the making of the epic series while knitting away on projects both inspired by and taken directly from the screen.

Whether you want to knit Quidditch socks (page 95) for your entire family or craft a Phoenix-inspired lace medallion blanket (page 195) to snuggle under during Harry Potter movie marathons, your next project awaits within these pages. Grab your needles and yarn – it's time to make some knitting magic.

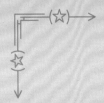
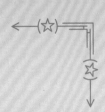

CRAFTY CREATURES

'COME ON, HARRY. THESE ARE SERIOUSLY
MISUNDERSTOOD CREATURES.'

Rubeus Hagrid, *Harry Potter and the Goblet of Fire*

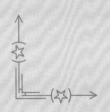
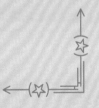

Cornish Pixie

Designed by **SUSAN CLAUDINO**

SKILL LEVEL ⚡⚡

While they might appear cute and harmless, Cornish pixies enjoy wreaking havoc and stirring up general mayhem wherever they go. Electric-blue creatures with large, pointed ears, antennae, big eyes and gossamer wings, they can carry a human with ease, as poor Neville Longbottom finds out in Professor Lockhart's disastrous Defence Against the Dark Arts class in *Harry Potter and the Chamber of Secrets.*

This trouble-free Cornish pixie is knit in pieces in the round for minimal finishing. The body and head are marked with purls for easy placement and attachment. For even stuffing, we recommend adding small bits of stuffing as the pieces are worked. Simple embroidery allows the maker to create a mischievous facial expression, while safety eyes make this a perfect toy for all ages.

SIZE
One size

FINISHED MEASUREMENTS
Height: 30.5 cm / 12 in.
Wingspan: 23 cm / 9 in.

YARN
Colour A: Aran weight (medium #4) yarn, shown in Berroco *Comfort* (50% super fine acrylic, 50% super fine nylon; 193 m / 210 yd. per 100 g / 3½ oz. skein) in colour #9735 Delft Blue, 1 skein

Colour B: 3 ply weight (super fine #1) yarn, shown in Lang Yarns *Alpaca Superlight* (54% superfine alpaca, 24% nylon, 22% fine merino wool; 199 m / 218 yd. per 25 g / 0.88 oz. ball) in colour #749.0021 Light Blue, 1 ball

NEEDLES
- 3.75 mm / US 5, 100 cm / 40 in. long circular needle for Magic Loop, or size needed to obtain correct tension

NOTIONS
- One pair of 12 mm / 7⁄16 in. black safety eyes
- Polyester stuffing
- Black embroidery thread
- Waste yarn
- Stitch marker (optional)
- Tapestry needle

TENSION
Approx 24 sts and 30 rnds = 10 cm / 4 in. in St st with colour A

To produce a dense fabric so the stuffing does not show through, use needles at least one or two sizes smaller than the smallest needle size recommended on the yarn label.

Continued on page 12

- All pieces are worked in the round for minimal finishing. The body and head are marked with purl stitches to take the guesswork out of limb, eye and ear placement. The body and head are worked as one piece, beginning at the base of the body and ending at the top of the head. Because of this construction, you need to stuff the toy as it is knit. The limbs are worked from leg/arm to foot/hand. Wings are knit in two pieces from end to end, so you will stuff as you go.
- This toy was designed using the Magic Loop method for working in the round. The beginning of the round runs along the side. If you are using another method, please make sure to use a stitch marker to mark the beginning of the round.
- When casting on or off, leave a tail long enough for weaving in or finishing, as indicated in the pattern.
- Keep your work in progress neat and tidy by weaving in ends as you go. The polyester stuffing helps to keep them hidden inside.

BODY & HEAD
BODY

With colour A, CO 4 sts. Join to work in the rnd, being careful not to twist sts.

SHAPE BOTTOM

Rnd 1 (inc): [K1f&b] around – 8 sts.
Rnd 2 (inc): [K1, k1f&b] around – 12 sts.
Rnd 3 (inc): [K2, k1f&b] around – 16 sts.
Rnd 4 (inc): [K3, k1f&b] around – 20 sts.
Rnd 5 (inc): [K4, k1f&b] around – 24 sts.
Rnd 6: Knit.
Rnd 7: K1, p3, k4, p3, k13. The purl sts mark leg placement.
Rnds 8–27: Knit.

SHAPE UPPER BODY

Rnd 28 (dec): [Ssk, k10] twice – 22 sts rem.
Rnd 29 (dec): [K9, k2tog] twice – 20 sts rem.
Rnd 30: Knit.
Rnd 31 (dec): [Ssk, k8] twice – 18 sts rem.
Rnd 32 (dec): [K7, k2tog] twice – 16 sts rem.
Rnd 33: Knit.
Rnd 34 (dec): [Ssk, k4, k2tog] twice – 12 sts rem.

Rnd 35: P1, k4, p2, k4, p1. The purl sts mark arm placement.
Rnd 36: Knit.
Stuff with polyester stuffing and cont stuffing as you go.

HEAD

Rnd 37 (inc): [K1f&b] around – 24 sts.
Rnd 38 (inc): [K1, k1f&b] around – 36 sts.
Rnds 39–43: Knit.
Rnd 44: K5, p1, k6, p1, k23. The purl sts mark eye placement.
Rnds 45–52: K18, p1, k16, p1. The purl sts mark ear placement.
Rnds 52–54: Knit.
Rnd 55 (dec): [K4, k2tog] around – 30 sts rem.
Rnd 56: Knit.
Rnd 57 (dec): [K3, k2tog] around – 24 sts rem.
Rnd 58: Knit.
Insert safety eyes at purl sts on Rnd 44 according to package instructions. Stuff head and cont stuffing as you go.
Rnd 59 (dec): [K2, k2tog] around – 18 sts rem.
Rnd 60: Knit.
Rnd 61 (dec): [K1, k2tog] around – 12 sts rem.
Rnd 62 (dec): [K2tog] around – 6 sts rem.
Cut yarn and thread tail through rem sts. Pull tight to close hole, then pull tail to inside. Thread CO tail through edge and pull tight to close hole, then pull tail to inside.

LEGS (MAKE 2)

With colour A, CO 8 sts leaving a tail 25.5 cm / 10 in. long. Join to work in the rnd, being careful not to twist sts.
Rnds 1–14: Knit.

LEFT: Cornish pixies wreak havoc during Professor Lockhart's Defence Against the Dark Arts class in *Harry Potter and the Chamber of Secrets*.

KNEE

Rnd 15 (inc): K1, [k1f&b] twice, k5 – 10 sts.

Rnds 16–18: Knit.

Rnd 19 (dec): K1, ssk, k2tog, k5 – 8 sts rem.

LOWER LEG

Rnds 20–31: Knit.

FOOT

Rnd 32 (inc): K1, [k1f&b] twice, k2, [k1f&b] twice, k1 – 12 sts.

Rnd 33 (inc): K1, [k1f&b, k2] 3 times, k1f&b, k1 – 16 sts.

Rnds 34–38: Knit.

TOES

Rnd 39: K4, slip next 8 sts to waste yarn, k4 – 8 sts rem. Join to work in the rnd.

Rnds 40–42: Knit.

Rnd 43 (dec): [Ssk, k2tog] twice – 4 sts rem.

Rnd 44 (dec): [Ssk] twice – 2 sts rem. Cut yarn and thread tail through rem sts. Pull tight to close hole, then pull tail to inside.

Place 8 held sts on needle and join to work in the rnd.

Join yarn, leaving a tail to close hole between toes, and rep Rnds 40–44 for 2nd toe.

Cut yarn and thread tail through rem sts. Pull tight to close hole, then pull tail to inside.

Lightly stuff the foot and toes. Using tail used to work 2nd toe, close the hole between the toes with a few whipstitches. Weave in ends.

ARMS (MAKE 2)

With colour A, CO 6 sts, leaving a tail 25.5 cm / 10 in. long. Join to work in the rnd, being careful not to twist sts.

Rnds 1–28: Knit.

HAND

Rnd 29 (inc): K1, k1f&b, k2, k1f&b, k1 – 8 sts.

Rnd 30 (inc): K1, [k1f&b] twice, k2, [k1f&b] twice, k1 – 12 sts.

Rnds 31–33: Knit.

FINGERS

Rnd 34: K2, slip next 8 sts to waste yarn, k2 – 4 sts rem. Join to work in the rnd.

Rnd 35: Knit.

Rnd 36 (dec): [Ssk] twice – 2 sts rem. Cut yarn and thread tail through rem sts. Pull tight to close hole, then pull tail to inside.

Place first 2 sts and last 2 sts back on needle for second finger and leave rem 4 sts on waste yarn. Join yarn, leaving a tail to close hole between fingers – 4 sts. Join to work in the rnd.

Rep Rnds 35 and 36. Cut yarn and fasten off sts same as for first finger.

Place rem 4 sts on needles. Join to work in the rnd. Join yarn.

Rep Rnds 35 and 36. Cut yarn and fasten off sts same as for first finger.

Using tails between fingers, close holes same as for toes. Weave in ends.

WINGS (MAKE 2)

With two strands of colour B held tog, CO 4 sts, leaving a 25.5 cm / 10 in. tail. Join to work in the rnd, being careful not to twist sts.

Rnd 1 (inc): [K1f&b] around – 8 sts.

Rnd 2 (inc): [K1f&b] around – 16 sts.

Rnds 3–14: Knit.

Lightly stuff piece and cont to lightly stuff as you go.

Rnd 15 (dec): K1, ssk, k10, k2tog, k1 – 14 sts rem.

Rnds 16–24: Knit.

Rnd 25 (dec): K1, ssk, k8, k2tog, k1 – 12 sts rem.

Rnds 26–32: Knit.

Rnd 33 (dec): K1, ssk, k6, k2tog, k1 – 10 sts rem.

Rnds 34–38: Knit.

Rnd 39 (dec): K1, ssk, k4, k2tog, k1 – 8 sts rem.

Rnds 40–42: Knit.

Rnd 43 (inc): K1, k1f&b, k4, k1f&b, k1 – 10 sts.

Rnds 44–48: Knit.

Rnd 49 (inc): K1, k1f&b, k6, k1f&b, k1 – 12 sts.

Rnds 50–56: Knit.

Rnd 57 (inc): K1, k1f&b, k8, k1f&b, k1 – 14 sts.

Rnds 58–66: Knit.

Rnd 67 (inc): K1, k1f&b, k10, k1f&b, k1 – 16 sts.

Rnds 68–79: Knit.

Rnd 80 (dec): [K2tog] around – 8 sts rem.

Rnd 81 (dec): [K2tog] around – 4 sts rem.

Cut yarn and thread tail through rem sts. Pull tight to close hole, then pull tail to inside.

Weave in ends.

EARS (MAKE 2)

With colour A, CO 32 sts, leaving a tail 30.5 cm / 12 in. long. Pm and join to work in the rnd, being careful not to twist sts.

Rnds 1–3: Knit.

Rnd 4 (dec): K1, ssk, k26, k2tog, k1 – 30 sts rem.

Rnd 5 (dec): K1, ssk, k24, k2tog, k1 – 28 sts rem.

Rnd 6 (dec): K1, ssk, k22, k2tog, k1 – 26 sts rem.

Rnd 7 (dec): K1, ssk, k20, k2tog, k1 – 24 sts rem.

Rnd 8 (dec): K1, ssk, k18, k2tog, k1 – 22 sts rem.

Rnd 9 (dec): K1, ssk, k16, k2tog, k1 – 20 sts rem.

Rnd 10: Knit.

Rnd 11 (dec): [K1, ssk, k4, k2tog, k1] twice – 16 sts rem.

Rnds 12–13: Knit.

Rnd 14 (dec): [K1, ssk, k2, k2tog, k1] twice – 12 sts rem.

Rnds 15–17: Knit.

Rnd 18 (dec): [K1, ssk, k2tog, k1] twice –
8 sts rem.

Rnd 19: Knit.

Rnd 20 (dec): [Ssk, k2tog] twice –
4 sts rem.

Rnd 21: Knit.

Rnd 22 (dec): [Ssk] twice – 2 sts rem.
Cut yarn and thread tail through rem
sts. Pull tight to close hole, then pull
tail to inside.

SHAPE EAR

With dec edge (Rnds 4–9) at top, fold
top 3rd of ear to front. Using CO
tail, whipstitch it in place along CO
edge, making sure to go through all
4 layers, leaving tail for attaching ear.
Holding 2nd ear with pointed end in
the opposite direction, rep shaping.

ANTENNAE
(MAKE 2)

With colour A, CO 3 sts, leaving a tail
25.5 cm / 10 in. long. Work I-cord
(see p. 203) for 10 rnds.
Cut yarn and thread tail through sts.
Pull tight to close, then pull tail
to inside.

FINISHING

Starting with legs, sew pieces to body at
purl st markers using yarn tails. Make
sure pieces cover the purl bumps
completely.

Sew antennae to top of head.

Lay wings with one over the other to
form an *X*, and sew tog where they
cross. Sew wings securely to
upper back.

Weave in rem ends.

Use black embroidery thread to add
facial features, using French knots
for nostrils and straight sts for
eyes and mouth. Refer to photos
to help with the embroidery stitch
placement.

'LAUGH IF YOU WILL, MR FINNEGAN. THESE PIXIES
CAN BE DEVILISHLY TRICKY LITTLE BLIGHTERS.
LET'S SEE WHAT YOU MAKE OF THEM!'

Gilderoy Lockhart, *Harry Potter and the Chamber of Secrets*

BEHIND THE MAGIC

The pixies' vibrant blue colour in the films
was based on Cornish blue roosters, Cornish
pottery and Cornish blue cheese.

TOP: Concept art of the Cornish pixie in flight by an unknown artist for *Harry Potter and the Chamber of Secrets*. ABOVE: Hermione Granger
freezes the freed pixies by casting *Immobulus*.

FLUFFY THE THREE-HEADED DOG

Designed by **SARA ELIZABETH KELLNER**

SKILL LEVEL ⚡⚡⚡⚡⚡

I n one memorable scene from *Harry Potter and the Philosopher's Stone*, Harry, Ron and Hermione find themselves in the forbidden third-floor corridor, a place that Professor Dumbledore has warned is 'off limits to anyone not wishing to die a most painful death'. The reason for his warning is immediately clear to the three first-year wizards: Guarding the corridor is Fluffy, a massive three-headed dog. The film designers modelled Fluffy's heads on that of a Staffordshire bull terrier. Each of the three heads moves independently of the others and has its own personality: one sleepy, one smart and one alert. Only the middle head is collared, but all have enormous, snapping teeth.

   Made both flat and in the round, Fluffy has short rows for shaping and stitches that are picked up and knit to create new body parts. You'll begin with the chest, followed by the legs, body, back and tail. The centre head is next, followed by an additional head on either side. Add a quick I-cord collar (see p. 203) and embroidered eyes, noses and teeth, and Fluffy will be ready to guard your most prized possessions.

SIZE
One size

FINISHED MEASUREMENTS
Length: 20.5 cm / 8 in.
Height: 20.5 cm / 8 in.

YARN
Aran weight (medium #4) yarn, shown in O-Wool *Balance* (50% certified organic merino wool, 50% certified organic cotton; 120 m / 130 yd. per 50 g / 1¾ oz. hank) in colour Smoky Quartz, 1 hank

NEEDLES
• 3.5 mm / US 4 straight needles and set of 4 or 5 double-pointed needles or size needed for correct tension

NOTIONS
• Waste yarn or small stitch holder
• Small amounts of black, white and medium-brown 2 ply weight yarn for eyes, nose, teeth and collar
• Polyester stuffing
• Tapestry needle

TENSION
21 sts and 30 rows = 10 cm / 4 in. in St st
Tension is not critical for a toy; just ensure the stitches are tight enough so the stuffing will not show through your finished project.

SPECIAL ABBREVIATION
K1fb&f: Knit into the front, back, then front again of the same stitch – 2 sts inc'd.

Continued on page 18

BODY
CHEST

With straight needles, CO 42 sts.

Row 1 and all other WS rows: Purl.

Row 2 (RS): Knit.

Row 4 (dec): K12, ssk, k14, k2tog, k12 – 40 sts rem.

Row 6: Knit.

Row 8 (dec): K12, ssk, k12, k2tog, k12 – 38 sts rem.

Row 10: Knit.

Row 12 (dec): K12, ssk, k10, k2tog, k12 – 36 sts rem.

Row 14: Knit.

Row 16 (dec): K12, ssk, k8, k2tog, k12 – 34 sts rem.

Row 18: Knit.

Row 20 (dec): K12, ssk, k6, k2tog, k12 – 32 sts rem.

Rows 22 and 24: Knit. Do not turn after Row 24.

FRONT LEFT LEG

With RS facing, divide first 14 sts over 3 dpn, and leave rem 18 sts on waste yarn. Pm and join to work in the rnd – 14 sts rem.

Rnds 1–2: Knit.

Rnd 3 (dec): K2tog, k10, ssk – 12 sts rem.

Rnds 4–15: Knit.

Rnd 16 (dec): K2tog, k8, ssk – 10 sts rem.

Rnd 17 (inc): K2, [k1fb&f] 3 times, k5 – 16 sts.

Rnds 18–21: Knit.

Cut yarn and thread tail through sts. Pull tight to close hole. Stuff leg, shaping leg and paw as you fill it.

FRONT RIGHT LEG

Return last 14 of the sts onto 3 dpn, leaving 4 sts at centre of chest on hold.

With RS facing, rejoin yarn and knit 1 row. Pm and join to work in the rnd.

Rep Rnds 2–16 of front left leg – 10 sts rem.

Rnd 17 (inc): k5, [k1fb&f] 3 times, k2 – 16 sts.

Rnds 18–21: Knit.

Cut yarn and thread tail through sts. Pull tight to close hole. Stuff leg, shaping leg and paw as you fill it.

BODY

Using CO tail, sew first st and last st tog for first 3 rows to form a circle.

With RS facing and first dpn, pick up and knit 17 sts along right back from seam to holder (approx 4 sts for every 5 rows); with 2nd dpn, pick up and knit 2 sts along inside of right leg, knit held 4 centre sts, then pick up and knit 2 sts along inside of left leg; with 3rd dpn, pick up and knit 17 sts along left back from gap to seam – 42 sts. Pm and join to work in the rnd.

Rnds 1–10: Knit.

Rnd 11 (dec): K18, ssk, k2, k2tog, k18 – 40 sts rem.

Rnd 12 and all other even-numbered rnds: Knit.

Rnd 13 (dec): K17, ssk, k2, k2tog, k17 – 38 sts rem.

Rnd 15 (dec): K16, ssk, k2, k2tog, k16 – 36 sts rem.

Rnd 17 (dec): K15, ssk, k2, k2tog, k15 – 34 sts rem.

Rnd 19 (dec): K14, ssk, k2, k2tog, k14 – 32 sts rem.

Rnd 21 (dec): K13, ssk, k2, k2tog, k13 – 30 sts rem.

Rnd 23 (dec): K12, ssk, k2, k2tog, k12 – 28 sts rem.

Rnd 24: Knit.

REAR

Rnd 1 (inc): [K3, RL1] 3 times, k10, [RL1, k3] 3 times – 34 sts.

Rnd 2 (short rows): K6, w&t, p12, w&t, k6.

Rnd 3 (short rows): K7, w&t, p14, w&t, k6.

Rnd 4 (short rows): Place next 2 sts on waste yarn for tail, k7, w&t, p14, w&t, k7 – 32 sts rem.

Rnd 5 (short rows): K8, w&t, p16, w&t, k8.

Rnd 6 (short rows): K9, w&t, p18, w&t, k9.

Rnd 7: Knit.

Rnd 8 (short rows): K3, w&t, p6, w&t, k3.

Rnd 9 (short rows): K4, w&t, p8, w&t, k4.

BACK RIGHT LEG

Dividing rnd: K16, place rem 16 sts on waste yarn for left leg, CO 2 sts using Backward Loop method – 18 sts. Arrange sts evenly over 3 dpn. Pm and join to work in the rnd.

Rnds 1–2: Knit.

Rnd 3 (dec): K2tog, k14, ssk – 16 sts rem.

Rnd 4: Knit.

Rnd 5 (dec): K2tog, k12, ssk – 14 sts rem.

Rnd 6: Knit.

Rnd 7 (dec): K2tog, k10, ssk – 12 sts rem.

Rnds 8–12: Knit.

Rnd 13 (dec): K2tog, k8, ssk – 10 sts rem.

Rnd 14 (inc): K5, [k1fb&f] 3 times, k2 – 16 sts.

Rnds 15–18: Knit.

Cut yarn and thread tail through sts. Pull tight to close hole. Stuff leg, shaping leg and paw as you fill it.

BACK LEFT LEG

With WS facing, place 16 held sts onto 3 dpn, make slip knot and place on dpn after held sts, then CO 1 more st on same needle – 18 sts.

Next row (RS): Knit. Pm and join to work in the rnd.

Work Rows 1–13 same as back right leg – 10 sts rem.

Rnd 14 (inc): K1, [k1fb&f] 3 times, k6 – 16 sts.

Rnds 15–18: Knit.

Cut yarn and thread tail through sts. Pull tight to close hole. Stuff leg, shaping leg and paw as you fill it.

Stuff chest and body firmly through opening between legs; leave opening between legs open.

TAIL

Return held 2 sts to dpn, then pick up and knit 4 sts evenly along hole below tail – 6 sts. Divide sts evenly over 3 dpn so rnds beg between 2 held sts. Pm and join to work in the rnd.

Rnds 1–2: Knit.

Cut yarn and thread tail through sts. Pull tight to close hole. Weave in ends.

CENTRE HEAD

With RS facing and first dpn, beg at centre back seam, pick up and knit 4 sts in CO edge (1 in each st), then CO 7 sts using Backward Loop method (see p. 202); with 2nd dpn, skip next 14 sts along CO edge, then pick up and knit 6 sts along neck CO edge; with 3rd dpn, CO 7 sts, skip next 14 sts along CO edge, then pick up and knit 4 sts in rem sts – 28 sts. Pm and join to work in the rnd. The skipped stitches on each side of the centre head will be used for the side heads.

Rnds 1–5: Knit.

Rnd 6 (short rows): K5, w&t, p10, w&t, k5.

Rnd 7 (short rows): K6, w&t, p12, w&t, k6.

Rnd 8 (short rows): K7, w&t, p14, w&t, k7.

Rnd 9 (short rows): K8, w&t, p16, w&t, k8.

Rnd 10: Knit.

Rnd 11 (inc): K4, [RL1, k4] 6 times – 34 sts.

Rnd 12: Knit.

Rnd 13 (inc): K5, [RL1, k4] 6 times, RL1, k5 – 41 sts.

Rnd 14 (short rows): K4, w&t, p8, w&t, k4.

Rnd 15 (short rows): K6, w&t, p12, w&t, k6.

Rnd 16 (short rows): K8, w&t, p16, w&t, k8.

Rnd 17 (short rows): K10, w&t, p20, w&t, k10.

Rnd 18 (dec and short rows): K3, ssk, k2tog, k5, w&t, p13, p2tog, p2tog-tbl, p5, w&t, k10 – 37 sts rem.

Rnd 19 (dec and short rows): K2, ssk, k2tog, k5, w&t, p11, p2tog, p2tog-tbl, p5, w&t, k9 – 33 sts rem.

Rnd 20 (dec): K1, ssk, k2tog, k6, ssk, k2tog, k3, ssk, k2tog, k6, ssk, k2tog, k1 – 25 sts rem.

Rnd 21: Knit.

Rnd 22 (dec): Ssk, k2tog, k4, ssk, k2tog, k1, ssk, k2tog, k4, ssk, k2tog – 17 sts rem.

Rnd 23: Knit.

Rnd 24 (short rows): K3, w&t, p6, w&t, k3.

Rnd 25 (short rows): K2, w&t, p4, w&t, k2.

Rnd 26 (short rows): K1, w&t, p2, w&t, k1.

Rnd 27 (dec): K2tog, k13, ssk – 15 sts rem.

Slip first st to 3rd dpn, lift last st of last rnd over slipped st and off needle – 14 sts rem.

Rnds 28–34: Knit.

Rnd 35: Knit, then k2 more sts. Arrange sts over 2 dpn with 7 sts on each needle.

Join sts using Kitchener stitch (p. 203).

LEFT HEAD

With RS facing and first dpn, beg in last st of centre head at back of neck pick-up, then pick up and knit 10 sts along chest CO edge; with 2nd dpn, pick up and knit 4 sts in chest CO edge, then [CO 1 using Backward Loop method, pick up 1 st] twice; with 3rd dpn, pick up and knit 10 sts along CO edge of centre head – 28 sts. Pm and join to work in the rnd.

Work Rnds 6–35 same as for centre head – 14 sts rem. Arrange sts over 2 dpn with 7 sts on each needle. Join sts using Kitchener stitch.

Stuff left head, leaving centre head unstuffed.

RIGHT HEAD

With RS facing and first dpn, beg in first st of centre head next to opening, then pick up and knit 10 sts along CO edge of centre head; with 2nd dpn, [CO 1, pick up 1 st in rem CO edge] twice, then pick up

and knit 6 sts in chest CO edge; then with 3rd dpn, pick up and knit 8 sts along chest CO edge, ending at join with centre head – 28 sts. Pm and join to work in the rnd.

Work Rnds 6–35 same as for centre head – 14 sts rem.

Working through mouth of right head, stuff centre head and right head. Join sts using Kitchener stitch.

EARS (MAKE 6)

CO 8 sts. Divide sts evenly over 3 dpn. Pm and join to work in the rnd, being careful not to twist sts.

Rnd 1: Knit.

Rnd 2 (dec): [K2tog, k2] twice – 6 sts rem.

Rnd 3: Knit.

Cut yarn and thread tail through rem sts. Pull tight to close hole, then fasten off on WS.

Sew an ear to side of all heads at first dec to shape face.

COLLAR

With 1 dpn, CO 3 sts. Work an I-cord (see p. 203) long enough to fit snugly around neck of centre head.

Cut yarn and thread tail through sts. Pull to secure sts.

Cut a piece of white yarn approx 30.5 cm / 12 in. long. Sew a line of running sts along length of collar so yarn shows on both sides, then fasten off.

Place collar around neck of centre head and use CO tail to sew ends tog.

FINISHING

Adjust stuffing as needed through hole between back legs so Fluffy is firmly stuffed, especially the front legs to support the weight of the heads. Use tip of dpn if needed to help sculpt the pieces.

Sew rem hole closed. Sew top half of back legs together to keep them from spreading apart.

For eyes, with black yarn, embroider a couple of short straight sts near top of each head between ears on a dec rnd. Then, with main yarn, work a couple of straight sts above eyes to form eyebrows.

For nose, tuck in seamed edge of each head to form the mouth. With black yarn, sew several straight sts covering 2 or 3 rows at short rows just above mouth of each head.

For teeth, with white yarn, sew a few sts inside each mouth, adjusting tension so teeth show.

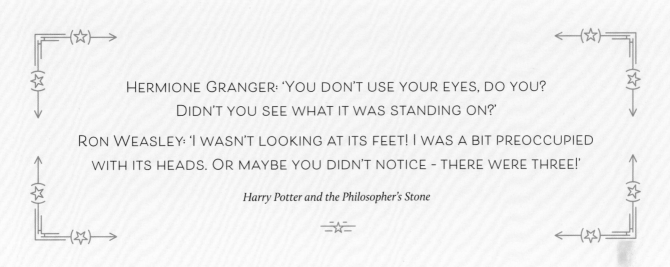

HERMIONE GRANGER: 'YOU DON'T USE YOUR EYES, DO YOU?
DIDN'T YOU SEE WHAT IT WAS STANDING ON?'

RON WEASLEY: 'I WASN'T LOOKING AT ITS FEET! I WAS A BIT PREOCCUPIED
WITH ITS HEADS. OR MAYBE YOU DIDN'T NOTICE - THERE WERE THREE!'

Harry Potter and the Philosopher's Stone

ABOVE: Fluffy guards the trapdoor in the third-floor corridor in *Harry Potter and the Philosopher's Stone*.

HEDWIG

Designed by **SARA ELIZABETH KELLNER**

SKILL LEVEL ⚡⚡⚡

Given to Harry by Hagrid as a birthday present in *Harry Potter and the Philosopher's Stone*, Hedwig is a large snowy owl with spotted wings. Owls are common companions for wizards, with the bonus of being excellent messengers. Hedwig is one of Harry's closest friends and allies for the first six films. At the beginning of *Harry Potter and the Deathly Hallows – Part 1*, she sacrifices herself to protect Harry from a Death Eater.

Worked predominantly in the round, short rows add shaping to Hedwig's chest area, while stitches are picked up and knit to create the legs and head. The tops of the wings are worked in stocking stitch and the bottom is ribbed with a row of scallops made diagonally across the bottom edges. Her wings and tail feathers extend beyond the body to provide balance, while the legs support her weight. All pieces are stuffed at the end, and safety eyes and an embroidered beak add detail to this cuddly replica of Harry's devoted friend.

SIZE
One size

FINISHED MEASUREMENTS
Height: 25 cm / 9¾ in.

YARN
Aran weight (medium #4) yarn, shown in Wool and the Gang *Shiny Happy Cotton* (100% cotton; 142 m / 155 yd. per 100 g / 3½ oz. ball)
Colour A: White Noise, 1 ball
Colour B: 101 Spots, 1 ball

NEEDLES
- 3.5 mm / US 4 straight needles and set of 4 or 5 double-pointed needles or size needed to obtain correct tension

NOTIONS
- Stitch marker
- Waste yarn or small stitch holders
- 4.5 m / 5 yd. DK or finer-weight black yarn
- Polyester stuffing
- Pair of 14 mm / 1½ in. yellow safety eyes
- Tapestry needle
- Sewing needle and white thread (optional)

TENSION
21 sts and 28 rows = 10 cm / 4 in. in St st
To produce a dense fabric so the stuffing does not show through, use needles smaller than the smallest needle size recommended on the yarn label.

Continued on page 24

NOTES

- Hedwig is a stuffed toy that is worked primarily in the round. Short rows add shaping to several areas and stitches are picked up to create the legs and head. The wings are worked separately, then sewn on.

- Hedwig was designed to be freestanding on hard, flat surfaces. The wings and tail feathers extend beyond the body to provide balance, while the legs support the weight. For ease in knitting, leave the entire project unstuffed until the head has been knitted.

SPECIAL ABBREVIATIONS

k1b&f: Knit into the back then the front of the same stitch – 2 sts inc'd.

sp2p: Slip 1 st purlwise, p2tog, then pass slipped st over – 2 sts dec'd.

PATTERN STITCH

Stocking Stitch (any number of sts)

Worked back and forth: knit RS rows, purl WS rows.

Worked in the round: knit every round.

RIGHT: Art by Dermot Power, created for *Harry Potter and the Chamber of Secrets*.

BODY

With dpn and colour A, CO 42 sts. Distribute sts evenly over 3 dpn with 14 sts on each needle. Pm and join to work in the rnd, taking care not to twist sts.

Rnds 1–2: Knit.
Rnd 3 (inc): [K1, M1L, k12, M1R, k1] 3 times – 48 sts.
Rnds 4–7: Knit.
Rnd 8 (inc): [K1, M1L, k14, M1R, k1] 3 times – 54 sts.
Rnds 9–12: Knit.
Rnd 13 (inc): [K1, M1L, k16, M1R, k1] 3 times – 60 sts.
Rnds 14–17: Knit.
Rnd 18 (inc): [K1, M1L, k18, M1R, k1] 3 times – 66 sts.
Rnds 19–22: Knit.
Rnd 23 (short rows): K52, w&t, p38, w&t, knit to end of rnd.
Rnds 24–25: Knit.
Rnd 26 (short rows): K54, w&t, p42, w&t, knit to end of rnd.
Rnds 27–28: Knit.
Rnd 29 (short rows): K56, w&t, p46, w&t, knit to end of rnd.

Rnds 30–31: Knit.
Rnd 32 (short rows): K58, w&t, p50, w&t, knit to end of rnd.
Rnds 33–34: Knit.
Rnd 35 (dec): K31, ssk, k2tog, k31 – 64 sts rem.
Rnd 36: Knit.
Rnd 37 (dec): K30, ssk, k2tog, k30 – 62 sts rem.
Rnd 38: Knit.
Rnd 39 (dec): K29, ssk, k2tog, k29 – 60 sts rem.
Rnd 40: Knit.
Rnd 41 (dec): K28, ssk, k2tog, k28 – 58 sts rem.
Rnd 42: Knit.
Rnd 43 (dec): K27, ssk, k2tog, k27 – 56 sts rem.

DIVIDE FOR LEGS AND TAIL

Rnd 44: K17, place next 9 sts on waste yarn, CO 6 sts using Backward Loop method (see p. 202), k4, place next 9 sts on waste yarn, CO 6 sts, k17 – 50 sts rem.

TAIL

Rnd 45: Knit.
Rnd 46 (dec): K23, ssk, k2tog, k23 – 48 sts rem.
Rnd 47: Knit.
Rnd 48 (dec): K22, ssk, k2tog, k22 – 46 sts rem.
Rnd 49: Knit.
Rnd 50 (dec): K21, ssk, k2tog, k21 – 44 sts rem.
Rnd 51: Knit.
Rnd 52 (dec): K20, ssk, k2tog, k20 – 42 sts rem.
Rnd 53: Knit.
Rnd 54 (dec): K19, ssk, k2tog, k19 – 40 sts rem.
Rnd 55: Knit.
Rnd 56 (dec): K18, ssk, k2tog, k18 – 38 sts rem.
Rnd 57: Knit.
Rnd 58 (dec): K17, ssk, k2tog, k17 – 36 sts rem.
Rnd 59: Knit.

TAIL FEATHERS

Next rnd: K9, place rem 27 sts on waste yarn. Rearrange 9 sts over 3 dpn. Join to work in the rnd.

Cont even in St st until piece measures approx 7.5 cm / 3 in. from division.

Dec rnd: [K2tog, k1] 3 times – 6 sts rem.

Next rnd: Knit.

Cut yarn and thread tail through rem sts. Pull tight to close hole.

Return next 9 sts on 3 dpn. Rejoin yarn and work 2nd tail feather same as first. Work 2 more tail feathers same as the last one. Weave in ends, leaving hole between tail feathers open.

LEGS

Return held 9 sts for one leg onto a dpn. With RS facing and colour A, k9, then with 2 more dpn, pick up and knit 9 sts along CO edge below opening – 18 sts. Rearrange sts over 3 dpn, making sure rnds beg and end at beg of 9 held sts.

Rnds 1–4: Knit.

Rnd 5 (dec): [K4, k2tog] 3 times – 15 sts rem.

Rnd 6: Knit.

Rnd 7 (dec): [K3, k2tog] 3 times – 12 sts rem.

Rnd 8: Knit.

Rnd 9 (dec): [K2, k2tog] 3 times – 9 sts rem.

Rnd 10: Knit.

TOES

Rnd 11: [K1f&b] 3 times, place rem 6 sts on waste yarn. Rearrange 6 sts over 3 dpn. Join to work in the rnd.

Rnd 12: Knit.

Rnd 13 (inc): [K1f&b, k1] 3 times – 9 sts.

Rnd 14: Knit.

Rnd 15 (dec): [K1, k2tog] 3 times – 6 sts rem.

Rnd 16: Knit.

Rnd 17 (dec): [K2tog] 3 times – 3 sts rem. Place all sts on one dpn.

Cut colour A. Join black yarn.

Work 3 rows of 3-st I-cord.

Cut and thread tail through sts. Pull tight to close hole. Fasten off and pull yarn to inside.

Return next 3 sts to dpn and work 2nd toe same as first. Rep with rem sts for 3rd toe.

Use one colour A tail to close hole at bottom of foot.

HEAD

You can face the head sideways or forwards. For a side-facing head, count 8 sts to the left of the first CO st and begin picking up sts there. For a front-facing head, begin in the first CO st when picking up stitches. After that, both head positions are worked the same. The 14 knit sts in the middle of Rnd 2 mark the location of the face.

With dpn, colour A and RS facing, pick up and knit 1 in each CO st – 42 sts. Pm and join to work in the rnd.

Rnd 1: Knit.

Rnd 2 (inc): K2, RL1, [k4, RL1] 3 times, k14, [RL1, k4] 3 times, RL1, k2 – 50 sts.

Rnds 3–17: Knit.

Cast off all sts.

RIGHT WING
UPPER WING

With straight needles and colour B, CO 9 sts.

Row 1 and all other WS rows to Row 17: Purl.

Row 2 (inc): K1f&b, knit to end of row – 10 sts.

Row 4 (inc): K1f&b, knit to end of row – 11 sts.

Row 6 (inc): K1f&b, knit to end of row – 12 sts.

Row 8 (inc): K1f&b, knit to end of row – 13 sts.

Row 10 (inc): K1f&b, knit to end of row – 14 sts.

Row 12 (inc): K1f&b, knit to end of row – 15 sts.

Row 14 (inc): K1f&b, knit to end of row – 16 sts.

Row 16 (inc): K1f&b, knit to end of row – 17 sts.

Row 18 (inc): K1f&b, knit to end of row – 18 sts.

Right Wing Scallop: P3, turn, k3, turn, sp2p, [pick up and purl 1 st along left edge of scallop, pass first st over st just picked up] twice, p1, lift first st over st just worked – 15 sts rem.

Row 19 (WS): Purl.

Row 20 (inc): K1f&b, knit to end of row – 16 sts.

Work Right Wing Scallop – 13 sts rem.

Row 21: Purl.

Row 22 (inc): K1f&b, knit to end of row – 14 sts.

Work Right Wing Scallop – 11 sts rem.

Row 23: Purl.

Row 24 (inc): K1f&b, knit to end of row – 12 sts.

Work Right Wing Scallop – 9 sts rem.

Row 25: Purl.

Row 26: Knit.

Work Right Wing Scallop – 6 sts rem.

Row 27: Purl.

Row 28: Knit.

Work Right Wing Scallop – 3 sts rem.

Row 29: Purl.

Row 30: Knit.

Final Right Wing Scallop: P3, turn, k3, turn, sp2p – 1 st rem. Fasten off rem st.

LOWER WING

With straight needles and colour B, CO 33 sts.

Row 1 (WS): [P2, k1] to end of row.

Row 2 (RS): [P1, k2] to end of row.

Rows 3–4: Rep Rows 1 and 2.

*Work Right Wing Scallop – 3 sts dec'd.

Row 5: P1, k1, [p2, k1] to end of row.

Work 3 more rows even in established patt.

Rep from * 9 times more – 3 sts rem.

Work 3 rows even.

Final Right Wing Scallop: P3, turn, k3, turn, sp2p – 1 st rem. Fasten off rem st.

LEFT WING
UPPER WING

With straight needles and colour B, CO 9 sts.

Row 1 and all other WS rows to Row 17: Purl.

Row 2 (RS): Knit to last st, k1b&f – 10 sts.

Row 4: Knit to last st, k1b&f – 11 sts.

Row 6: Knit to last st, k1b&f – 12 sts.

Row 8: Knit to last st, k1b&f – 13 sts.

Row 10: Knit to last st, k1b&f – 14 sts.

Row 12: Knit to last st, k1b&f – 15 sts.

Row 14: Knit to last st, k1b&f – 16 sts.

Row 16: Knit to last st, k1b&f – 17 sts.

Row 18: Knit to last st, k1b&f – 18 sts.

Row 19: Purl.

Left Wing Scallop: K3, turn, p3, turn, sk2p, [pick up and knit 1 st along left edge of scallop, pass first st over st just picked up] twice, k1, lift first st over st just worked – 15 sts rem.

Row 20 (inc): Knit to last st, k1b&f – 16 sts.

Row 21: Purl.

Work Left Wing Scallop – 13 sts rem.

Row 22 (inc): Knit to last st, k1b&f – 14 sts.

Row 23: Purl.

Work Left Wing Scallop – 11 sts rem.

Row 24 (inc): Knit to last st, k1b&f – 12 sts.

Row 25: Purl.

Work Left Wing Scallop – 9 sts rem.

Row 26: Knit.

Row 27: Purl.

Work Left Wing Scallop – 6 sts rem.

Row 28: Knit.

Row 29: Purl.

Work Left Wing Scallop – 3 sts rem.

Row 30: Knit.

Row 31: Purl.

Final Left Wing Scallop: K3, turn, p3, turn, sk2p – 1 st rem. Fasten off rem st.

LOWER WING

With straight needles and colour B, CO 33 sts.

Row 1 (RS): [K2, p1] to end of row.

Row 2 (WS): [K1, p2] to end of row.

Rows 3–4: Rep Rows 1 and 2.

*Work Left Wing Scallop – 3 sts dec'd.

Row 5: K1, p1, [k2, p1] to end of row.

Work 3 more rows even in established patt.

Rep from * 9 more times – 3 sts rem.

Work 2 rows even.

Final Left Wing Scallop: K3, turn, p3, turn, sk2p – 1 st rem. Fasten off rem st.

FINISHING

Weave in ends. Stuff body carefully, being careful not to overstuff; do not stuff tail feathers. Stuff legs very firmly.

With a strand of colour A threaded in tapestry needle, thread yarn through base of each tail feather. Pull tight to gather tail feathers together and close hole, then fasten off, keeping tail flattened.

SHAPE HEAD

Stuff head about halfway. Fold front (face) edge down onto stuffing so front edge almost touches the back of the head. Fold left and right sides of head down on top of front piece so the side edges meet in the middle of the head and a little pointed 'hood' is formed at the back of the head.

Sew side edges together from front to point at back (approx 7.5 cm / 3 in.), adding additional stuffing to hood as needed. Pull point forwards and over face, about 2.5 cm / 1 in. above neck; excess fabric on each side of face is used to shape face and eyelids. Sew tip to front of head.

EYES

Insert safety eyes under 2 legs of one stitch in space next to 'hood' from centre of face towards side. Turn post of eye to inside of head. Fabric above eye can be brought down slightly over top of eye at inner corner and sewn to form a small tuck with optional sewing needle and thread to create a more realistic eye.

BEAK

With tapestry needle threaded with black yarn, make 3 or 4 straight sts in same place between neck and about 0.5 cm / ¼ in. below point of hood, making sure sts are slightly loose. Adjust by pulling them outwards slightly if needed. Wrap yarn around sts several times until they are completely covered. Thread tapestry needle down into bottom of beak and out back of head. Cut yarn.

WINGS

Sew both pieces of each wing together, with scallops of upper wing over CO edge of lower wing. Tack left and right wings together along back edges from just above the upper scallops to halfway to lower edge.

Sew upper wings to sides of body, with top of wings approx 1.3 cm / ½ in. below neck and centring seam on the back of body. Remove tacking and sew left and right wings together along back edges as tacked, adjusting seam at back of wings if needed so wings separate just above the bottom of the tail feathers.

'RIGHT SMART BIRD YOU'VE GOT THERE, MR POTTER. IT ARRIVED HERE JUST FIVE MINUTES BEFORE YOURSELF.'

Tom, landlord of the Leaky Cauldron, *Harry Potter and the Prisoner of Azkaban*

Behind the Magic

During filming, Hedwig was often portrayed by a radio-controlled animatronic puppet that could turn its head in any direction – just like a real owl.

ABOVE: Hedwig keeps Harry company in *Harry Potter and the Prisoner of Azkaban*.

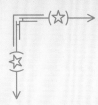
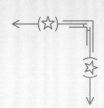

Wizarding Wardrobe

'You two better change into your robes.
I expect we'll be arriving soon.'

Hermione Granger, *Harry Potter and the Philosopher's Stone*

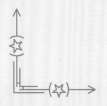
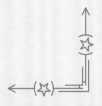

Mrs Weasley's Home-Knit Christmas Jumpers

Designed by **MARTASCHMARTA**

SKILL LEVEL ⚡⚡⚡

Some of the most iconic costumes from the Harry Potter films, Mrs Weasley's knitted jumpers first appear in *Harry Potter and the Philosopher's Stone*. Mrs Weasley, a prolific knitter and family-oriented witch, makes one for each of her children as a Christmas gift. She also makes one for Ron's new best friend, Harry. Ron grumbles, but Harry, who never gets presents, accepts it with delight.

A Weasley jumper can be a warm gift, a clever costume or a fashion statement. Make one, make a pair, make a set for the whole family! Worked flat in stocking stitch from the bottom up in pieces, the front and back are shaped to fit in drop sleeves. Shoulder seams are joined with a three-needle cast off, and sleeves are worked flat, seamed up and fitted in. The collar is then picked up and knit in 2 × 2 ribbing once the sweater is seamed together. Choose your initial or the lucky recipient's initial to duplicate stitch onto the front. A complete alphabet chart is included in the instructions.

SIZES
XS (S, M, L, XL, 2XL, 3XL, 4XL, 5XL, 6XL) Shown in size M.
Instructions are written for the smallest size, with larger sizes given in parentheses; when only one number is given, it applies to all sizes.

FINISHED MEASUREMENTS
Bust/Chest: 92.5 (98, 108, 117.5, 129.5, 138.5, 148.5, 157.5, 167.5, 178) cm / 36½ (38½, 42½, 47, 51, 54½, 57½, 62, 66, 70) in.

Length: 58.5 (61, 62, 65, 66, 68.5, 70, 71, 72.5, 73.5) cm / 23 (24, 24½, 25½, 26, 27, 27½, 28, 28½, 29) in.

YARN
Main Colour (MC): Aran weight (medium #4) yarn, shown in The Green Mountain Spinnery *Mountain Mohair* (40% fine western wool, 30% medium wool, 30% fine mohair; 128 m / 140 yd. per 57 g / 2 oz. hank) in colour Claret, 7 (8, 9, 10, 10, 11, 12, 13, 14, 15) hanks

Contrast Colour (CC): Aran weight (medium #4) yarn, shown in The Green Mountain Spinnery *Weekend Wool* (100% wool; 128 m / 140 yd. per 57 g / 2 oz. hank) in colour Pollen, 1 hank

NEEDLES
• 5.5 mm / US 9 straight needles or size needed to obtain correct tension
• 4.5 mm / US 7 straight needles and 40 cm / 16 in. long circular or two sizes smaller than needle needed to obtain correct tension

Continued on page 34

NOTIONS

- Stitch markers
- Stitch holders or scrap yarn
- Tapestry needle

TENSION

15 sts and 24 rows = 10 cm / 4 in. in St st

Be sure to check your tension.

NOTES

- The initial on the front of this sweater is added using duplicate stitch embroidery (see p. 202). If desired, you can add the initial when knitting the front using the intarsia technique, beginning to work the chart for your desired initial when the front measures approximately 36 (37.5, 38.5, 41.5, 41.5, 44, 44, 45, 45, 45) cm / 14¼ (14¾, 15¼, 16¼, 16¼, 17¼, 17¼, 17¾, 17¾, 17¾) in. from the cast-on edge, centring the chart on the front.

PATTERN STITCHES

K2, P2 Rib (multiple of 4 sts)

Row 1 (RS): *K2, p2; rep from * to end of row.

Row 2 (WS): *K2, p2; rep from * to end of row.

Rep Rows 1 and 2 for patt.

BACK

With smaller needles and MC, CO 68 (72, 80, 88, 96, 104, 112, 116, 124, 132) sts.

Work in K2, P2 Rib for 4.5 cm / 1¾ in., ending with a WS row.

Change to larger needles.

Next row (RS): Knit and dec 0 (0, 0, 2, 2, 2, 4, 0, 0, 0) sts evenly spaced – 68 (72, 80, 86, 94, 102, 108, 116, 124, 132) sts rem.

Cont in St st until piece measures 35.5 (37, 37, 38, 38, 39.5, 39.5, 39.5, 39.5, 39.5) cm / 14 (14½, 14½, 15, 15, 15½, 15½, 15½, 15½, 15½) in. from beg, ending with a WS row.

SHAPE ARMHOLES

Cast off 5 (5, 7, 7, 8, 9, 12, 15, 19, 22) sts at beg of next 2 rows – 58 (62, 66, 72, 78, 84, 84, 86, 86, 88) sts rem.

Cont even until armholes measure 23 (24, 25.5, 26.5, 28, 29, 30.5, 31.5, 33, 34.5) cm / 9 (9½, 10, 10½, 11, 11½, 12, 12½, 13, 13½) in., ending with a WS row.

Next row (RS): K17 (18, 20, 22, 23, 25, 25, 25, 25, 25) and slip to holder for shoulder, cast off next 24 (26, 26, 28, 32, 34, 34, 36, 36, 38) sts for neck, then knit to end and slip rem 17 (18, 20, 22, 23, 25, 25, 25, 25, 25) sts to holder for shoulder.

FRONT

Work as for back until armholes measure approx 18 (18, 19, 20.5, 20.5, 21.5, 21.5, 23, 23, 24) cm / 7 (7, 7½, 8, 8, 8½, 8½, 9, 9, 9½) in., ending with a WS row.

SHAPE NECK

Next row (RS): K22 (24, 26, 28, 31, 33, 33, 33, 33, 34) sts, join a second ball of yarn, and cast off 14 (14, 14, 16, 16, 18, 18, 20, 20, 20) sts for neck, then knit to end of row – 22 (24, 26, 28, 31, 33, 33, 33, 33, 34) sts rem for each side.

Working each side at the same time with separate balls of yarn, cast off at each neck edge 3 sts 0 (0, 0, 0, 1, 1, 1, 1, 1, 1) time(s), then 2 sts 1 (2, 2, 2, 1, 1, 1, 1, 1, 1) time(s), then dec 1 st every RS row 3 (2, 2, 2, 3, 3, 3, 3, 3, 4) times – 17 (18, 20, 22, 23, 25, 25, 25, 25, 25) sts rem for each side.

Cont even until armholes measure 23 (24, 25.5, 26.5, 28, 29, 30.5, 31.5, 33, 34.5) cm. / 9 (9½, 10, 10½, 11, 11½, 12, 12½, 13, 13½) in.

Slip rem sts to holders.

EMBROIDERY

Place a marker at centre of front, then place a second marker approx 4 cm / 1½ in. down from neck edge.

With RS facing, use CC and duplicate stitch (see p 202) to work appropriate chart (charts 1–26), with the initial centred on front and top edge placed at marker below neck edge.

BEHIND THE MAGIC

The Weasleys' costumes were all designed to have a crafty feel and imbued with 'woolly elements' to reflect Mrs Weasley's love of knitting.

'WE WENT ON A WOOLLEN TWEED ADVENTURE!'

Lindy Hemming, costume designer for *Harry Potter and the Chamber of Secrets*

ABOVE: Harry and Ron dressed in their Weasley jumpers in *Harry Potter and the Philosopher's Stone*. TOP RIGHT: Costume sketches for Mrs Weasley for *Harry Potter and the Order of the Phoenix*. RIGHT: Julie Walters as Mrs Weasley in a publicity shot for *Harry Potter and the Half-Blood Prince*.

SLEEVES

With smaller needles and MC, CO 32 (36, 40, 40, 44, 44, 48, 48, 52, 52) sts.
Work in K2, P2 Rib for 6.5 cm / 2½ in., ending with a WS row.
Change to larger needles.

Next row (RS): Knit and dec 0 (1, 1, 1, 0, 0, 0, 0, 0, 0) st(s) at centre of row – 32 (35, 39, 39, 44, 44, 48, 48, 52, 52) sts.
Cont in St st and work 3 (3, 3, 3, 3, 3, 3, 1, 1, 1) row(s) even.

Inc row (RS): K1, M1, knit to last st, M1, k1 – 2 sts inc.
Rep Inc row every RS row 0 (0, 0, 0, 0, 0, 0, 3, 8) times, every 4 rows 7 (7, 8, 11, 9, 14, 14, 22, 19, 16) more times, then every 6 rows 10 (10, 9, 8, 9, 6, 6, 0, 0, 0) times – 68 (71, 75, 79, 82, 86, 90, 94, 98, 102) sts.
Cont even until piece measures 49.5 (51, 51, 50, 49.5, 49.5, 49.5, 47, 45.5, 44.5) cm / 19½ (20, 20, 19¾, 19½, 19½, 19½, 18½, 18, 17½) in. from beg.
Pm each end of last row for armhole placement. Cont even for 3 (3, 4.5, 4.5, 5.5, 6.5, 8.5, 10, 12.5, 14.5) cm / 1¼ (1¼, 1¾, 1¾, 2¼, 2½, 3¼, 4, 5, 5¾) in.
Cast off all sts.

FINISHING

Weave in ends. Block pieces to finished measurements.
Join shoulders using Three-Needle Cast off (see p. 204).

NECKBAND

With cir needle, MC and RS facing, pick up and knit 68 (72, 72, 76, 80, 88, 88, 96, 96, 100) sts evenly along neck edge. Pm and join to work in the rnd.
Next rnd: *K2, p2; rep from * around.
Rep last rnd until neckband measures 2.5 cm / 1 in. Cast off loosely in rib.

Sew in sleeves. Sew side and sleeve seams.

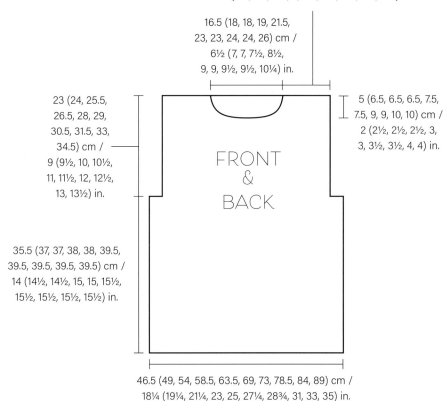

11.5 (12, 13.5, 14.5, 16, 17, 17, 17, 17, 17) cm / 4½ (4¾, 5¼, 5¾, 6, 6¾, 6¾, 6¾, 6¾, 6¾) in.

16.5 (18, 18, 19, 21.5, 23, 23, 24, 24, 26) cm / 6½ (7, 7, 7½, 8½, 9, 9, 9½, 9½, 10¼) in.

23 (24, 25.5, 26.5, 28, 29, 30.5, 31.5, 33, 34.5) cm / 9 (9½, 10, 10½, 11, 11½, 12, 12½, 13, 13½) in.

5 (6.5, 6.5, 6.5, 7.5, 7.5, 9, 9, 10, 10) cm / 2 (2½, 2½, 2½, 3, 3, 3½, 3½, 4, 4) in.

FRONT & BACK

35.5 (37, 37, 38, 38, 39.5, 39.5, 39.5, 39.5, 39.5) cm / 14 (14½, 14½, 15, 15, 15½, 15½, 15½, 15½, 15½) in.

46.5 (49, 54, 58.5, 63.5, 69, 73, 78.5, 84, 89) cm / 18¼ (19¼, 21¼, 23, 25, 27¼, 28¾, 31, 33, 35) in.

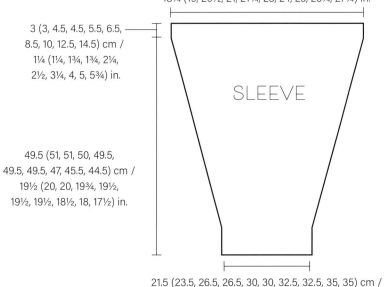

46.5 (48.5, 51.5, 53.5, 55, 58.5, 61, 63.5, 66.5, 69) cm / 18¼ (19, 20½, 21, 21¾, 23, 24, 25, 26¼, 27¼) in.

3 (3, 4.5, 4.5, 5.5, 6.5, 8.5, 10, 12.5, 14.5) cm / 1¼ (1¼, 1¾, 1¾, 2¼, 2½, 3¼, 4, 5, 5¾) in.

SLEEVE

49.5 (51, 51, 50, 49.5, 49.5, 49.5, 47, 45.5, 44.5) cm / 19½ (20, 20, 19¾, 19½, 19½, 19½, 18½, 18, 17½) in.

21.5 (23.5, 26.5, 26.5, 30, 30, 32.5, 32.5, 35, 35) cm / 8½ (9¼, 10½, 10½, 11¾, 11¾, 12¾, 12¾, 13¾, 13¾) in.

FIG. 1

ALPHABET CHARTS

☐ MC

▨ CC

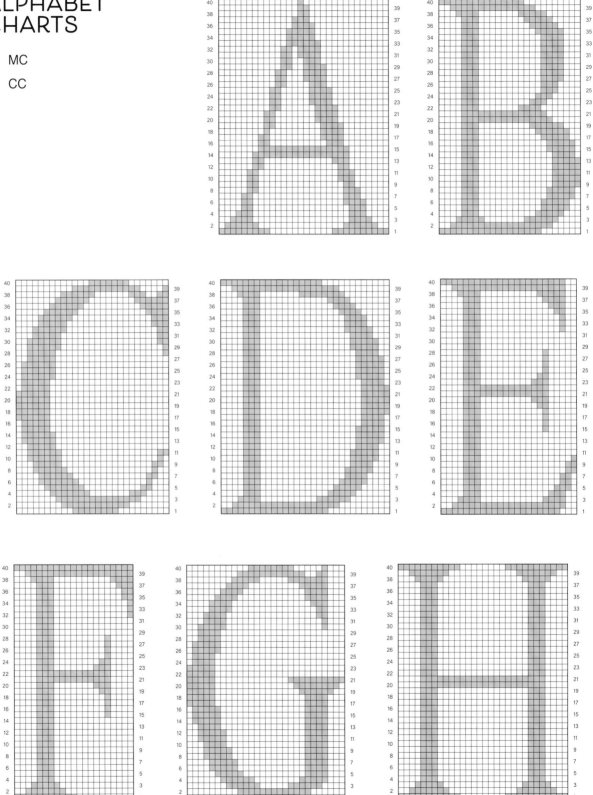

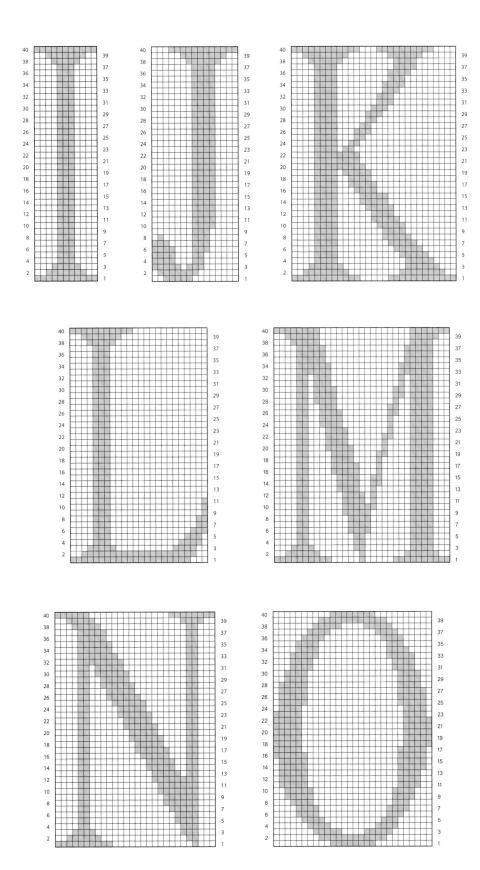

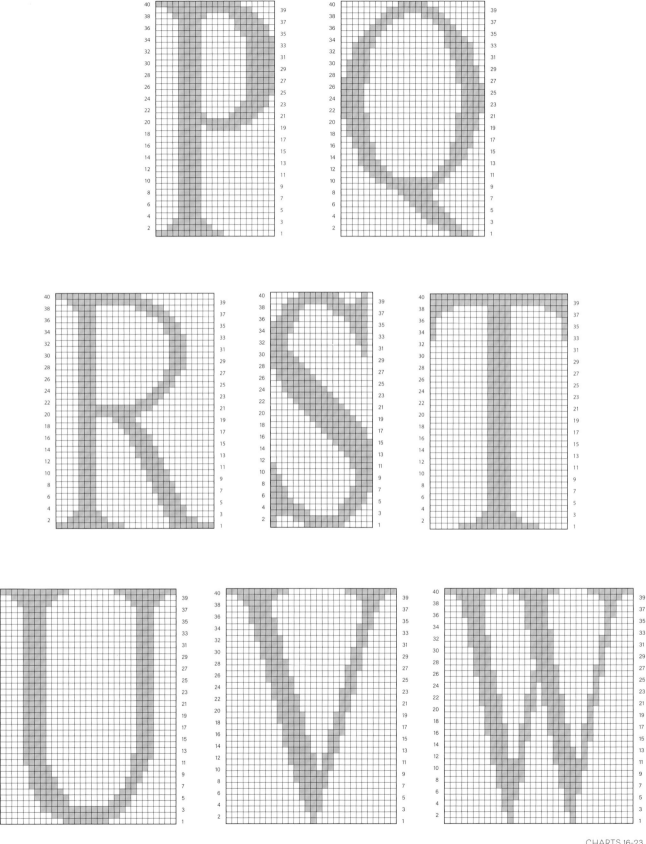

CHARTS 16-23

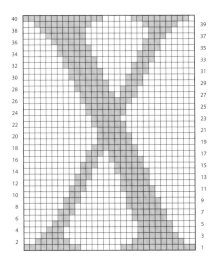
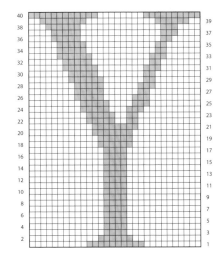
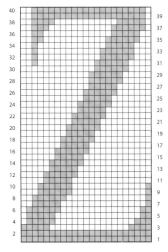

BEHIND THE MAGIC

Costume designers for the films went to vintage wool merchants to source the wool used for the knitted aspects of the Weasleys' costumes.

ABOVE LEFT: The Weasley family heads to the Quidditch World Cup in *Harry Potter and the Goblet of Fire*. ABOVE RIGHT: Mark Williams as Arthur Weasley sporting some cosy knitwear in *Harry Potter and the Half-Blood Prince*.

HOGWARTS HOUSE SCARVES

Designed by **TANIS GRAY**

SKILL LEVEL ⚡⚡

On Harry's first night at Hogwarts in *Harry Potter and the Philosopher's Stone*, Professor McGonagall says, 'While you're here, your house will be like your family'. This becomes especially true for Harry, as his friends and classmates in Gryffindor become the first true family he's ever known. Students at Hogwarts show their house pride in a variety of ways: earning house points, cheering for their team at Quidditch games and, of course, wearing their house colours. Among the most popular pieces of house-themed apparel are the classic house scarves.

This design is worked in the round from the bottom up with no purling. The easy tubular construction means there's no wrong side and the length is easy to adjust. The clean jogless stripes (see p. 203) give this scarf a classic prep-school feel and quick fringe decorates both edges for a playful touch. Whether you're a Gryffindor, Hufflepuff, Ravenclaw or Slytherin, a house scarf is a must-do project for any knitter who's ever dreamed of going to Hogwarts.

SIZE
One size

FINISHED MEASUREMENTS
Circumference: 45.5 cm / 18 in.
Length: 198 cm / 78 in., excluding fringe

YARN
Aran weight (medium #4) yarn, shown in Brown Sheep Company *Lamb's Pride Worsted* (85% wool, 15% mohair; 174 m / 190 yd. per 113 g / 4 oz. skein), colour A, 5 skeins; colour B, 2 skeins

Colourways:
Gryffindor: #M101 Bing Cherry (A) and #M155 Lemondrop (B)
Ravenclaw: #M82 Blue Flannel (A) and #M03 Grey Heather (B)
Hufflepuff: #M14 Sunburst Gold (A) and #M05 Onyx (B)
Slytherin: #M172 Deep Pine (A) and #M03 Grey Heather (B)

NEEDLES
- 5 mm / US 8, 40 cm / 16 in. long circular needles or size needed to obtain correct tension

NOTIONS
- Stitch marker
- 6 mm / US J-10 crochet hook
- Tapestry needle

TENSION
18 sts and 23 rnds = 10 cm / 4 in. in St st
Be sure to check your tension.

Continued on page 44

NOTES

- Scarf is worked in the round in one piece from the bottom up. Work stripes using Jogless Join method (p. 203). When attaching fringe, be sure to have both layers held together to flatten the tube into scarf.

STITCH PATTERNS

Stocking Stitch (any number of sts)

Worked in the round, knit every rnd.

House Colour Stripes (see charts for correct colours)

Knit 5 rnds with colour B, 5 rnds with colour A, then 5 rnds with colour B.

SCARF

With colour A, CO 80 sts. Pm and join to work in the rnd, being careful not to twist sts.

*Knit 27 rnds, or for approx 12 cm / 4¾ in.

Work Rnds 1–15 of appropriate House Colours Chart (chart 27).

Rep from * 9 more times, then knit 27 rnds in A, or until piece measures approx 198 cm / 78 in. from CO edge, or desired length.

Cast off kwise.

FINISHING

Weave in ends. Block to measurements. Cut 80 pieces of colour A, each approx 10 cm / 4 in. long. Using crochet hook and working through both layers of cast-on or cast-off edge, attach a piece of yarn in each pair of sts across both edges. Trim to 4 cm / 1½ in. long.

CHARTS

GRYFFINDOR

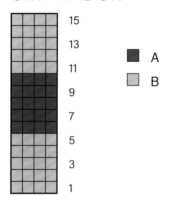

HUFFLEPUFF

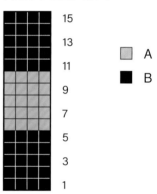

SLYTHERIN

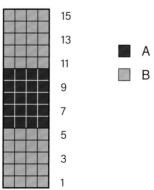

RAVENCLAW

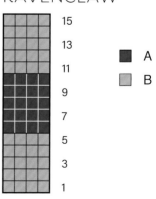

CHART 27

'BEFORE YOU CAN TAKE YOUR SEATS, YOU MUST BE SORTED INTO YOUR HOUSES.
THEY ARE GRYFFINDOR, HUFFLEPUFF, RAVENCLAW, AND SLYTHERIN.'

Professor McGonagall, *Harry Potter and the Philosopher's Stone*

TOP: Daniel Radcliffe sporting a Gryffindor scarf while shooting a scene for *Harry Potter and the Goblet of Fire*. ABOVE: Katie Leung as Cho Chang in a blue-and-silver Ravenclaw scarf for *Harry Potter and the Goblet of Fire*.

HOGWARTS HOUSE CARDIGANS

Designed by **MARTASCHMARTA**

SKILL LEVEL ⚡⚡

School uniforms at Hogwarts consist of a white collared shirt, formal skirt or trousers and robes, with the option of a pullover, cardigan or tank top. The uniforms, originally designed by Judianna Makovsky for *Harry Potter and the Philosopher's Stone* and re-imagined by Jany Temime for *Harry Potter and the Prisoner of Azkaban*, are mostly grey or black and embellished with each student's house colours. The knits show off house colours with piping around the neck and hemline.

Knit your own Hogwarts cardigan to show your affection for the famous school of magic. Knit flat in pieces with set-in sleeves, this simple stocking-stitch cardigan has gentle armhole and neck shaping. A unisex cardigan, with no waist shaping, this button-up jumper makes a fun addition to any fan's wardrobe.

Continued on page 48

NEEDLES

- 5 mm / US 8 straight needles or size needed to obtain correct tension
- 4 mm / US 6 straight needles and 100 cm / 40 in. long circular needle or two sizes smaller than size needed to obtain correct tension

NOTIONS

- Stitch markers
- Stitch holders
- Tapestry needle
- 6 (6, 6, 7, 7, 7, 7, 7, 7) buttons, approx 25 mm / 1 in. diameter

TENSION

15½ sts and 26 rows = 10 cm / 4 in. in St st

Be sure to check your tension.

NOTE

- This unisex cardigan is worked in pieces from the bottom up, then sewn together.

PATTERN STITCHES

Stocking Stitch (any number of sts)
Knit on RS rows; purl on WS rows.

K1, P1 Rib (even number of sts)

Row 1: *K1, p1; rep from * to end of row.

Rep Row 1 for patt.

BACK

With smaller needles and MC, CO 64 (72, 80, 88, 96, 104, 110, 118, 126, 134) sts.
Work in K1, P1 Rib for 6.5 cm / 2½ in., ending with a WS row.
Change to larger needles.
Work in St st for 2 rows. Cut yarn.

STRIPE PATTERN

Next row (RS): Join CC1 and knit. Cut yarn.

Next row (WS): Join CC2 and purl. Cut yarn.

Next row: Join CC1 and knit. Cut yarn.
Rejoin MC and work even in St st until piece measures 38 (37.5, 38, 39.5, 40.5, 42, 43, 43, 43, 43) cm / 15 (14¾, 15, 15½, 16, 16½, 17, 17, 17, 17) in. from beg, ending with a WS row.

SHAPE ARMHOLES

Cast off 3 (3, 4, 5, 7, 9, 10, 12, 13, 15) sts at beg of next 2 rows, 3 sts at beg of next 0 (2, 2, 2, 2, 2, 2, 2, 4, 4) rows, then 2 sts at beg of next 2 (0, 0, 0, 0, 2, 2, 4, 2, 4) rows – 54 (60, 66, 72, 76, 76, 80, 80, 84, 84) sts rem.

Dec row (RS): K1, ssk, knit to last 3 sts, k2tog, k1 – 2 sts dec'd.
Rep Dec row every RS row 1 (2, 3, 4, 5, 4, 5, 5, 6, 6) more time(s) – 50 (54, 58, 62, 64, 66, 68, 68, 70, 70) sts rem.
Cont even until armholes measure 20.5 (22, 24, 25.5, 26.5, 28, 29, 30.5, 31.5, 33) cm / 8 (8¾, 9½, 10, 10½, 11, 11½, 12, 12½, 13) in., ending with a WS row.

SHAPE SHOULDERS

Cast off 4 (4, 5, 5, 5, 5, 5, 5, 5, 5) sts at beg of next 4 (2, 6, 4, 4, 4, 4, 4, 4, 4) rows, then 5 (5, 0, 6, 6, 6, 6, 6, 6, 6) sts at beg of next 2 (4, 0, 2, 2, 2, 2, 2, 2, 2) rows – 24 (26, 28, 30, 32, 34, 36, 36, 38, 38) sts rem.
Cast off rem sts.

LEFT FRONT

With smaller needles and MC, CO 32 (36, 40, 44, 48, 52, 56, 60, 64, 68) sts.
Work in K1, P1 Rib for 6.5 cm / 2½ in., ending with a WS row, and dec 0 (0, 0, 0, 0, 0, 1, 1, 1, 1) st(s) on last row – 32 (36, 40, 44, 48, 52, 55, 59, 63, 67) sts.
Change to larger needles.
Cont same as back until piece measures 38 (37.5, 38, 39.5, 40.5, 42, 43, 43, 43, 43) cm / 15 (14¾, 15, 15½, 16, 16½, 17, 17, 17, 17) in. from beg, ending with a WS row.

SHAPE ARMHOLE AND NECK

Cast off at beg of RS rows 3 (3, 4, 5, 7, 9, 10, 12, 13, 15) sts once, 3 sts 0 (1, 1, 1, 1, 1, 1, 1, 2, 2) time(s), then 2 sts 1 (0, 0, 0, 0, 1, 1, 2, 1, 2) time(s) – 27 (30, 33, 36, 38, 38, 40, 40, 42, 42) sts rem.
Work 1 WS row even.

Dec row (RS): K1, ssk, knit to last 3 sts, k2tog, k1 – 2 sts dec'd.
Rep dec at beg of every RS row 1 (2, 3, 4, 5, 4, 5, 5, 6, 6) more time(s), and *at the same time*, dec at end of every 4 rows 11 (12, 13, 14, 15, 16, 17, 17, 18, 18) more times – 13 (14, 15, 16, 16, 16, 16, 16, 16, 16) sts rem.
Cont even until armhole measures 20.5 (22, 24, 25.5, 26.5, 28, 29, 30.5, 31.5, 33) cm / 8 (8¾, 9½, 10, 10½, 11, 11½, 12, 12½, 13) in., ending with a WS row.

SHAPE SHOULDER

Cast off at beg of every RS row 4 sts 2 (1, 0, 0, 0, 0, 0, 0, 0, 0) time(s), 5 sts 1 (2, 3, 2, 2, 2, 2, 2, 2, 2) time(s), then 6 sts 0 (0, 0, 1, 1, 1, 1, 1, 1, 1) time(s).

RIGHT FRONT

Work same as left front until piece measures 38 (37.5, 38, 39.5, 40.5, 42, 43, 43, 43, 43) cm / 15 (14¾, 15, 15½, 16, 16½, 17, 17, 17, 17) in. from beg, ending with a RS row.

HOUSE COLOURWAYS

RAVENCLAW

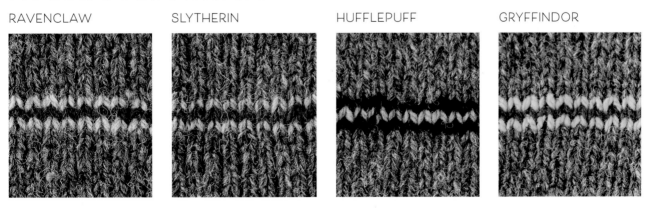

SLYTHERIN

HUFFLEPUFF

GRYFFINDOR

SHAPE ARMHOLE AND NECK

Cast off at beg of WS rows 3 (3, 4, 5, 7, 9, 10, 12, 13, 15) sts once, 3 sts 0 (1, 1, 1, 1, 1, 1, 1, 2, 2) time(s), then 2 sts 1 (0, 0, 0, 0, 1, 1, 2, 1, 2) time(s) – 27 (30, 33, 36, 38, 38, 40, 40, 42, 42) sts rem.

Dec row (RS): K1, ssk, knit to last 3 sts, k2tog, k1 – 2 sts dec'd.

Rep dec at end of every RS row 1 (2, 3, 4, 5, 4, 5, 5, 6, 6) more time(s), and *at the same time*, dec at beg of every 4 rows 11 (12, 13, 14, 15, 16, 17, 17, 18, 18) more times – 13 (14, 15, 16, 16, 16, 16, 16, 16, 16) sts rem.

Cont even until armhole measures 20.5 (22, 24, 25.5, 26.5, 28, 29, 30.5, 31.5, 33) cm / 8 (8¾, 9½, 10, 10½, 11, 11½, 12, 12½, 13) in., ending with a RS row.

SHAPE SHOULDER

Cast off at beg of every WS row 4 sts 2 (1, 0, 0, 0, 0, 0, 0, 0, 0) time(s), 5 sts 1 (2, 3, 2, 2, 2, 2, 2, 2, 2) time(s), then 6 sts 0 (0, 0, 1, 1, 1, 1, 1, 1, 1) time(s).

SLEEVES

With smaller needles and MC, CO 34 (38, 40, 42, 44, 46, 48, 50, 52, 54) sts.
Work in K1, P1 Rib for 6.5 cm / 2½ in., ending with a WS row.
Change to larger needles.
Work in St st for 2 rows. Cut yarn.

STRIPE PATTERN

Next row (RS): Join CC1 and knit. Cut yarn.
Next row (WS): Join CC2 and purl. Cut yarn.
Next row: Join CC1 and knit. Cut yarn.
Rejoin MC and work 1 WS row even.
Inc row (RS): K1, M1, knit to last st, M1, k1 – 2 sts inc'd.

WOMEN'S CARDIGAN ONLY

Rep Inc row every 4 rows 0 (0, 0, 0, 5, 7, 7, 8, 12, 15) times, every 6 rows 2 (2, 5, 10, 9, 8, 9, 9, 6, 4) times, then every 8 rows 8 (8, 6, 2, 0, 0, 0, 0, 0, 0) times – 56 (60, 64, 68, 74, 78, 82, 86, 90, 84) sts.

Cont even until piece measures 42 (42, 42, 42.5, 42.5, 43, 44.5, 44.5, 44.5, 44.5) cm / 16½ (16½, 16½, 16¾, 16¾, 17, 17½, 17½, 17½, 17½) in. from beg, ending with a WS row.

MEN'S CARDIGAN ONLY

Rep Inc row every 4 rows 0 (0, 0, 0, 0, 0, 0, 0, 2, 5) times, every 6 rows 0 (0, 0, 0, 8, 15, 12, 17, 16, 14) times, every 8 rows 5 (5, 7, 12, 6, 0, 4, 0, 0, 0) times, then every 10 rows 5 (5, 4, 0, 0, 0, 0, 0, 0, 0) times – 56 (60, 64, 68, 74, 78, 82, 86, 90, 94) sts.

Cont even until piece measures 49.5 (49.5, 49.5, 50, 50, 51, 52, 52, 52, 52) cm / 19½ (19½, 19½, 19¾, 19¾, 20, 20½, 20½, 20½, 20½) in. from beg, ending with a WS row.

BOTH CARDIGANS
SHAPE CAP

Cast off 3 (3, 4, 5, 7, 9, 10, 12, 13, 15) sts at beg of next 2 rows, 3 sts at beg of next 0 (2, 2, 2, 2, 2, 2, 2, 4, 4) rows, then 2 sts at beg of next 2 (0, 0, 0, 0, 2, 2, 4, 2, 4) rows – 46 (48, 50, 52, 54, 50, 52, 48, 48, 44) sts rem.

Dec row (RS): K1, ssk, knit to last 3 sts, k2tog, k1 – 2 sts dec'd.

Rep Dec row every RS row 10 (11, 9, 8, 9, 5, 4, 1, 2, 1) more time(s), then every 4 rows 0 (0, 2, 3, 3, 5, 6, 7, 7, 7) times – 24 (24, 26, 28, 28, 28, 30, 30, 28, 26) sts rem.

Cast off 2 sts at beg of next 2 rows, then 3 (3, 3, 3, 3, 3, 3, 2, 2) sts at beg of next 2 rows – 14 (14, 16, 18, 18, 18, 20, 20, 20, 18) sts rem.

Cast off rem sts.

FINISHING

Weave in ends. Block pieces to measurements.
Sew shoulder seams.

NECKBAND

On left front for Men's Cardigan and right front for Women's Cardigan, pm for 6 (6, 6, 7, 7, 7, 7, 7, 7) buttonholes, placing bottom marker approx 1.3 cm / ½ in. from bottom edge and top marker at beg of the neck shaping, while evenly spacing rem markers in between.

With cir needle, MC and with RS facing, pick up and knit 68 (66, 68, 70, 72, 74, 76, 76, 76, 76) sts along right front to beg of neck shaping, 38 (42, 44, 48, 50, 52, 54, 56, 58, 60) sts along right front neck, 25 (27, 29, 31, 33, 35, 37, 39, 41, 43) sts across back neck, 38 (42, 44, 48, 50, 52, 54, 56, 58, 60) sts along left front neck, then 68 (66, 68, 70, 72, 74, 76, 76, 76, 76) sts along left front edge – 237 (243, 253, 267, 277, 287, 297, 303, 309, 315) sts. Do not join.

Row 1 (WS): P1, *k1, p1; rep from * to end of row.
Cont in established ribbing for 2 more rows.

Buttonhole row (RS): *Work in established ribbing to 1 st before buttonhole marker, work One-Row Buttonhole over next 3 sts; rep from * 5 (5, 5, 6, 6, 6, 6, 6, 6) more times, then work in rib to end of row.
Cont in established ribbing until neckband measures 2.5 cm / 1 in.
Cast off in patt.
Sew in sleeves. Sew side and sleeve seams. Sew buttons to front opposite buttonholes.

BEHIND THE MAGIC

Jany Temime, costume designer for the last six films, allowed the actors playing the Hogwarts students to style their own uniforms to some extent. This allowed each character's personality to show through little touches such as untucked shirts or loosened neckties.

TOP LEFT: Katie Leung in her Hogwarts school uniform as Cho Chang in a publicity image for *Harry Potter and the Order of the Phoenix*.
TOP RIGHT: A costume sketch of the girls' Hogwarts school uniform, designed by Jany Temime and sketched by Laurent Guinci.
ABOVE: The members of Dumbledore's Army line up in their school uniforms during DA practice in *Harry Potter and the Order of the Phoenix*.

BEHIND THE MAGIC

More than twenty-five thousand items of clothing were created for the eight Harry Potter films, including over six hundred school uniforms.

RIGHT FRONT

21.5 (23.5, 25.5, 26.5, 28, 29, 30.5, 31.5, 33, 34.5) cm /
8½ (9¼, 10, 10½, 11, 11½, 12, 12½, 13, 13½) in.

21 (23.5, 26, 28.5, 32, 34.5, 36, 38.5, 41.5, 44) cm /
8¼ (9¼, 10¼, 11¼, 12½, 13½, 14¼, 15¼, 16¼, 17¼) in.

16 (17, 18.5, 19.5, 21, 22, 23.5, 23.5, 25, 25) cm /
6¼ (6¾, 7¼, 7¾, 8¼, 8¾, 9¼, 9¼, 9¾, 9¾) in.

8.5 (9, 9.5, 11, 11, 11, 11, 11, 11, 11) cm /
3¼ (3½, 3¾, 4¼, 4¼, 4¼, 4¼, 4¼, 4¼, 4¼) in.

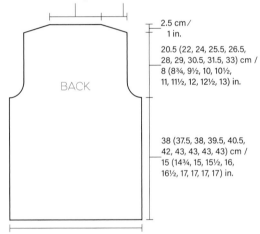

2.5 cm /
1 in.

20.5 (22, 24, 25.5, 26.5, 28, 29, 30.5, 31.5, 33) cm /
8 (8¾, 9½, 10, 10½, 11, 11½, 12, 12½, 13) in.

BACK

38 (37.5, 38, 39.5, 40.5, 42, 43, 43, 43, 43) cm /
15 (14¾, 15, 15½, 16, 16½, 17, 17, 17, 17) in.

42 (47, 52.5, 58, 63, 68, 72.5, 77.5, 82.5, 87.5) cm /
16½ (18½, 20¾, 22¾, 24¾, 26¾, 28½, 30½, 32½, 34½) in.

37 (39.5, 42, 44.5, 48.5, 51.5, 54, 56.5, 59, 61.5) cm /
14½ (15½, 16½, 17½, 19, 20¼, 21¼, 22¼, 23¼, 24¼) in.

11.5 (12.5, 14, 14.5, 16, 16.5, 17, 17, 18, 18) cm /
4½ (5, 5½, 5¾, 6¼, 6½, 6¾, 6¾, 7, 7) in.

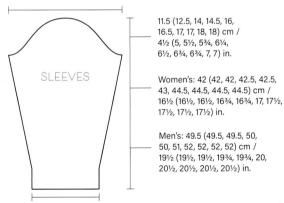

SLEEVES

Women's: 42 (42, 42, 42.5, 42.5, 43, 44.5, 44.5, 44.5, 44.5) cm /
16½ (16½, 16½, 16¾, 16¾, 17, 17½, 17½, 17½, 17½) in.

Men's: 49.5 (49.5, 49.5, 50, 50, 51, 52, 52, 52, 52) cm /
19½ (19½, 19½, 19¾, 19¾, 20, 20½, 20½, 20½, 20½) in.

22 (25, 26, 27.5, 28.5, 30, 31.5, 33, 34.5, 35.5) cm /
8¾ (9¾, 10¼, 10¾, 11¼, 11¾, 12½, 13, 13½, 14) in.

FIG. 2

ABOVE: Hermione Granger (Emma Watson) wearing her Hogwarts cardigan in *Harry Potter and the Order of the Phoenix*.

PROFESSOR UMBRIDGE'S CAT SCARF

Designed by **HEATHER ZOPPETTI**

SKILL LEVEL ⚡⚡⚡

The Defence Against the Dark Arts post at Hogwarts is a tough job to fill. Seven different teachers take the post across the eight films, starting with the stuttering Professor Quirrell and ending with the sadistic Professor Carrow (who teaches Dark Arts, rather than defence). But there is perhaps none so universally despised as Dolores Umbridge, who joins the school in *Harry Potter and the Order of the Phoenix*. Brought to life in the films by Imelda Staunton, who calls her character 'just a delicious baddie', Professor Umbridge is a pink-wearing, cat-loving Ministry spy masquerading as a teacher. Costume designer Jany Temime says, 'I wanted her costumes to appear serious, but always have one detail that was just a bit too much.'

Is this cat scarf a bit too much? You decide. Knit in the round from the tail up, this costume replica takes form with increases and simple wrap-and-turn short-row shaping and stuffing. After the nose is grafted, ear stitches are picked up and knit from waste yarns placed earlier. A clever hook-and-eye clasp keeps the scarf wrapped around the wearer's neck, while button eyes and duplicate stitching bring this kitty to life. Meow!

SIZE
One size

FINISHED MEASUREMENTS
Circumference: 19 cm / 7½ in.
Length: 101.5 cm / 40 in.

YARN
DK weight (light #3) yarn, shown in The Alpaca Yarn Company *Classic Alpaca* (100% baby alpaca; 101 m / 110 yd. per 50 g / 1¾ oz. skein)
Colour A: #2019 Petal Pink, 3 skeins
Colour B: #100 White House, 1 skein

NEEDLES
- 3.75 mm / US 5 set of 4 or 5 double-pointed needles or size needed to obtain correct tension
- 3.5 mm / US 4 set of 4 or 5 double-pointed needles
- 3.25 mm / US 3 set of 4 or 5 double-pointed needles

NOTIONS
- Stitch markers
- Waste yarn
- Tapestry needle
- Two 9.5 mm / ⅜ in. half-dome buttons
- One hook from hook-and-eye closure
- Small amounts of charcoal grey and dark pink yarn for the eyes, nose and mouth
- Polyester stuffing

TENSION
27 sts and 38 rnds = 10 cm / 4 in. in St st with largest needles
Be sure to check your tension.

Continued on page 56

NOTES

- Short rows, lifted increases, make-one increases and standard k2tog/ssk decreases are used to shape the scarf. The body is worked in a Bias Stocking pattern (see below), pairing lifted increases with k2tog and ssk. When working short rows, make sure you hide the wraps when you come to them.

- The face embroidery is done using a scrap of dark yarn in charcoal colour; this project shows Coyote Yellowstone by Stitch Sprouts, but any lightweight dark yarn is acceptable. The dark pink yarn is The Alpaca Yarn Company *Classic Alpaca* in colour #2061 Pretty in Pink.

PATTERN STITCH

Bias Stocking Stitch (multiple of 27 sts)

Rnd 1: *K2tog, k11, RLI, knit to marker; rep from * once more.

Rnd 2: Knit.

Rnd 3: *K14, LLI, k11, skp; rep from * once.

Rnd 4: Knit.

Rep Rnds 1–4 for patt.

SCARF
TAIL

With largest dpn and colour B, CO 10 sts, leaving a tail approx 20.5 cm / 8 in. long. Divide sts evenly over 3 or 4 dpn. Pm and join to work in the rnd, being careful not to twist sts.

Setup rnd: K5, pm, k5.

Next rnd: Knit.

Inc rnd: *K1, M1R, knit to 1 st before marker, M1L, k1; rep from * once – 4 sts inc'd.

Next rnd: Knit.

Rep last 2 rnds 10 more times – 54 sts.

Short Row 1 (RS): K1, w&t.

Short Row 2 (WS): P2, w&t.

Short Row 3: Knit to 1 st past last wrap, w&t.

Short Row 4: Purl to 1 st past last wrap, w&t.

Short Rows 5–6: Rep last 2 short rows once more.

Short Row 7: Knit to 2 sts past last wrap, w&t.

Short Row 8: Purl to 2 sts past last wrap, w&t.

Short Row 9: Knit to 3 sts past last wrap, w&t.

Short Row 10: Purl to 3 sts past last wrap, w&t.

Short Row 11: Knit to next marker, do not turn.

Rep Short Rows 1–11 once more.

Knit 1 rnd. Cut colour B and join colour A.

BODY

Knit 1 rnd.

Short Row 1 (RS): Knit to 6 sts before marker, w&t.

Short Row 2 (WS): Purl to 6 sts before marker, w&t.

Short Row 3: Knit to 4 sts before last wrap, w&t.

Short Row 4: Purl to 4 sts before last wrap, w&t.

Short Row 5: Knit to 3 sts before last wrap, w&t.

Short Row 6: Purl to 3 sts before last wrap, w&t.

Short Row 7: Knit to next marker, do not turn.

Rep Short Rows 1–7 once more.

Knit 4 rnds.

Work in Bias St st for 28 rnds.

Change to middle-size dpn.

Work 20 rnds in established patt.

BEHIND THE MAGIC

Forty different cats and kittens modelled for the decorative plates that adorned Professor Umbridge's office in *Harry Potter and the Order of the Phoenix*. The plates were digitally composited by Hattie Storey.

ABOVE: Imelda Staunton as Dolores Umbridge, complete with cat scarf, in *Harry Potter and the Deathly Hallows – Part 1*. RIGHT: A publicity shot of Dolores Umbridge for *Harry Potter and the Order of the Phoenix*. BELOW: Costume sketches for Professor Umbridge in *Harry Potter and the Order of the Phoenix*. Design by Jany Temime. Sketched by Mauricio Carneiro.

Change to smallest dpn.

Work 212 rnds in established patt, or until piece measures approx 91.5 cm / 36 in. from tip of tail, ending with Rnd 4 of patt.

Using CO tail, sew tip of tail closed. Weave in ends. Steam block body and tail. Stuff body to within a few inches below dpn, leaving tail empty. Cont adding stuffing as you go.

HEAD

Knit 4 rnds even.

Inc rnd: *K1, LL1, knit to 1 st before marker, RL1, k1; rep from * once – 4 sts inc'd.

Knit 2 rnds even.

Rep last 3 rnds once more – 62 sts.

PLACE EARS

Next rnd: K3, k8 with waste yarn, slip 8 sts just worked back to LH needle and k8 with colour A, k9, k8 with waste yarn, slip 8 sts just worked back to LH needle and k8 with colour A, then knit to end of rnd.

SHAPE HEAD

Rnd 1 (inc): K15, RL1, k1, LL1, knit to end of rnd – 64 sts.

Rnd 2: Knit.

Rnd 3 (inc): K6, RL1, k4, skp, k3, RL1, k3, LL1, k3, k2tog, k4, LL1, k6, knit to end of rnd – 66 sts.

Rnds 4–6: Knit.

Rnd 7 (dec): K2tog, k9, skp, k9, k2tog, k9, skp, k2tog, knit to last 2 sts, skp – 60 sts rem.

Rnd 8: Knit.

Rnd 9 (dec): K2tog, k8, skp, k7, k2tog, k8, skp, k2tog, knit to last 2 sts, skp – 54 sts rem.

Rnd 10: Knit.

Rnd 11 (dec): K2tog, k7, skp, k5, k2tog, k7, skp, k2tog, knit to last 2 sts, skp – 48 sts rem.

Rnd 12: Knit.

Rnd 13 (dec): K8, skp, k3, k2tog, knit to end of rnd – 46 sts rem.

Rnds 14–15: Knit.

Rnd 16 (dec): K7, k2tog, k3, skp, knit to end of rnd – 44 sts rem.

Rnd 17: Knit.

Rnd 18 (dec): K6, k2tog, RL1, k3, LL1, skp, k17, skp, k2tog, knit to end of rnd – 42 sts rem.

Rnd 19: Knit.

Rnd 20 (dec): K5, k2tog, RL1, k5, LL1, skp, k15, skp, k2tog, knit to end of rnd – 40 sts rem.

Rnd 21: Knit.

Rnd 22 (dec): K2tog, k14, skp, k2tog, k7, skp, k2tog, k7, skp – 34 sts rem.

Rnd 23: Knit.

Rnd 24 (dec): K2tog, k1, k2tog, k6, skp, k1, skp, k2tog, k5, skp, k2tog, k5, skp – 26 sts rem.

Rnd 25: Knit.

Rnd 26 (dec): S2kp, k6, s2kp, k2tog, k3, skp, k2tog, k3, skp – 18 sts rem.

NOSE

Short Row 1 (RS): Knit to last 2 sts, turn.

Short Row 2 (WS): Sl 1, p4, p2tog, turn – 1 st dec'd.

Short Row 3: Sl 1, k4, ssk, turn – 1 st dec'd.

Rep last Short Rows 2 and 3 twice more – 12 sts rem.

Cut yarn, leaving a long tail. Add rem stuffing. Divide rem sts over 2 dpn, with 6 sts from top of head on one needle and 6 sts from belly on 2nd needle.

Using Kitchener st, graft sts tog, then wrap top of nose, using whip st to create a nose bump over grafted sts. Fasten off.

EARS (MAKE 2)

Carefully remove waste yarn from one ear opening, and place 16 sts onto needles. Divide sts evenly over 4 dpn. Pm and join to work in the rnd.

Join colour A.

Setup rnd: K8, pick up and knit 1 st in gap at corner, pm, k8, pick up and knit 1 st in gap at corner – 18 sts.

Knit 2 rnds even.

Dec rnd: *Ssk, knit to 2 sts before marker, k2tog; rep from * once – 4 sts dec'd.

Next rnd: Knit.

Rep last 2 rnds twice more – 6 sts rem. Switch to 3 dpn when there are not enough sts to work dec over 4 dpn.

Dec rnd: [S2kp] twice – 2 sts rem.

Place both sts on same dpn, lift 1 st over the other, cut yarn and fasten off rem st.

Pull tail through ear to base and baste along base of ear to keep it flat.

Rep for 2nd ear.

FINISHING

Embroider eye details with dark pink yarn, using photos as a guide. Sew buttons to head for eyes.

With colour B in tapestry needle, Duplicate st (see p. 202) over front of ears, making sure to leave a border along the sides and top of each ear.

With grey yarn, embroider mouth and nose details, using photos as a guide.

Sew hook under chin with colour A.

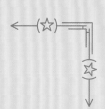

Inspired
Apparel

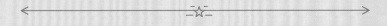

'Dear Mr Potter, we are pleased to inform you that you have been accepted at Hogwarts School of Witchcraft and Wizardry.'

Harry Potter, *Harry Potter and the Philosopher's Stone*

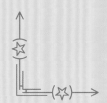
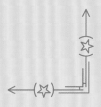

Harry Potter 'Wizarding World' Jumper

Designed by **CASAPINKA**

SKILL LEVEL ⚡⚡⚡⚡⚡

S how your love of the Wizarding World with this gorgeous jumper featuring recognisable themes and motifs from the Harry Potter films. A challenging project celebrating the on-screen world, this jumper features repeating patterns of wizarding iconography including the Sorting Hat, the Golden Snitch, Mrs Norris, the Triwizard Cup, Harry's glasses and a bubbling cauldron.

Worked from the top down in the round, this spellbinding pullover is covered in magical stranded colourwork motifs. Increases are worked across the yoke at intervals between the motifs, and the sleeves are separated and worked later. Working from the top down means that the torso and sleeve lengths are easily adjustable.

SIZES

XS (S, M, L, XL, 2XL, 3XL, 4XL, 5XL, 6XL)
Shown in size S.

FINISHED MEASUREMENTS

Bust: 84 (93.5, 102, 112, 121.5, 132, 142, 152.5, 162.5, 172.5) cm / 33 (36¾, 40¼, 44, 47¾, 52, 56, 60, 64, 68) in.

Length: 54.5 (57, 58.5, 61, 63.5, 65, 67.5, 68.5, 70, 71) cm / 21½ (22½, 23, 24, 25, 25½, 26½, 27, 27½, 28) in.

YARN

DK weight (light #3) yarn, shown in Dragonfly Fibers *Traveller DK* (100% superwash merino wool; 256 m / 280 yd. per 113 g / 4 oz. hank)

Main Colour (MC): Blue Velvet, 4 (4, 5, 5, 6, 7, 7, 8, 8, 9) hanks

Contrast Colour (CC): Golden Compass, 1 (1, 2, 2, 2, 2, 2, 2, 2, 3) hank(s)

NEEDLES

• 4 mm / US 6 circular needles, 40 cm / 16 in. and 60 cm / 24 in. long, and set of 4 or 5 double-pointed needles or size needed to obtain correct tension

NOTIONS

• Stitch marker
• Stitch holders or waste yarn
• Tapestry needle

TENSION

24 sts and 29 rnds = 10 cm / 4 in. in St st
Be sure to check your tension.

Continued on page 64

NOTES

- This jumper is worked in the round from the top down, with the pattern worked using stranded colourwork. Most knitters will tend to knit stranded colourwork more tightly than regular stocking stitch; be sure to check your tension over the charted patterns, too, and adjust your needle size as needed. The number of stitches is adjusted for each chart to accommodate the full repeat into the round.

PATTERN STITCHES

Stocking Stitch (any number of sts)
Knit every rnd.

K2, P2 Rib (multiple of 4 sts)
All rnds: *K2, p2; rep from * to end of rnd.

YOKE

With shorter cir needle and MC, CO 96 (100, 104, 108, 112, 116, 120, 124, 128, 132) sts. Pm and join to work in the rnd, being careful not to twist sts.
Work in K2, P2 Rib for 6 rnds. Change to longer cir needle when there are too many sts to work comfortably on shorter cir needle.

SIZES XS (S, M, XL, 2XL, 3XL) ONLY

Inc rnd 1: K2 (1, 1, 1, 0, 4), [(M1R, k1) 1 (1, 1, 1, 4, 14) time(s), (M1R, k2) 3 (2, 3, 1, 2, 1) time(s)] 11 (19, 13, 30, 14, 7) times, [M1R, k2 (1, 1, 1, 1, 1)] 8 (3, 12, 20, 4, 1) time(s), k1 (1, 0, 1, 0, 3) – 148 (160, 168, 192, 204, 226) sts.

SIZES L (4XL, 5XL, 6XL) ONLY

Inc rnd 1: K3 (0, 1, 2), [(M1R, k1) 3 (7, 5, 8) times, (M1R, k2) 3 (2, 1, 1) time(s)] 11 (11, 18, 13) times, [M1, k3 (1, 1, 0)] 2 (3, 1, 0) time(s) – 176 (226, 237, 249) sts.

ALL SIZES

Knit 2 (3, 4, 4, 5, 6, 7, 8, 9, 9) rnds and inc 5 (0, 2, 0, 0, 0, 2, 8, 10, 3) sts evenly spaced on last rnd – 153 (160, 170, 176, 192, 204, 228, 234, 247, 252) sts.
Join CC.
Next rnd: Working Rnd 1 of Sorting Hat Chart (chart 29), *work 13 sts of chart, k4 (3, 4, 3, 3, 4, 6, 5, 6, 5) sts with MC; rep from * to end of rnd.
Work Rnds 2–13 of chart as established. Cut CC.
With MC only, knit 2 (2, 3, 3, 4, 4, 4, 5, 5, 5) rnds even.

SIZE XS ONLY

Inc rnd 2: K3, [M1R, k3] 50 times – 203 sts.

SIZES S (XL, 2XL, 3XL) ONLY

Inc rnd 2: K1 (1, 1, 2), [(M1R, k3) 6 (1, 1, 1) time(s), (M1R, k2) 1 (1, 2, 1) time(s)] 7 (36, 28, 43) times, [M1R, k3 (2, 2, 3)] 6 (5, 3, 3) times, M1R, k1 (1, 1, 2) – 216 (270, 292, 318) sts.

SIZES M (4XL, 6XL) ONLY

Inc rnd 2: K2 (3, 0), [(M1R, k3) 4 (1, 1) time(s), (M1R, k2) 1 (2, 3) time(s)] 12 (33, 28) times – 230 (333, 364) sts.

SIZES L (5XL) ONLY

Inc rnd 2: K2 (0), [M1R, k2, M1R, k3] 30 (49) times, [M1R, k3 (2)] 8 (1) time(s) – 244 (346) sts.

ALL SIZES

Knit 3 (4, 4, 5, 5, 6, 6, 6, 7, 7) rnds and dec 3 (dec 0, dec 0, inc 6, dec 0, dec 4, dec 6, dec 8, inc 4, inc 0) sts on last rnd – 200 (216, 230, 250, 270, 288, 312, 325, 350, 364) sts.
Join CC.
Next rnd: Working Rnd 1 of Golden Snitch Chart (chart 31), *work 21 sts of chart, k4 (3, 2, 4, 6, 3, 3, 4, 4, 5) sts with MC; rep from * to end of rnd.
Work Rnds 2–7 of chart as established. Cut CC.
With MC only, knit 2 (3, 3, 4, 4, 5, 5, 5, 5, 6) rnds even.

SIZES XS (L, 4XL) ONLY

Inc rnd 3: K2 (3, 1), [M1R, k4 (4, 3)] 49 (61, 108) times, [M1R, k2 (3, 0)] 1 (1, 0) time(s) – 250 (312, 433) sts.

SIZES S (M, XL, 3XL) ONLY

Inc rnd 3: K2 (3, 2, 1), [M1R, k3, (M1R, k4) 5 (3, 1, 1) time(s)] 8 (15, 36, 36) times, [M1R, k4 (0, 3, 3)] 7 (0, 5, 19) times, M1R, k2 (2, 1, 2) – 272 (291, 348, 404) sts.

'YOU'RE A WIZARD, HARRY.'

Hagrid, *Harry Potter and the Philosopher's Stone*

TOP: Harry has his first flying lesson in *Harry Potter and the Philosopher's Stone*. ABOVE: Harry visits Diagon Alley in his first foray into the Wizarding World. Scene from *Harry Potter and the Philosopher's Stone*.

SIZES 2XL (5XL) ONLY

Inc rnd 3: K2 (0), [(M1R, k3) 4 (2) times, M1R, k4] 17 (35) times, [(M1R, k3) 4 times, M1R, k2] 1 (0) time(s) – 378 (455) sts.

SIZE 6XL ONLY

Inc rnd 3: [(M1R, k3) 3 times, M1R, k4] 28 times, M1R – 477 sts.

ALL SIZES

Knit 3 (3, 4, 4, 5, 5, 6, 6, 7, 7) rnds and inc 2 (inc 0, dec 2, inc 8, inc 4, inc 0, inc 4, dec 1, inc 1, dec 2) sts evenly spaced across last rnd – 252 (272, 289, 320, 352, 378, 408, 432, 456, 475) sts.
Join CC.
Next rnd: Working Rnd 1 of Mrs. Norris Chart (chart 34), *work 10 sts of chart, k8 (7, 7, 6, 6, 8, 7, 8, 9, 9) with MC; rep from * to end of rnd.
Work Rnds 2–13 of chart as established. Cut CC.
With MC only, knit 1 (1, 2, 2, 3, 3, 4, 5, 6, 7) rnd(s) even.

SIZE XS ONLY

Inc rnd 4: K3, [M1R, k5, M1R, k6] 22 times, M1R, k5, M1R, k2 – 298 sts.

SIZES S (M) ONLY

Inc rnd 4: K2, [(M1R, k5) 6 (1) time(s), (M1R, k4) 1 (2) time(s)] 7 (18) times, [M1R, k5] 6 (10) times, M1R, k2 (3) – 328 (354) sts.

SIZE L ONLY

Inc rnd 4: [(M1R, k5) twice, M1R, k6] 20 times – 380 sts.

SIZE XL ONLY

Inc rnd 4: [(M1R, k5) 3 times, M1R, k4] 18 times, [M1R, k5] twice – 426 sts.

SIZE 2XL ONLY

Inc rnd 4: [M1R, k5, (M1R, k4) 4 times] 18 times – 468 sts.

SIZE 3XL ONLY

Inc rnd 4: [(M1R, k5) twice, M1R, k4] 24 times, [M1R, k5, M1R, k4] 8 times – 496 sts.

SIZES 4XL (6XL) ONLY

Inc rnd 4: K0 (5), [M1R, k4] 108 (117) times, k0 (2) – 540 (592) sts.

SIZE 5XL ONLY

Inc rnd 4: K5, [(M1R, k4) 5 times, M1R, k5] 18 times, k1 – 564 sts.

ALL SIZES

Cont even until piece measures 20.5 (21.5, 23, 24, 25.5, 26.5, 28, 29, 30.5, 31.5) cm / 8 (8½, 9, 9½, 10, 10½, 11, 11½, 12, 12½) in. from beg.

DIVIDE BODY AND SLEEVES

Next rnd: K93 (104, 113, 122, 133, 144, 154, 166, 174, 184), place next 56 (60, 64, 68, 80, 90, 94, 104, 108, 112) sts on holder or waste yarn for sleeve, CO 6 (6, 8, 10, 10, 12, 14, 14, 18, 20) sts using Backward Loop method (p. 202) for underarm, k93 (104, 113, 122, 133, 144, 154, 166, 174, 184) sts, place next 56 (60, 64, 68, 80, 90, 94, 104, 108, 112) sts on holder or waste yarn for sleeve, then CO 6 (6, 8, 10, 10, 12, 14, 14, 18, 20) sts for underarm – 198 (220, 242, 264, 286, 312, 336, 360, 384, 408) sts rem.

BODY

Knit 9 (9, 10, 10, 11, 11, 12, 12, 12, 12) rnds and inc 2 (inc 0, dec 2, inc 2, dec 1, inc 3, inc 0, dec 3, dec 4, inc 6) sts evenly across last rnd – 200 (220, 240, 266, 285, 315, 336, 357, 380, 414) sts.
Join CC.

Next rnd: Working Rnd 1 of Triwizard Cup Chart (chart 32), *work 13 sts of chart, k7 (7, 7, 6, 6, 8, 8, 8, 7, 10) with MC; rep from * to end of rnd.
Work Rnds 2–17 of chart as established. Cut CC.
Knit 1 rnd with MC and dec 2 (dec 0, inc 2, dec 2, inc 1, dec 3, dec 0, inc 3, inc 4, dec 6) sts evenly spaced – 198 (220, 242, 264, 286, 312, 336, 360, 384, 408) sts.
Knit 10 (11, 11, 12, 12, 13, 13, 14, 14, 15) more rnds and inc 2 (0, 0, 0, 0, 0, 0, 0, 0, 0) sts evenly spaced across last rnd – 200 (220, 242, 264, 286, 312, 336, 360, 384, 408) sts.
Join CC.
Next rnd: Working Rnd 1 of Harry Potter Glasses Chart (chart 30), *work 18 sts of chart, k2 (2, 4, 4, 4, 6, 6, 6, 6, 6) sts with MC; rep from * to end of rnd.
Knit 1 rnd and dec 2 (0, 0, 0, 0, 0, 0, 0, 0, 0) sts evenly spaced – 198 (220, 242, 264, 286, 312, 336, 360, 384, 408) sts.
Knit 19 (21, 21, 23, 23, 25, 25, 25, 27, 27) more rounds and inc 2 (inc 0, dec 2, inc 2, dec 1, inc 3, inc 0, inc 0, dec 4, inc 6) sts evenly across last rnd – 200 (220, 240, 266, 285, 315, 336, 360, 380, 414) sts.
Join CC.
Next rnd: Working Rnd 1 of Cauldron Chart (chart 33), *work 11 sts of chart, k9 (9, 9, 8, 8, 10, 10, 9, 9, 7) with MC; rep from * to end of rnd.
Work Rnds 2–15 of chart as established. Cut CC.
Knit 1 rnd with MC and dec 0 (dec 0, inc 2, inc 3, inc 1, dec 0, dec 0, inc 4, dec 6) sts evenly spaced – 200 (220, 240, 268, 288, 316, 336, 360, 384, 408) sts.
Cont even until piece measures 30.5 (31.5, 31.5, 33, 34.5, 37, 35.5, 35.5, 35.5, 35.5) cm / 12 (12½, 12½, 13, 13½, 14½, 14, 14, 14, 14) in. from armhole.
Work in K2, P2 Rib for 10 rnds.
Cast off loosely in rib.

SLEEVES

With shorter cir needle or dpn and MC, beg at centre of armhole CO, pick up and knit 3 (3, 4, 5, 5, 6, 7, 7, 9, 10) sts along CO edge, knit 56 (60, 64, 68, 80, 90, 94, 104, 108, 112) sts from holder, then pick up and knit 3 (3, 4, 5, 5, 6, 7, 7, 9, 10) along rem CO edge – 62 (66, 72, 78, 90, 102, 108, 120, 126, 132) sts. Pm and join to work in the rnd.

Knit 17 (17, 17, 14, 7, 2, 2, 2, 2, 2) rnds even.

Dec rnd: K2tog, knit to last 2 sts, ssk – 2 sts dec'd.

Rep Dec rnd every 18 (18, 18, 14, 8, 6, 6, 5, 4, 4) rnds 2 (2, 2, 4, 8, 11, 11, 14, 16, 17) more times – 56 (60, 66, 68, 72, 78, 84, 88, 92, 96) sts rem. Change to dpn when there are too few sts to work comfortably on short cir needle.

Cont even until sleeve measures 25.5 (26.5, 26.5, 28, 28, 28, 28, 28, 26.5, 26.5) cm / 10 (10½, 10½, 11, 11, 11, 11, 11, 10½, 10½) in., and dec 2 (dec 0, dec 3, inc 2, inc 0, inc 2, dec 3, dec 0, dec 2, inc 3) sts evenly across last rnd – 54 (60, 63, 70, 72, 80, 81, 88, 90, 99) sts.

Join CC.

Next rnd: Working Rnd 1 of Lightning Bolt Chart (chart 28), *work 5 sts of chart, k4 (5, 4, 5, 4, 5, 4, 6, 5, 6) sts with MC; rep from * to end of rnd.

Work Rnds 2–9 of chart as established. Cut CC.

With MC only, knit 1 rnd and inc 2 (inc 0, inc 1, dec 2, inc 0, dec 4, dec 5, dec 8, dec 6, dec 7) sts evenly spaced – 56 (60, 64, 68, 72, 76, 76, 80, 84, 92) sts.

Cont even until sleeve measures 30.5 (31.5, 31.5, 33, 33, 33, 33, 33, 31.5, 31.5) cm / 12 (12½, 12½, 13, 13, 13, 13, 13, 12½, 12½) in. from armhole.

Work in K2, P2 Rib for 10 rnds. Cast off loosely in patt.

FINISHING

Weave in ends. Wet block to measurements.

CHARTS

KEY

■ MC

□ CC

LIGHTNING BOLT

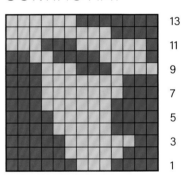

5 sts

9
7
5
3
1

CHART 28

SORTING HAT

13 sts

13
11
9
7
5
3
1

CHART 29

ʙEHIND THE ᴍAGIC

Harry Potter's iconic lightning bolt scar was applied daily to Daniel Radcliffe's forehead using a fixed template and prosthetics.

HARRY POTTER GLASSES

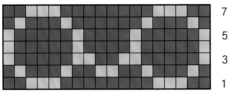

18 sts

CHART 30

GOLDEN SNITCH

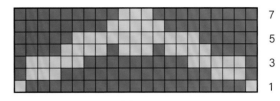

21 sts

CHART 31

TRIWIZARD CUP

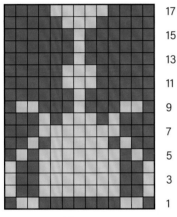

13 sts

CHART 32

CAULDRON

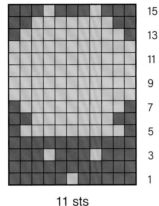

11 sts

CHART 33

MRS NORRIS

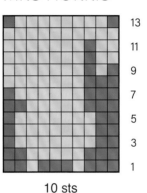

10 sts

CHART 34

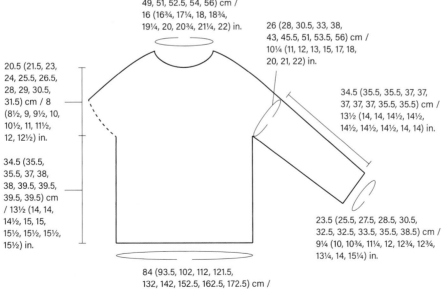

40.5 (42.5, 44, 45.5, 47.5, 49, 51, 52.5, 54, 56) cm / 16 (16¾, 17¼, 18, 18¾, 19¼, 20, 20¾, 21¼, 22) in.

26 (28, 30.5, 33, 38, 43, 45.5, 51, 53.5, 56) cm / 10¼ (11, 12, 13, 15, 17, 18, 20, 21, 22) in.

34.5 (35.5, 35.5, 37, 37, 37, 37, 37, 35.5, 35.5) cm / 13½ (14, 14, 14½, 14½, 14½, 14½, 14½, 14, 14) in.

20.5 (21.5, 23, 24, 25.5, 26.5, 28, 29, 30.5, 31.5) cm / 8 (8½, 9, 9½, 10, 10½, 11, 11½, 12, 12½) in.

34.5 (35.5, 35.5, 37, 38, 38, 39.5, 39.5, 39.5, 39.5) cm / 13½ (14, 14, 14½, 15, 15, 15½, 15½, 15½, 15½) in.

23.5 (25.5, 27.5, 28.5, 30.5, 32.5, 32.5, 33.5, 35.5, 38.5) cm / 9¼ (10, 10¾, 11¼, 12, 12¾, 12¾, 13¼, 14, 15¼) in.

84 (93.5, 102, 112, 121.5, 132, 142, 152.5, 162.5, 172.5) cm / 33 (36¾, 40¼, 44, 47¾, 52, 56, 60, 64, 68) in.

FIG. 3

Mirror of Erised Cabled Cowl

Designed by **TANIS GRAY**

SKILL LEVEL ⚡⚡⚡

While sneaking around Hogwarts in *Harry Potter and the Philosopher's Stone*, Harry stumbles upon the Mirror of Erised, a large Gothic-style mirror with an interlocking golden frame (similar to a cabled motif). When Harry looks in the mirror, he sees himself with his mother and father. Later, Dumbledore tells Harry the truth about that mirror: 'It shows us nothing more or less than the deepest and most desperate desires of our hearts.'

Inspired by the mirror's stunning golden frame, this cowl can be lengthened or shortened according to your preference. After a provisional cast on (see p. 202), six different ribs intertwine up the panel in a golden yarn. The cast on is then removed and joined with a three-needle cast off (see p. 204), completing this lovely homage to a key prop from the films.

SIZE
One size

FINISHED MEASUREMENTS
Width: 23 cm / 9 in. wide
Circumference: 91.5 cm / 36 in.

YARN
Aran weight (medium #4) yarn, shown in Cascade Yarns *Luminosa* (52% viscose, 44% baby alpaca, 4% merino wool; 220 m / 240 yd. per 100 g / 3½ oz. hank) in colour #02 Tiger's Eye, 2 hanks

NEEDLES
- 4.5 mm / US 7, 60 cm / 24 in. long circular needle or size needed to obtain correct tension

NOTIONS
- Cable needle
- Stitch markers
- Waste yarn
- 6 mm / US J-10 crochet hook
- Spare 4.5 mm / US size 7 circular needle
- Tapestry needle

TENSION
21 sts and 25 rows = 10 cm / 4 in. in Cable Pattern
Be sure to check your tension.

Continued on page 72

NOTES

- Cowl is begun with a provisional cast (see p. 202) on using waste yarn and crochet hook, then worked back and forth in rows. The ends are joined using Three-Needle Cast Off (see p. 204).

SPECIAL ABBREVIATIONS

2/1 LPC (2 over 1 left purl cross): Sl 2 sts to cn and hold at front, p1, k2 from cn.

2/1 RPC (2 over 1 right purl cross): Sl 1 st to cn and hold at back, k2, p1 from cn.

2/2 LC (2 over 2 left cross): Sl 2 sts to cn and hold at front, k2, k2 from cn.

2/2 RC (2 over 2 right cross): Sl 2 sts to cn and hold at back, k2, k2 from cn.

2/2 LPC (2 over 2 left purl cross): Sl 2 sts to cn and hold at front, p2, k2 from cn.

2/2 RPC (2 over 2 right purl cross): Sl 2 sts to cn and hold at back, k2, p2 from cn.

COWL

With waste yarn, CO 48 sts using a provisional method. Do not join.

Work from Cable Chart (chart 35), or as follows:

Rows 1, 3, 5, 7, and 9 (RS): K2, p3, [k2, p5] twice, k2, p6, [k2, p5] twice, k2, p3, k2.

Rows 2, 4, 6, 8, and 10 (WS): [K5, p2] 3 times, k6, [p2, k5] 3 times.

Row 11: K2, p3, [k2, p5] twice, 2/1 LPC, p4, 2/1 RPC, [p5, k2] twice, p3, k2.

Row 12: [K5, p2] twice, k6, p2, k4, p2, k6, [p2, k5] twice.

Row 13: K2, p3, k2, p5, k2, p6, 2/1 LPC, p2, 2/1 RPC, p6, k2, p5, k2, p3, k2.

Row 14: [K5, p2] twice, k7, p2, k2, p2, k7, [p2, k5] twice.

Row 15: K2, p3, k2, p5, k2, p7, 2/1 LPC, 2/1 RPC, p7, k2, p5, k2, p3, k2.

Rows 16 and 18: [K5, p2] twice, k8, p4, k8, [p2, k5] twice.

Row 17: K2, p3, k2, p5, k2, p8, 2/2 RC, p8, k2, p5, k2, p3, k2.

Row 19: K2, p3, k2, p5, 2/2 LPC, p4, 2/2 RPC, 2/2 LPC, p4, 2/2 RPC, p5, k2, p3, k2.

Row 20: K5, p2, k7, p2, [k4, p2] 3 times, k7, p2, k5.

Row 21: K2, p3, k2, p7, 2/2 LPC, 2/2 RPC, p4, 2/2 LPC, 2/2 RPC, p7, k2, p3, k2.

Rows 22 and 24: K5, p2, k9, p4, k8, p4, k9, p2, k5.

Row 23: K2, p3, k2, p9, 2/2 LC, p8, 2/2 RC, p9, k2, p3, k2.

Row 25: K2, p3, k2, p7, 2/2 RPC, 2/2 LPC, p4, 2/2 LPC, 2/2 RPC, p7, k2, p3, k2.

Row 26: Rep Row 20.

Row 27: K2, p3, k2, p5, [2/2 RPC, p4, 2/2 LPC] twice, p5, k2, p3, k2.

Rows 28 and 30: [K5, p2] twice, k8, p4, k8, [p2, k5] twice.

Row 29: K2, p3, k2, p5, k2, p8, 2/2 RC, p8, k2, p5, k2, p3, k2.

Row 31: K2, p3, k2, p5, [2/2 LPC, p4, 2/2 RPC] twice, p5, k2, p3, k2.

Row 32: Rep Row 20.

BEHIND THE MAGIC

The writing on the top of the Mirror of Erised reads *Erised stra ehru oyt ube cafru oyt on wohsi*, which, read backwards, says, 'I show not your face but your heart's desire'.

ABOVE: Harry looks into the Mirror of Erised and sees himself holding the Philosopher's Stone.

Row 33: K2, p3, k2, p7, 2/2 LPC, 2/2 RPC, p4, 2/2 LPC, 2/2 RPC, p7, k2, p3, k2.

Rows 34 and 36: Rep Row 22.

Row 35: Rep Row 23.

Row 37: Rep Row 25.

Row 38: Rep Row 20.

Row 39: Rep Row 27.

Rows 40 and 42: Rep Row 16.

Row 41: Rep Row 17.

Row 43: K2, p3, k2, p5, k2, p7, 2/1 RPC, 2/1 LPC, p7, k2, p5, k2, p3, k2.

Row 44: Rep Row 14.

Row 45: K2, p3, k2, p5, k2, p6, 2/1 RPC, p2, 2/1 LPC, p6, k2, p5, k2, p3, k2.

Row 46: Rep Row 12.

Row 47: K2, p3, [k2, p5] twice, 2/1 RPC, p4, 2/1 LPC, [p5, k2] twice, p3, k2.

Rows 48–56: Rep Row 2, then rep Rows 1 and 2 eight times.

Rep Rows 1–56 three more times.

FINISHING

Carefully remove provisional CO and place 48 sts on spare needle.

Join sts using Three-Needle Cast Off.

Weave in ends. Block to finished measurements.

LEFT: The Mirror of Erised, created for *Harry Potter and the Philosopher's Stone.*

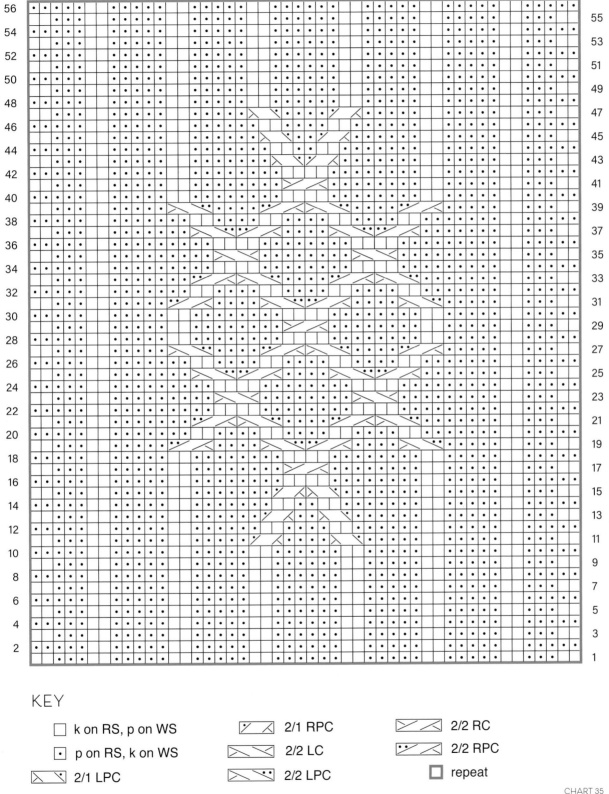

KEY

☐ k on RS, p on WS		2/1 RPC	2/2 RC
• p on RS, k on WS		2/2 LC	2/2 RPC
2/1 LPC		2/2 LPC	☐ repeat

CHART 35

Golden Snitch Socks and Mittens

Designed by **SPILLYJANE**

SKILL LEVEL ⚡⚡⚡

The Golden Snitch is the most valuable ball in the game of Quidditch – worth 150 points to the Seeker who catches it. Concept artists went through many drafts to get the Golden Snitch just right for the films. Moth wings and fish fins were some of the first concepts for the wings, while crustacean and shell looks were considered for the ball. Eventually an Art Nouveau theme was chosen for the ball, with delicate, feathering wings that can fold into the ball when not in flight.

Show your sporting spirit with Golden Snitch socks and mittens. The socks are worked in the round from the cuff down, beginning with a 2 × 2 twisted rib. Once the cuff is complete, the easy stranded colourwork chart is worked over the leg. An afterthought heel is made to interrupt the colourwork as little as possible and is worked after the toe has been grafted.

The stranded colourwork mittens are worked from the bottom up in the round, beginning with a twisted rib cuff. Spiralling decreases bring the top to a close, while a solid-coloured afterthought thumb is worked at the end to maintain the colourwork pattern in the body of the mitten.

SIZE
One size

FINISHED MEASUREMENTS
SOCKS
Foot Circumference: 20.5 cm / 8 in.
Leg Length: 23 cm / 9 in.

MITTENS
Hand Circumference: 20.5 cm / 8 in.
Length: 25.5 cm / 10 in.

YARN
3 ply weight (super fine #1) yarn, shown in Cascade Yarns *Heritage* (75% superwash merino wool, 25% nylon; 400 m / 437 yd. per 100 g / 3½ oz. hank)

Main Colour (MC): #5615 Royal, 1 hank (2 hanks if making both socks and mittens)
Contrast Colour 1 (CC1): #5682 White, 1 hank
Contrast Colour 2 (CC2): #5723 Gold Fusion, 1 hank

NEEDLES
- 2.75 mm / US 2 set of 5 double-pointed needles or size needed to obtain correct tension

NOTIONS
- Stitch marker
- Waste yarn
- Tapestry needle

TENSION
32 sts and 40 rnds = 10 cm / 4 in. in chart pattern
Be sure to check your tension.

Continued on page 78

- The socks are worked in the round from the top down. The pattern uses an afterthought heel to avoid interrupting the chart pattern. The heel will be worked after the main part of the sock is complete.
- The mittens are worked in the round from the bottom up. The pattern uses a peasant (afterthought) thumb to avoid interrupting the chart pattern. The peasant thumb will be worked after the main part of the mitten is complete.
- To reduce the number of ends to weave in, do not cut the CCs at the end of each round but carry the colour loosely up along the WS until needed again.

STITCH PATTERNS

Stocking Stitch (any number of sts)

Worked back and forth, knit RS rows, purl WS rows.

Worked in the round, knit every rnd.

K2, P2 Twisted Rib (multiple of 4 sts)

All rnds: *K2 tbl, p2; rep from * around.

SOCKS

LEG

With MC, CO 64 sts. Divide sts evenly over 4 dpn with 16 sts on each needle. Pm and join to work in the rnd, being careful not to twist sts.

Work in K2, P2 Twisted Rib for 10 rnds.

Knit 2 rnds.

From Socks Chart (chart 36), work Rows 1–16 three times, then work Rows 1–13 again.

HEEL PLACEMENT

Next rnd: K32 sts with waste yarn for heel, then return to beg of rnd, work next rnd of chart.

FOOT

Cont in established patt until foot is approx 5 cm / 2 in. short of desired length, ending with Rnd 2 or 10 of chart if possible. Cut CC1 and CC2.

TOE

With MC only, knit 2 rnds.

Dec rnd: Needle 1, k1, ssk, knit to end of dpn; Needle 2, knit to last 3 sts on dpn, k2tog, k1; Needle 3, k1, ssk, knit to end of dpn; Needle 4, knit to last 3 sts on dpn, k2tog, k1 – 4 sts dec'd.

Knit 1 rnd even.

Rep last 2 rnds 10 more times – 20 sts rem.

Next rnd: Knit to end of Needle 1.

Sl sts from Needle 2 to Needle 1, and sts from Needle 4 to Needle 3. Using Kitchener st, graft toe closed.

HEEL

Holding sock with foot towards you, carefully remove waste yarn from heel and place resulting 64 sts on dpn. Distribute sts evenly over 4 dpn with 16 sts on each needle, and beg rnds at side of heel (beg/end of rnds for leg). Pm and join to work in the rnd.

Next rnd: With MC and Needle 1, pick up and knit 1 st in gap between dpn, k16; with Needle 2, k16, pick up and knit 1 st in gap between dpn; with Needle 3, pick up and knit 1 st in gap between dpn, k16; with Needle 4, knit to end of rnd, then pick up and knit 1 st in gap between dpn – 68 sts.

Knit 1 rnd even.

Dec rnd: Needle 1, k1, ssk, knit to end of dpn; Needle 2, knit to last 3 sts on dpn, k2tog, k1; Needle 3, k1, ssk, knit to end of dpn; Needle 4, knit to last 3 sts on dpn, k2tog, k1 – 4 sts dec'd.

Knit 1 rnd even.

Rep Dec rnd on next rnd, every other rnd 5 more times, then every rnd twice – 32 sts rem.

Next rnd: Knit to end of Needle 1.

Sl sts from Needle 2 to Needle 1 and sts from Needle 4 to Needle 3. Using Kitchener st, graft heel closed.

FINISHING

Weave in ends. Block to measurements.

MITTENS

With MC, CO 64 sts. Divide sts evenly over 4 dpn, with 16 sts on each needle. Pm and join to work in the rnd, being careful not to twist sts.

Work in K2, P2 Twisted Rib for 10 rnds.

Knit 2 rnds.

From Mittens Chart (chart 37), work Rnds 1–16 twice, then work Rnds 1–4 once more.

THUMB PLACEMENT

LEFT MITTEN ONLY

Next rnd: K51, knit next 10 sts with waste yarn, slip these sts back to LH needle, then knit to end of rnd with MC.

RIGHT MITTEN ONLY

Next rnd: K35, knit next 10 sts with waste yarn, slip these sts back to LH needle, then knit to end of rnd with MC.

BOTH MITTENS

Cont in established patt until piece measures 21 cm / 8¼ in. from beg, or 4.5 cm / 1¾ in. short of desired length, ending with Rnd 2 or 10 of chart. Cut CC1 and CC2.

SHAPE TOP

Dec rnd: [Knit to last 2 sts on needle, k2tog] 4 times – 4 sts dec'd.

Rep Dec rnd every rnd 13 more times – 8 sts rem.

Cut yarn and thread tail through rem sts. Pull tight to close hole, and fasten securely on WS.

THUMB

Carefully remove waste yarn and place resulting 20 sts on dpn. Divide sts evenly over 4 dpn, with 5 sts on each needle. Pm and join to work in the rnd.

Next rnd: With MC, beg at one end of thumb opening, with Needle 1, pick up and knit 1 st in gap, k5; with Needle 2, k5, pick up and knit 1 st in gap; with Needle 3, pick up and knit 1 st in gap, k5; then with Needle 4, k5, pick up and knit 1 st in gap – 24 sts.

Cont even in St st with MC only until thumb measures 1.3 cm / ½ in. short of desired length.

Dec rnd: [Knit to last 2 sts on needle, k2tog] 4 times – 4 sts dec'd.

Rep Dec rnd 3 more times – 8 sts rem.

Cut yarn and thread tail through rem sts. Pull tight to close hole, and fasten securely on WS.

FINISHING

Weave in ends. Block to measurements.

SOCKS

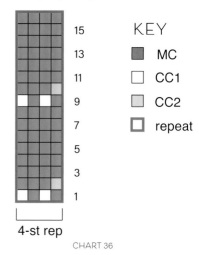

KEY

- ■ MC
- □ CC1
- ▨ CC2
- ☐ repeat

4-st rep

CHART 36

MITTENS

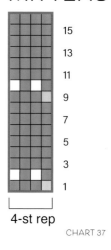

4-st rep

CHART 37

TOP: Harry and Draco race to catch the Golden Snitch in concept art by Adam Brockbank for *Harry Potter and the Chamber of Secrets*.
ABOVE: Harry holds the Golden Snitch in *Harry Potter and the Philosopher's Stone*

Wizarding Transportation Scarf

Designed by **TANIS GRAY**

SKILL LEVEL ⚡⚡⚡

The Harry Potter films feature many modes of magical transportation, from flying broomsticks to Floo powder to the famous Hogwarts Express. Creating all these artifacts was the responsibility of a massive team of artists, designers and prop makers, all working under the direction of production designer Stuart Craig. Some of the items, like the broomsticks, simply required a new take on a magical classic, while others, like the zany purple Knight Bus from *Harry Potter and the Prisoner of Azkaban*, had to be imagined and built from scratch.

This scarf is an ode to all the magical methods the wizarding world uses to get from A to B. Stitched in the round so there is no visible wrong side, this extra-warm scarf is adorned with broomsticks, Knight Bus motifs and the symbol for platform nine and three-quarters – where student wizards catch the Hogwarts Express. The scarf length is easily adjustable depending on the number of pattern repeats. Multicoloured fringing is worked on both ends with a crochet hook, fusing the edges of the tube closed.

SIZE
One size

FINISHED MEASUREMENTS
Circumference: 38 cm / 15 in.
Length: 233.5 cm / 91 in., excluding fringe

YARN
Aran weight (medium #4) yarn, shown in
  Tanis Fiber Arts *PureWash Worsted* (100%
  organic superwash merino wool; 187 m /
  205 yd. per 113 g / 4 oz. hank)
Main Colour (MC): Smoke, 5 hanks
Contrast Colour 1 (CC1): Plum, 2 hanks
Contrast Colour 2 (CC2): Chestnut, 1 hank
Contrast Colour 3 (CC3): Charcoal, 1 hank

NEEDLES
• 5 mm / US 8, 40 cm / 16 in. long circular
  needle or size needed to obtain correct
  tension
•

NOTIONS
• Stitch marker
• 6 mm / US J-10 crochet hook
• Tapestry needle

TENSION
23½ sts and 20 rnds = 10 cm / 4 in.
  in chart patt.
Be sure to check your tension.

NOTES
• This scarf is worked in the round in one
  piece. When attaching the fringe, be sure
  to hold both layers together to flatten the
  tube into a scarf.

Behind the Magic

Transporting the Knight Bus around London was a major logistical headache for the filmmakers. The top of the bus had to be removed with a crane, the two halves transported separately, and the pieces reassembled on site every time they started filming.

THIS PAGE: Art for the Knight Bus (*top*) and the Hogwarts Express at platform nine and three-quarters (*above*)

SCARF

With CC1, CO 88 sts. Pm and join to work in the rnd, being careful not to twist sts.

Working from charts, *work Rnds 1–53 of the Knight Bus Chart (chart 38), Rnds 1–32 of the Broomstick Chart (chart 39), then Rnds 1–29 of the Platform Nine and Three-quarters Chart (chart 40); rep from * 3 more times, then work Rnds 1–5 of the Knight Bus chart once more. Piece should measure approx 233.5 cm / 92 in. long.

Cast off knitwise with CC1.

FINISHING

Weave in ends. Block to measurements.

FRINGE

Cut 80 pieces each of CC1, CC2 and CC3, each approx 30.5 cm / 12 in. long.

Holding 10 strands of one colour tog, use crochet hook to attach fringes to cast-on and cast-off edges, alternating colours across edge, with 12 groups of fringe (4 of each colour) evenly spaced along each edge. Trim to even length.

CHARTS

KNIGHT BUS

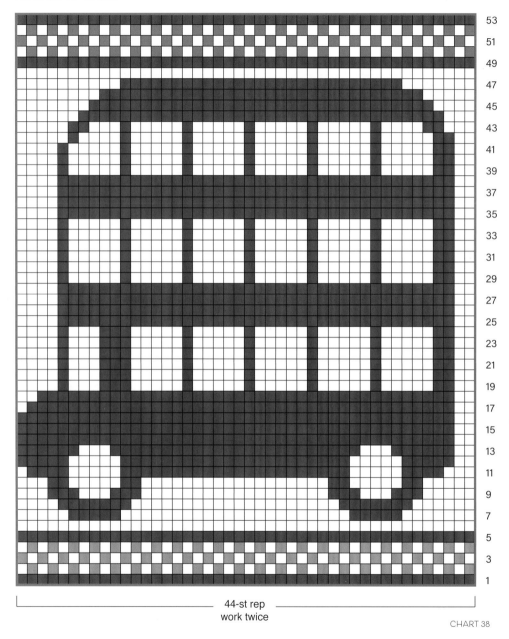

53
51
49
47
45
43
41
39
37
35
33
31
29
27
25
23
21
19
17
15
13
11
9
7
5
3
1

44-st rep
work twice

CHART 38

BROOMSTICKS

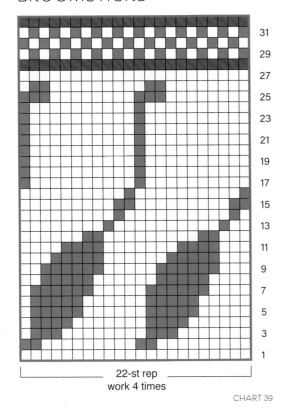

31
29
27
25
23
21
19
17
15
13
11
9
7
5
3
1

22-st rep
work 4 times

CHART 39

BEHIND THE MAGIC

The broomsticks the actors performed with during flying scenes were outfitted with moulded bicycle seats and extra padding for comfort.

ABOVE: Concept art for the Firebolt.

PLATFORM NINE AND THREE-QUARTERS

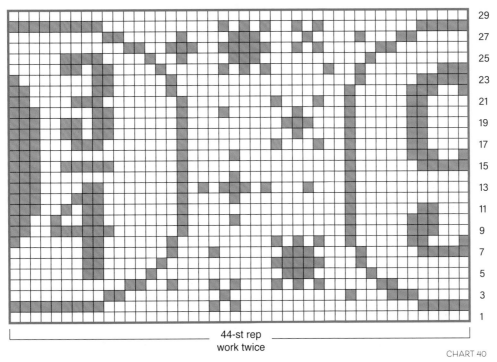

29
27
25
23
21
19
17
15
13
11
9
7
5
3
1

44-st rep
work twice

CHART 40

Hogwarts Dueling Club Fingerless Mitts

Designed by **TANIS GRAY**

SKILL LEVEL ⚡⚡⚡

Formed to teach students how to defend themselves in a magical confrontation, the Duelling Club is presided over by Professor Lockhart and Professor Snape in *Harry Potter and the Chamber of Secrets*. It is there that Harry and his fellow students learn he can speak Parseltongue. The scene takes place in the Great Hall, where the professors use a long table, covered in a beautiful runner showing the phases of the moon, as a stage for demonstrations.

Featuring the lunar motif from this gorgeous set piece, these fingerless mitts are knit back and forth in garter stitch from the bottom up. The stretchiness of the finished fabric and gentle shaping at the inside edge ensures a fit that works for a variety of knitters. The edges are mattress stitched together, leaving an opening for the thumb, and the pre-strung beads create the moon motif centred down the front of the arm.

SIZE
One Size

FINISHED MEASUREMENTS
Hand Circumference: 18 cm / 7 in.
Length: 35.5 cm / 14 in.

YARN
3 ply weight (super fine #1) yarn, shown in The Lemonade Shop *Simple Sock* (80% superwash merino wool, 20% nylon); 366 m / 400 yd. per 100 g / 3½ oz. hank) in colour Duelling Club, 1 hank

NEEDLES
- 2 mm / US 0 straight needles or 40 cm / 16 in. long circular needle or size needed to obtain correct tension

NOTIONS
- Stitch markers
- Wire bead threader
- Tapestry needle
- Beads: 1556 3 mm (size 8/0) Miyuki glass beads in Silverlined Gold

TENSION
34 sts and 73 rows = 10 cm / 4 in. in Garter st
Be sure to check your tension.

STITCH PATTERNS
Garter Stitch (any number of sts)
Worked back and forth, knit every row.

Continued on page 90

NOTES

- All WS rows are knit straight across and are not charted. These fingerless mitts are worked back and forth from the forearm down to the fingers, with shaping at the inside edge. Edges are then sewn together with mattress stitch, leaving a thumb opening.

SPECIAL TERMS

Place Bead: String all beads onto yarn with a wire bead threader (adding a few extra, just in case) before casting on stitches. When working a bead, push a bead snug against the back of the work, then knit the stitch. The bead will lie between the stitches and will favour the WS side, even though beads are placed on RS rows only. The bead and the knit stitch worked immediately after placing the bead equal the *B* square on the Lunar Phase Chart (chart 41). Do not use a small crochet hook – the beads will become lost in the garter stitch and will not be seen.

RIGHT MITT

String half of the beads onto yarn.
CO 80 sts. Do not join.
Knit 10 rows.
Setup row (RS): K18, pm, work Row 1 of Lunar Phase Chart (chart 41) across next 13 sts, pm, knit to end of row.
Next row (WS): Knit.
Cont as established and *at the same time*, when piece measures 4.5 cm / 1¾ in. from CO edge, end with a WS row.

SHAPE FOREARM

Dec row 1 (RS): K1, [k2tog] 3 times, work to last 7 sts, [ssk] 3 times, k1 – 6 sts dec'd.
Work even until piece measures 8.5 cm / 3¼ in. from CO edge, ending with a WS row.
Rep Dec row 1 – 68 sts rem.
Work even until piece measures 12.5 cm / 5 in. from CO edge, ending with a WS row.
Rep Dec row 1 – 62 sts rem.
Work even until piece measures 17 cm / 6¾ in. from CO edge, ending with a WS row.

Dec row 2: K1, k2tog, work to last 3 sts, ssk, k1 – 60 sts rem.
When chart is complete, knit 10 rows even.
Cast off kwise, leaving a long tail.

LEFT MITT

String rem beads onto yarn.
CO 80 sts. Do not join.
Knit 10 rows.
Setup row (RS): K49, pm, work Row 1 of Lunar Phase Chart (chart 41) across next 13 sts, pm, knit to end of row.
Next Row (WS): Knit.
Cont same as for right fingerless mitt.

FINISHING

Fold piece in half lengthwise. With long tail and tapestry needle, beg from cast-off edge, sew side edges tog using mattress stitch (see p. 203) for 4.5 cm / 1¾ in.. Leave an opening for thumb 5 cm / 2 in. long, then sew rem edge closed.
Weave in ends. Block to measurements.

'IN LIGHT OF THE DARK EVENTS OF RECENT WEEKS, PROFESSOR DUMBLEDORE HAS GRANTED ME PERMISSION TO START THIS LITTLE DUELLING CLUB TO TRAIN YOU ALL UP IN CASE YOU EVER NEED TO DEFEND YOURSELVES AS I MYSELF HAVE DONE ON COUNTLESS OCCASIONS. FOR FULL DETAILS, SEE MY PUBLISHED WORKS.'

Gilderoy Lockhart, *Harry Potter and the Chamber of Secrets*

BEHIND THE MAGIC

Lockhart actor Kenneth Branagh brought a great deal of consideration to the way he handled his wand during his duel with Professor Snape in the Duelling Club scene: 'If you're down the other end of the platform from Alan Rickman, and he's got a wand, you've got to be very good to be noticed down at your end.'

OPPOSITE: Kenneth Branagh as Professor Gilderoy Lockhart. THIS PAGE: Professor Lockhart attempts to teach Harry and his peers how to duel in two images from *Harry Potter and the Chamber of Secrets*.

LUNAR PHASE

☐ Knit [B] Place Bead NOTE: Chart shows RS rows; knit all WS rows

				B		B		B					235
					B	B	B						233
				B	B	B	B	B					231
					B	B	B						229
				B		B		B					227
						B							225
						B							223
						B							221
			B			B			B				219
		B				B				B			217
	B					B					B		215
B	B					B					B	B	213
B	B					B					B	B	211
B	B					B					B	B	209
B	B					B					B	B	207
B	B	B				B				B	B	B	205
B	B	B	B	B	B	B	B	B	B	B	B	B	203
	B	B	B	B	B	B	B	B	B	B	B		201
		B	B	B	B	B	B	B	B	B			199
			B	B	B	B	B	B	B				197
						B							195
						B							193
						B							191
			B			B			B				189
		B				B				B			187
	B	B				B				B	B		185
B	B	B				B				B	B	B	183
B	B	B				B				B	B	B	181
B	B	B	B			B			B	B	B	B	179
B	B	B	B	B	B	B	B	B	B	B	B	B	177
B	B	B	B	B	B	B	B	B	B	B	B	B	175
B	B	B	B	B	B	B	B	B	B	B	B	B	173
	B	B	B	B	B	B	B	B	B	B	B		171
		B	B	B	B	B	B	B	B	B			169
			B	B	B	B	B	B	B				167
						B							165
						B							163
						B							161
			B			B			B				159
		B	B			B			B	B			157
	B	B	B			B			B	B	B		155
B	B	B	B	B		B		B	B	B	B	B	153
B	B	B	B	B	B	B	B	B	B	B	B	B	151
B	B	B	B	B	B	B	B	B	B	B	B	B	149
B	B	B	B	B	B	B	B	B	B	B	B	B	147
B	B	B	B	B	B	B	B	B	B	B	B	B	145
B	B	B	B	B	B	B	B	B	B	B	B	B	143
	B	B	B	B	B	B	B	B	B	B	B		141
		B	B	B	B	B	B	B	B	B			139
			B	B	B	B	B	B	B				137
						B							135
						B							133
						B							131
			B	B	B	B	B	B	B				129
		B	B	B	B	B	B	B	B	B			127
	B	B	B	B	B	B	B	B	B	B	B		125
B	B	B	B	B	B	B	B	B	B	B	B	B	123
B	B	B	B	B	B	B	B	B	B	B	B	B	121
B	B	B	B	B	B	B	B	B	B	B	B	B	119

B	B	B	B	B	B	B	B	B	B	B	B	B	117
B	B	B	B	B	B	B	B	B	B	B	B	B	115
B	B	B	B	B	B	B	B	B	B	B	B	B	113
	B	B	B	B	B	B	B	B	B	B	B		111
		B	B	B	B	B	B	B	B	B			109
			B	B	B	B	B	B	B				107
						B							105
						B							103
						B							101
			B	B	B	B	B	B	B				99
		B	B	B	B	B	B	B	B	B			97
	B	B	B	B	B	B	B	B	B	B	B		95
B	B	B	B	B	B	B	B	B	B	B	B	B	93
B	B	B	B	B	B	B	B	B	B	B	B	B	91
B	B	B	B	B	B	B	B	B	B	B	B	B	89
B	B	B	B	B	B	B	B	B	B	B	B	B	87
B	B	B	B	B	B	B	B	B	B	B	B	B	85
B	B	B	B	B		B		B	B	B	B	B	83
	B	B	B			B			B	B	B		81
		B	B			B			B	B			79
			B			B			B				77
						B							75
						B							73
						B							71
			B	B	B	B	B	B	B				69
		B	B	B	B	B	B	B	B	B			67
	B	B	B	B	B	B	B	B	B	B	B		65
B	B	B	B	B	B	B	B	B	B	B	B	B	63
B	B	B	B	B	B	B	B	B	B	B	B	B	61
B	B	B	B	B	B	B	B	B	B	B	B	B	59
B	B	B	B			B			B	B	B	B	57
B	B	B				B				B	B	B	55
B	B	B				B				B	B	B	53
	B	B				B				B	B		51
		B				B				B			49
			B			B			B				47
						B							45
						B							43
						B							41
			B	B	B	B	B	B	B				39
		B	B	B	B	B	B	B	B	B			37
	B	B	B	B	B	B	B	B	B	B	B		35
B	B	B	B	B	B	B	B	B	B	B	B	B	33
B	B	B				B				B	B	B	31
B	B					B					B	B	29
B	B					B					B	B	27
B	B					B					B	B	25
B	B					B					B	B	23
	B					B					B		21
		B				B				B			19
			B			B			B				17
						B							15
						B							13
						B							11
				B		B		B					9
					B	B	B						7
				B	B	B	B	B					5
					B	B	B						3
				B		B		B					1

CHART 41

'Show Your House Colours' Quidditch Socks

Designed by **SPILLYJANE**

SKILL LEVEL ⚡⚡⚡

The Quidditch Cup is an annual inter-house series of Quidditch matches played at Hogwarts for house points and house pride. Because of construction costs and special effects needs, the Quidditch pitch in *Harry Potter and the Philosopher's Stone* was one of the first Harry Potter sets created almost entirely in CGI. The final design highlights the competition's focus on the houses, showing a ring of stands with soaring towers draped in Slytherin, Gryffindor, Hufflepuff and Ravenclaw colours.

Inspired by the house-themed checkerboard pattern of the Quidditch pitch towers, these socks can be knit in the house colours of your choice. The top-down socks have an afterthought heel, designed to interrupt the colourful pattern as little as possible. The heel is worked at the end after completing the toe. Knit a matching pair, or mix and match to support your favourite houses.

SIZE
One size

FINISHED MEASUREMENTS
Foot Circumference: 19 cm / 7½ in.
Leg Length: 23.5 cm / 9¼ in.

YARN
3 ply weight (super fine #1) yarn, shown in Cascade Yarns *Heritage* (75% superwash merino wool, 25% nylon; 400 m / 437 yd. per 100 g / 3½ oz. hank), colour A, 1 hank; colour B, 1 hank

COLOURWAYS
Slytherin: #5612 Moss (A) and #5660 Grey (B)
Gryffindor: #5607 Red (A) and #5723 Gold Fusion (B)
Ravenclaw: #5636 Sapphire (A) and #5660 Grey (B)
Hufflepuff: #5644 Lemon (A) and #5672 Real Black (B)

NEEDLES
- 2.75 mm / US 2 set of 5 double-pointed needles or size needed to obtain correct tension

NOTIONS
- Stitch marker
- Waste yarn
- Tapestry needle

TENSION
34 sts and 34 rnds = 10 cm / 4 in. in chart patt
Be sure to check your tension.

Continued on page 96

NOTES

- These socks are worked in the round from the top down. The pattern uses an afterthought heel to avoid interrupting the chart pattern. The heel will be worked after the main part of the sock is complete.

STITCH PATTERNS

Stocking Stitch (any number of sts)
Worked in the round, knit every rnd.
K2, P2 Twisted Rib (multiple of 4 sts)
All rnds: *K2 tbl, p2; rep from * around.

SOCKS

LEG

With colour A, CO 64 sts. Divide sts evenly over 4 dpn, with 16 sts on each needle. Pm and join to work in the rnd, being careful not to twist sts.

Work in K2, P2 Rib for 10 rnds.

Knit 2 rnds.

Work Rows 1–8 of Sock Chart (chart 42) 7 times. Piece should measure approx 19 cm / 7½ in. from beg.

HEEL PLACEMENT

Next rnd: K32 sts with waste yarn for heel, then return to beg of rnd, work next rnd of chart.

FOOT

Cont in established patt until foot is approx 5 cm / 2 in. short of desired length, ending with Rnd 4 or 8 of chart if possible. Cut colour B.

TOE

With colour A, knit 2 rnds.

Dec rnd: Needle 1, k1, ssk, knit to end of dpn; Needle 2, knit to last 3 sts on dpn, k2tog, k1; Needle 3, k1, ssk, knit to end of dpn; Needle 4, knit to last 3 sts on dpn, k2tog, k1 – 4 sts dec'd.

Knit 1 rnd even.

Rep last 2 rnds 10 more times – 20 sts rem.

Sl sts from Needle 2 to Needle 1 and sts from Needle 4 to Needle 3. Using Kitchener st, graft toe closed.

HEEL

Holding sock with foot towards you, carefully remove waste yarn from heel and place resulting 64 sts on dpn. Distribute sts evenly over 4 dpn, with 16 sts on each needle, and beg rnds at side of heel (beg/end of rnds for leg). Pm and join to work in the rnd.

Next rnd: With colour B and Needle 1, pick up and knit 1 st in gap between dpn, k16; with Needle 2, k16, pick up and knit 1 st in gap between dpn; with Needle 3, pick up and knit 1 st in gap between dpn, k16; with Needle 4, knit to end of rnd, then pick and knit 1 st in gap between dpn – 68 sts.

Knit 1 rnd even.

Dec rnd: Needle 1, k1, ssk, knit to end of dpn; Needle 2, knit to last 3 sts on dpn, k2tog, k1; Needle 3, k1, ssk, knit to end of dpn; Needle 4, knit to last 3 sts on dpn, k2tog, k1 – 4 sts dec'd.

Knit 1 rnd even.

Rep Dec rnd on next rnd, every other rnd 5 more times, then every rnd twice – 32 sts rem.

Sl sts from Needle 2 to Needle 1 and sts from Needle 4 to Needle 3. Using Kitchener st, graft heel closed.

FINISHING

Weave in ends. Block to measurements.

SOCK CHART

KEY

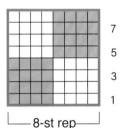

☐ A

▨ B

☐ repeat

7
5
3
1

└─ 8-st rep ─┘

CHART 42

OWL POST PULLOVER

Designed by **JOAN FORGIONE**

SKILL LEVEL ⚡⚡⚡

In the Harry Potter films, wizards use owls to send and receive letters, packages, and other mail. At Hogwarts, the post owls live in the Owlery – a set first seen in *Harry Potter and the Goblet of Fire*. While a live set was used for filming, some shots employed a highly detailed miniature replica that even included miniature owls of multiple sizes and species.

An ode to Owl Post, this pullover begins with the cable panel knit flat then joined to form a circle. Stitches are picked up along the top edge and worked in the round up to the neck to form the yoke. The bottom-edge stitches are picked up and worked in the round for the body and sleeves down to the hem, with a cabled owl motif surprise on one sleeve. The inner body hem is worked in a contrasting colour, with duplicate stitch (see p. 202) in the main colour for the secret message, 'By Owl Post'.

SIZES

XS (S, M, L, XL, 2XL, 3XL, 4XL, 5XL, 6XL)
Shown in size S.
Instructions are written for the smallest
    size, with larger sizes given in
    parentheses; when only one number
    is given, it applies to all sizes.

FINISHED MEASUREMENTS

Bust: 76 (86.5, 97, 107.5, 118, 128.5, 139,
    149, 162.5, 173.5) cm / 30 (34, 38¼, 42¼,
    46½, 50½, 54¾, 58¾, 64, 68¼) in.
Front Length: 53.5 (54.5, 56, 58.5, 61, 63.5,
    65, 67.5, 68.5, 70) cm / 21 (21½, 22, 23,
    24, 25, 25½, 26½, 27, 27½) in.

YARN

Aran weight (medium #4) yarn, shown
    in Rowan *Felted Tweed Aran*
    (50% lightly felted wool, 25% alpaca,
    25% viscose; 87 m / 95 yd. per
    50 g / 1¾ oz. ball)
Main Colour (MC): #777 Clay, 9 (10, 11,
    13, 14, 16, 17, 18, 19, 21) balls
Contrast Colour (CC): #719 Granite,
    1 ball

NEEDLES

5 mm / US 8 circular needles,
    40 cm / 16 in., 60 cm / 24 in. and
    80 cm / 32 in. long, and set of double-
    pointed needles or size needed to
    obtain correct tension.

Continued on page 100

NOTIONS

- Stitch markers
- Cable needle
- Waste yarn
- Tapestry needle

TENSIONS

15½ sts and 24 rnds = 10 cm / 4 in. in St st

30-st Yoke Cable panel = approx

10 cm / 4 in. wide and 27½ rows =

10 cm / 4 in.

Be sure to check your tensions.

NOTES

- The pullover begins with the cable panel worked flat, then joined to form a circle. Stitches are picked up along one edge and worked up to the neck for the upper yoke. Then stitches are picked up along the other edge to work the body and sleeves.
- The inner body hem is worked in a contrasting colour, then the message is added with the main colour using duplicate stitch embroidery.

SPECIAL ABBREVIATIONS

2/1 LPC (2 over 1 left purl cross):
Sl 2 sts to cn and hold at front, p1, k2 from cn.

2/1 RPC (2 over 1 right purl cross):
Sl 1 st to cn and hold at back, k2, p1 from cn.

2/2 LC (2 over 2 left cross): Sl 2 sts to cn and hold at front, k2, k2 from cn.

2/2 RC (2 over 2 right cross): Sl 2 sts to cn and hold at back, k2, k2 from cn.

PATTERN STICHES

Stocking Stitch (any number of sts)
Worked in the rnd, knit every rnd.

Yoke Cable Panel (30 sts)

Row 1 (RS): K1, p5, k2, 2/1 LPC, p2, 2/2 RC, p2, 2/1 RPC, k2, p5, k1.

Row 2 (WS): K6, p2, k1, p2, k2, p4, k2, p2, k1, p2, k6.

Row 3: K1, p5, k2, p1, [2/1 LPC, 2/1 RPC] twice, p1, k2, p5, k1.

Row 4: K6, p2, [k2, p4] twice, k2, p2, k6.

Row 5: K1, p5, k2, [p2, 2/2 LC] twice, p2, k2, p5, k1.

Row 6: Rep Row 4.

Row 7: K1, p5, k2, p1, [2/1 RPC, 2/1 LPC] twice, p1, k2, p5, k1.

Row 8: Rep Row 2.

Row 9: K1, p5, k2, 2/1 RPC, p2, 2/2 RC, p2, 2/1 LPC, k2, p5, k1.

Row 10: K6, [p4, k3] twice, p4, k6.

Row 11: K1, p5, 2/2 RC, p2, 2/1 RPC, 2/1 LPC, p2, 2/2 LC, p5, k1.

Row 12: K6, p4, [k2, p2] twice, k2, p4, k6.

Row 13: K1, p4, 2/1 RPC, 2/1 LPC, 2/1 RPC, p2, 2/1 LPC, 2/1 RPC, 2/1 LPC, p4, k1.

Row 14: K5, p2, k2, p4, k4, p4, k2, p2, k5.

Row 15: K1, p3, 2/1 RPC, p2, 2/2 RC, p4, 2/2 LC, p2, 2/1 LPC, p3, k1.

Row 16: K4, p2, k3, p4, k4, p4, k3, p2, k4.

Row 17: K1, p3, k2, p3, k4, p4, k4, p3, k2, p3, k1.

Row 18: Rep Row 16.

Row 19: K1, p3, 2/1 LPC, p2, 2/2 RC, p4, 2/2 LC, p2, 2/1 RPC, p3, k1.

Row 20: Rep Row 14.

Row 21: K1, p4, 2/1 LPC, 2/1 RPC, 2/1 LPC, p2, 2/1 RPC, 2/1 LPC, 2/1 RPC, p4, k1.

Row 22: Rep Row 12.

Row 23: K1, p5, 2/2 LC, p2, 2/1 LPC, 2/1 RPC, p2, 2/2 RC, p5, k1.

Row 24: Rep Row 10.

Rep Rows 1–24 for patt.

Owl Motif (14 sts)

Rnd 1: P3, 2/2 LC, 2/2 RC, p3.

Rnds 2–4: P3, k8, p3.

Rnd 5: Rep Rnd 1.

Rnds 6–12: Rep Rnd 2.

Rnd 13: Rep Rnd 1.

Rnds 14–15: Rep Rnd 2.

Rnds 16 and 18: P14.

Rnd 17: Rep Rnd 2.

I-Cord Edging

Using the Backward Loop method (see p. 202), CO 3 sts. With dpn, *k2, ssk (next st and one st from edge), slide the 3 sts just worked back to cir needle; rep from * until 3 sts rem, ssk – 2 sts rem. Cut yarn and pull through rem 2 sts. Sew end to CO end.

YOKE

CABLE PANEL

With shortest cir needle and MC, CO 30 sts.

Work Rows 1–24 of Yoke Cable Panel (chart 44) 11 (12, 13, 15, 16, 18, 20, 21, 23, 24) times, then work Rows 1–23 once more.

Cast off all sts in patt. Sew cast-on and cast-off edges tog, forming a circle.

UPPER YOKE

With longest cir needle and MC, beg at seam, pick up and knit 160 (172, 196, 212, 228, 252, 280, 300, 320, 336) sts evenly along one edge of cable panel. Pm and join to work in the rnd.
Change to shorter cir needle as number of sts dec.

Knit 2 (4, 6, 8, 10, 12, 14, 16, 18, 20) rnds even.

Dec rnd: *K2, k2tog; rep from * to end of rnd – 120 (129, 147, 159, 171, 189, 210, 225, 240, 252) sts rem.

Knit 11 (12, 13, 14, 15, 16, 17, 18, 19, 20) rnds even.

Dec rnd: *K1, k2tog; rep from * to end of rnd – 80 (86, 98, 106, 114, 126, 140, 150, 160, 168) sts rem.

Work 4 rnds even.

SHAPE BACK NECK

Short Row 1 (RS): K30 (32, 37, 40, 43, 47, 52, 56, 60, 63), w&t.

Short Row 2 (WS): P60 (64, 74, 80, 86, 94, 104, 112, 120, 126), w&t.

Short Row 3: Knit to 3 sts before last wrapped st, w&t.

Short Row 4: Purl to 3 sts before last wrapped st, w&t.

Rep Short Rows 3 and 4 once more.

Next short row: Knit to marker.

Knit 1 rnd, picking up wraps and knitting them together with the wrapped sts.

SIZE XS ONLY

Dec rnd: K2, *k2tog, k11; rep from * to end of rnd – 74 sts rem.

SIZE S ONLY

Dec rnd: K1, *k6, k2tog, k7, k2tog; rep from * to end of rnd – 76 sts rem.

SIZE M ONLY

Dec rnd: [K2, k2tog] twice, *k3, k2tog; rep from * to end of rnd – 78 sts rem.

SIZE L ONLY

Dec rnd: [K2, k2tog] 4 times, *k3, k2tog, k2, k2tog; rep from * to end of rnd – 82 sts rem.

SIZE XL ONLY

Dec rnd: *[K2, k2tog] 4 times, k1, k2tog; rep from * to end of rnd – 84 sts rem.

SIZE 2XL ONLY

Dec rnd: K1, *[k1, k2tog] 7 times, k2, k2tog; rep from * to end of rnd – 86 sts rem.

SIZE 3XL ONLY

Dec rnd: *[K1, k2tog] 4 times, k2tog; rep from * to end of rnd – 90 sts rem.

SIZE 4XL ONLY

Dec rnd: K2, [k2tog] twice, *[k1, k2tog] twice, k2tog; rep from * to end of rnd – 94 sts rem.

SIZE 5XL ONLY

Dec rnd: *K1, [k2tog] twice; rep from * to end of rnd – 96 sts rem.

SIZE 6XL ONLY

Dec rnd: K2tog, *[k2tog] twice, [k1, k2tog] twice; rep from * to last 6 sts, [k2tog] 3 times – 100 sts rem.

ALL SIZES

Knit 1 rnd even.
Work I-cord edging along neck edge.

LOWER BODY

With longest cir needle, MC and RS facing, beg at seam, pick up and knit 160 (172, 196, 212, 228, 252, 280, 300, 320, 336) sts evenly along rem edge of cable panel. Pm and join to work in the rnd.

Knit 3 rnds even.

DIVIDE BODY AND SLEEVES

Next rnd: K24 (27, 31, 34, 37, 40, 44, 47, 51, 54), using Backward Loop method CO 10 (12, 12, 14, 16, 18, 18, 20, 22, 24) sts for underarm, place next 32 (32, 36, 38, 40, 46, 52, 56, 58, 60) sts on waste yarn for left sleeve, k48 (54, 62, 68, 74, 80, 88, 94, 102, 108) sts for front, CO 10 (12, 12, 14, 16, 18, 18, 20, 22, 24) sts for underarm, place next 32 (32, 36, 38, 40, 46, 52, 56, 58, 60) sts on waste yarn for right sleeve, then k24 (27, 31, 34, 37, 40, 44, 47, 51, 54) – 116 (132, 148, 164, 180, 196, 212, 228, 248, 264) sts rem.

BODY

Work even in St st until piece measures 30.5 (30.5, 30.5, 32, 33, 34.5, 34.5, 35.5, 35.5, 35.5) cm / 12 (12, 12, 12½, 13, 13½, 13½, 14, 14, 14) in. from underarm.

Purl 1 rnd for fold line.

Change to CC. Work even in St st for 5 cm / 2 in. Place sts on waste yarn.

RIGHT SLEEVE

With RS facing, beg at centre of underarm, pick up and knit 5 (6, 6, 7, 8, 9, 9, 10, 11, 12) sts along CO edge, pm, knit 32 (32, 36, 38, 40, 46, 52, 56, 58, 60) held sleeve sts, then pick up and knit 5 (6, 6, 7, 8, 9, 9, 10, 11, 12) sts along rem CO edge – 42 (44, 48, 52, 56, 64, 70, 76, 80, 84) sts. Pm and join to work in the rnd.

VERNON DURSLEY: 'FINE DAY, SUNDAY.
IN MY OPINION, BEST DAY OF THE WEEK.
WHY IS THAT, DUDLEY?'

HARRY POTTER: 'BECAUSE THERE'S
NO POST ON SUNDAYS?'

VERNON DURSLEY: 'RIGHT YOU ARE, HARRY!
NO POST ON SUNDAY, HA! NO BLASTED
LETTERS TODAY, NO SIR! NOT ONE SINGLE
BLOODY LETTER. NOT ONE!'

Harry Potter and the Philosopher's Stone

ABOVE: Harry tries to grab one of his letters from the flood of mail arriving at number four, Privet Drive, in *Harry Potter and the Philosopher's Stone*.

Knit 3 rnds even.
Dec rnd: K2, k2tog, knit to last 4 sts, ssk, k2 – 2 sts dec'd.
Rep Dec rnd every 20 (20, 14, 12, 10, 7, 6, 5, 5, 5) rnds 4 (4, 6, 8, 9, 13, 16, 18, 18, 19) times – 32 (34, 34, 34, 36, 36, 36, 38, 42, 44) sts rem.
Cont even until sleeve measures 42 (43, 43, 43, 44.5, 44.5, 44.5, 45.5, 45.5, 45.5) cm / 16½ (17, 17, 17, 17½, 17½, 17½, 18, 18, 18) in. from underarm.
Work I-cord edging along cuff edge.

LEFT SLEEVE

Work same as right sleeve until sleeve measures 34.5 (35.5, 35.5, 35.5, 37, 37, 37, 38, 38, 38) cm / 13½ (14, 14, 14, 14½, 14½, 14½, 15, 15, 15) in. from underarm. Pm each side of centre 14 sts.
Cont rem shaping as established, work Owl Cable Chart (chart 43) between marked 14 sts.
Complete left sleeve same as for right sleeve.

FINISHING

Mark centre 47 sts of front hem.
With MC, work Hem Message Chart (chart 45) using duplicate stitch (see p. 202). Turn hem to inside along fold line. With MC, sew sts to WS, working into purl bumps on inside of body.
Weave in ends. Block to finished measurements.

CHARTS

KEY

☐	k on RS, p on WS	⧄ 2/1 LPC
⊡	p on RS, k on WS	⧄ 2/1 RPC
⧅	2/2 LC	☐ pattern repeat
⧄	2/2 RC	☐ MC
		▩ CC

YOKE

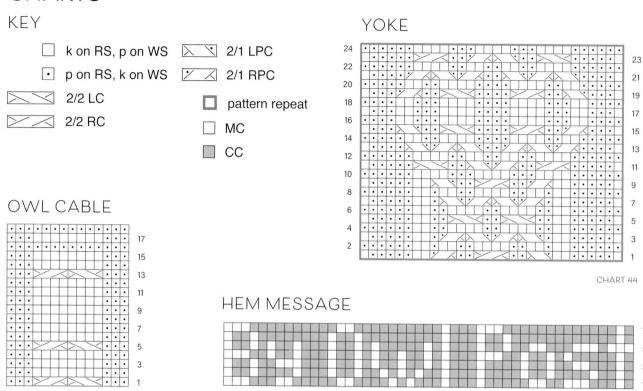

CHART 44

OWL CABLE

CHART 43

HEM MESSAGE

CHART 45

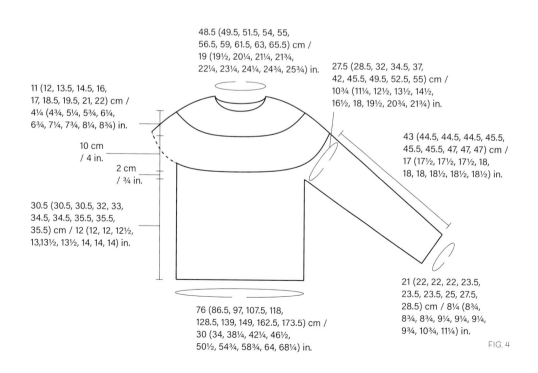

11 (12, 13.5, 14.5, 16, 17, 18.5, 19.5, 21, 22) cm / 4¼ (4¾, 5¼, 5¾, 6¼, 6¾, 7¼, 7¾, 8¼, 8¾) in.

48.5 (49.5, 51.5, 54, 55, 56.5, 59, 61.5, 63, 65.5) cm / 19 (19½, 20¼, 21¼, 21¾, 22¼, 23¼, 24¼, 24¾, 25¾) in.

27.5 (28.5, 32, 34.5, 37, 42, 45.5, 49.5, 52.5, 55) cm / 10¾ (11¼, 12½, 13½, 14½, 16½, 18, 19½, 20¾, 21¾) in.

10 cm / 4 in.

2 cm / ¾ in.

43 (44.5, 44.5, 44.5, 45.5, 45.5, 45.5, 47, 47, 47) cm / 17 (17½, 17½, 17½, 18, 18, 18, 18½, 18½, 18½) in.

30.5 (30.5, 30.5, 32, 33, 34.5, 34.5, 35.5, 35.5, 35.5) cm / 12 (12, 12, 12½, 13,13½, 13½, 14, 14, 14) in.

76 (86.5, 97, 107.5, 118, 128.5, 139, 149, 162.5, 173.5) cm / 30 (34, 38¼, 42¼, 46½, 50½, 54¾, 58¾, 64, 68¼) in.

21 (22, 22, 22, 23.5, 23.5, 23.5, 25, 27.5, 28.5) cm / 8¼ (8¾, 8¾, 8¾, 9¼, 9¼, 9¼, 9¾, 10¾, 11¼) in.

FIG. 4

EXPECTO PATRONUM! MITTENS

Designed by **DIANNA WALLA**

SKILL LEVEL ⚡⚡⚡⚡

First seen in *Harry Potter and the Prisoner of Azkaban*, the Patronus Charm is a highly advanced piece of defensive magic used to repel Dementors. The spell – *Expecto Patronum* – conjures a Patronus, which takes a unique form for each wizard and protects the wizard from the Dementor's ill effects. Harry's Patronus takes the form of a stag – just like his father's.

The body of the mittens are knit first for this enchanting pair, starting with a provisional cast on (p. 202) at the bottom cuff edge. The mittens are then worked with separate charts for the right and left, which form the complete *Expecto Patronum* spell and Harry's stag Patronus. For the linings, lace-weight yarn is held double, creating a cosy warm inner layer, also begun with a provisional cast on. Once both pieces are completed, the cast-on edges are joined with a three-needle cast off. When the wearer's hands are together, the complete scene is on display.

FINISHED MEASUREMENTS
Hand Circumference: 20.5 cm / 8 in.
Length: 23 cm / 9 in.

YARNS
4 ply weight (super fine #1) yarn, shown in Jamieson's *Shetland Spindrift* (100% Shetland wool; 105 m / 115 yd. per 25 g / ⅞ oz. skein)
Main Colour (MC): #999 Black, 2 skeins
Contrast Colour 1 (CC1): #135 Surf, 1 skein
Lace weight (lace #0) yarn, shown in Shibui Knits *Silk Cloud* (60% kid mohair, 40% silk; 302 m / 330 yd. per 25 g / ⅞ oz. hank)
Contrast Colour 2 (CC2): Bone, 1 hank

NEEDLES
- 2.25 mm / US 1 set of 5 double-pointed needles or size needed to obtain correct tension

NOTIONS
- Crochet hook for provisional cast on
- Waste yarn
- Stitch markers
- Stitch holders or waste yarn
- Spare set of 2.25 mm / US 1 double-pointed needles
- Tapestry needle

Continued on page 108

TENSIONS

36 sts and 41 rnds = 10 cm / 4 in.

in chart patt with 3 ply weight yarn

36 sts and 47 rnds = 10 cm / 4 in. in St

st with lace weight yarn held double

Be sure to check your tensions.

NOTES

- The outer mitten is worked using stranded colourwork, holding one strand of each colour. The lining is worked with two strands of the lace weight yarn held together.
- When working the outer mitten, to reduce the number of ends to weave in, do not cut the unused colour when working with only one colour but carry it loosely up along the wrong side until needed again.
- The mittens and liners are worked separately, each beginning with a provisional cast on. Once the knitting is complete, both sets of cast-on stitches are placed back on the needles, then the liners are joined to the mittens using three-needle cast off.

STITCH PATTERN

Stocking Stitch (any number of sts)
Worked in the round, knit every rnd.

RIGHT MITTEN

With crochet hook and waste yarn, ch 60 over cir needle so back bump of each ch is worked around needle. Do not join.

With dpn and CC1, k60. Divide sts evenly over 4 dpn with 15 sts on each needle. Pm and join to work in the rnd, being careful not to twist sts.

Knit 4 rnds.

Join MC. Work Rnds 1–6 of Right Cuff Chart (chart 48).

Knit 5 rnds with CC1 only.

Knit 1 rnd with MC.

Knit 1 rnd with CC1.

Knit 1 rnd with MC.

Inc rnd: *K30, M1L; rep from * once more – 62 sts.

Work Rnds 1–24 of Right Hand Chart (chart 51) – 72 sts.

Next rnd: Work next rnd in established patt over first 36 sts, place next 13 sts on waste yarn or stitch holder, CO 13 sts in patt using Backward Loop method, then work to end of rnd.

Cont in established patt through Rnd 75 of chart – 8 sts rem.

Cut yarns and thread tails through rem sts. Pull tight to close hole and fasten securely on WS.

THUMB

Place 13 held thumb sts on dpn.

Rnd 1: Working in patt from Row 1 of Right Thumb Chart (chart 46), pick up and knit 1 in gap between held sts and CO edge above thumb opening, 13 sts along CO edge of opening,

1 st in gap between CO edge and held sts, then work 13 thumb sts – 28 sts. Divide sts evenly over 4 dpn, with 7 sts on each needle. Pm and join to work in the rnd.

Work Rnds 2–27 of chart as established – 8 sts rem.

Cut yarns and thread tails through rem sts. Pull tight to close hole and fasten securely on WS.

RIGHT MITTEN LINER

With crochet hook and waste yarn, ch 60 over cir needle same as for right mitten. Do not join.

With dpn and 2 strands of CC2 held tog, k60. Divide sts evenly over 4 dpn, with 15 sts on each needle. Pm and join to work in the rnd, being careful not to twist sts.

Knit 24 rnds.

Setup rnd: K20, pm for thumb gusset, k1, pm for thumb gusset, knit to end of rnd.

Inc rnd: Knit to marker, sm, M1L, knit to marker, M1R, sm, knit to end – 2 sts inc'd.

Rep Inc rnd every 3 rnds once, every 4 rnds twice, then every 5 rnds once – 70 sts.

Knit 4 rnds even.

Next rnd: Knit to marker, remove gusset marker, place next 11 sts on waste yarn or stitch holder for thumb, remove gusset marker, CO 11 sts using Backward Loop method (see p. 202), then knit to end of rnd.

'A Patronus is a kind of positive force. For the wizard who can conjure one, it works something like a shield, with the Dementor feeding on it rather than him.'

Professor Lupin, *Harry Potter and the Prisoner of Azkaban*

BEHIND THE MAGIC

Aside from Harry's stag, other Patronuses developed for the film include a hare, chimpanzee, otter and dog. Many of these can be seen in one of the Dumbledore's Army scenes in *Harry Potter and the Order of the Phoenix*.

ABOVE: Members of Dumbledore's Army cast their Patronuses in concept art by Adam Brockbank for *Harry Potter and the Order of the Phoenix*.

Cont even until liner measures approx 20.5 cm / 8 in. from CO edge.
Setup rnd: K35, pm, k35.

SHAPE TOP

Dec rnd: *K1, ssk, knit to 3 sts before marker, k2tog, k1; rep from * once more – 4 sts dec'd.
Rep Dec rnd every rnd 14 more times – 10 sts rem.
Dec rnd: *K1, sk2p, k1; rep from * once more – 6 sts rem.
Cut yarn and thread tail through rem sts. Pull tight to close hole and fasten securely on WS.

RIGHT MITTEN LINER THUMB

Place 11 held thumb sts on dpn.
Rnd 1: With 2 strands of CC2 held tog, pick up and knit 1 st in gap between held sts and CO edge above thumb opening, 11 sts along CO edge of opening, 1 st in gap between CO edge and held sts, then knit 11 thumb sts – 24 sts. Divide sts evenly over 4 dpn, with 6 sts on each needle. Pm and join to work in the rnd.
Cont in St st until thumb is approx 1.3 cm / ½ in. short of desired length.
Next rnd: K12, pm, k12.
Dec rnd: *K1, ssk, knit to 3 sts before marker, k2tog, k1; rep from * once more – 4 sts dec'd.
Rep Dec rnd every rnd 3 more times – 8 sts rem.
Cut yarns and thread tail through rem sts. Pull tight to close hole, and fasten securely on WS.

LEFT MITTEN

CO and knit 4 rnds same as for right mitten.
Join MC. Work Rnds 1–6 of Left Cuff Chart (chart 49).
Knit 5 rnds with CC1 only.
Knit 1 rnd with MC.
Knit 1 rnd with CC1.
Knit 1 rnd with MC.
Inc rnd: *K30, M1L; rep from * once more – 62 sts.
Work Rnds 1–24 of Left Hand Chart (chart 50) – 72 sts.
Next rnd: Work next rnd in patt over first 20 sts, place next 13 sts on waste yarn or stitch holder, CO 13 sts in patt using Backward Loop method, then work to end of rnd.
Cont in established patt through Rnd 75 of chart – 8 sts rem.
Cut yarns and thread tails through rem sts. Pull tight to close hole, and fasten securely on WS.

THUMB

Place 13 held thumb sts on dpn.
Rnd 1: Working in patt from Row 1 of Left Thumb Chart (chart 47), pick up and knit 1 st in gap between held sts and CO edge above thumb opening, 13 sts along CO edge of opening, 1 st in gap between CO edge and held sts, then work 13 thumb sts – 28 sts. Divide sts evenly over 4 dpn, with 7 sts on each needle. Pm and join to work in the rnd.
Work Rnds 2–27 of chart as established – 8 sts rem.
Cut yarns and thread tails through rem sts. Pull tight to close hole and fasten securely on WS.

LEFT MITTEN LINER

CO and knit 24 rnds same as for right mitten liner.

Setup rnd: K39, pm, k1, pm, knit to end of rnd.

Inc rnd: Knit to marker, sm, M1L, knit to marker, M1R, sm, knit to end – 2 sts inc'd.

Complete left mitten liner same as for right mitten liner.

FINISHING

Weave in ends.

JOINING MITTENS AND LINERS

Carefully remove provisional CO from mitten and liner for one hand, and place resulting 60 sts for each piece on 2 sets of dpn. Divide sts for each piece evenly over 4 dpn, with 15 sts on each needle.

Turn liner with WS facing, then slip liner inside mitten, making sure liner thumb is inside mitten thumb.

Holding both sets of dpn tog, and with CC1, join sts using Three-Needle Cast Off (see p. 204).

Rep with rem mitten and liner.

Block to measurements.

CHARTS

KEY

- ■ MC
- ■ C1
- ■ no stitch
- □ knit
- ◪ k2tog
- ◪ ssk
- ◪ sk2p
- ◪ M1L
- ◪ M1R

RIGHT THUMB

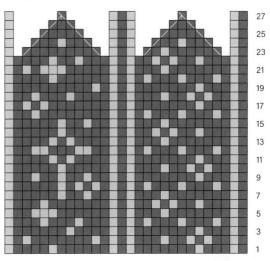

CHART 46

LEFT THUMB

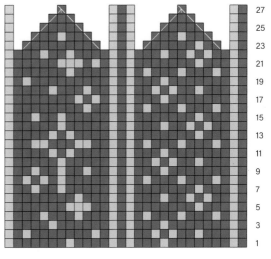

CHART 47

RIGHT CUFF

CHART 48

LEFT CUFF

CHART 49

LEFT HAND

75
73
71
69
67
65
63
61
59
57
55
53
51
49
47
45
43
41
39
37
35
33
31
29
27
25
23
21
19
17
15
13
11
9
7
5
3
1

CHART 50

RIGHT HAND

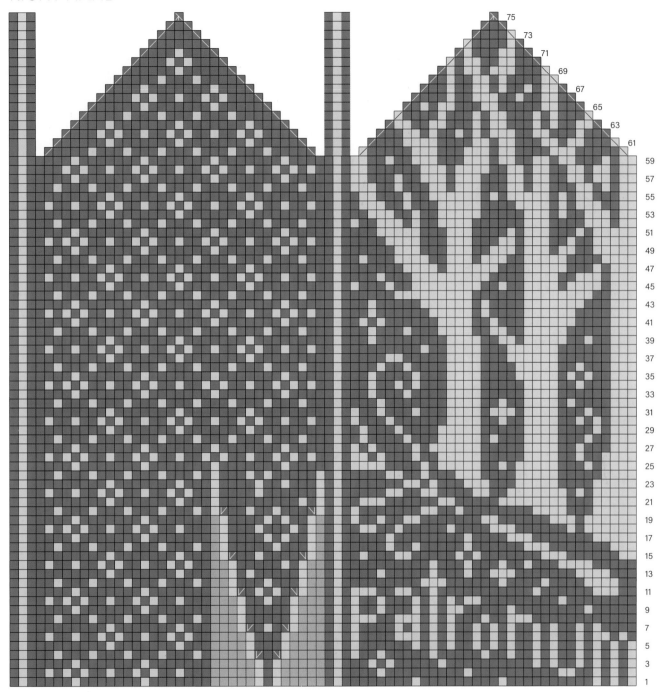

75
73
71
69
67
65
63
61
59
57
55
53
51
49
47
45
43
41
39
37
35
33
31
29
27
25
23
21
19
17
15
13
11
9
7
5
3
1

CHART 51

BUCKBEAK PULLOVER

Designed by **DANA WILLIAMS-JOHNSON**

SKILL LEVEL ⚡⚡⚡⚡

Half horse, half eagle, Hippogriffs are proud animals who demand respect. Film designers took great care in bringing this fan-favourite, mythology-inspired creature to life on-screen. They consulted veterinarians and physiologists, examining the mechanics of how birds fly and how horses gallop to make sure the Hippogriff's movements were as lifelike as possible. It was important to get the body proportions correct so that the animal could feasibly carry multiple humans on its back, as Buckbeak does in *Harry Potter and the Prisoner of Azkaban*. Buckbeak's wingspan is 8.5 metres (28 feet)!

Worked from the top down with minimal finishing, beginning with a ribbed collar, German short rows are used to gently raise up the back of this pullover inspired by Hagrid's beloved Hippogriff Buckbeak. A band of stranded colourwork feathers emphasises the collarbone area, while easy increases build out the yoke and body. Once the sleeves are separated, the feather motif is continued on. Waist and sleeve shaping create a flattering flared silhouette reminiscent of the creature's stunning wingspan.

SIZES

XS (S, M, L, XL, 2XL, 3XL, 4XL, 5XL, 6XL)
Shown in size S.

Instructions are written for the smallest size, with larger sizes given in parentheses; when only one number is given, it applies to all sizes.

FINISHED MEASUREMENTS

Bust: 79.5 (88.5, 97, 106, 115, 124, 141.5, 150.5, 158.5, 167.5) cm / 31¼ (34¾, 38¼, 41¾, 45¼, 48¾, 55¾, 59¼, 62½, 66) in.

Front Length: 58.5 (61, 63.5, 66, 68.5, 71, 72.5, 73.5, 75, 76) cm / 23 (24, 25, 26, 27, 28, 28½, 29, 29½, 30) in., including 4 cm / 1½ in. tall collar

YARN

DK weight (light #3) yarn, shown in Miss Babs *Yowza* (100% superwash merino wool; 512 m / 560 yd. per 227 g / 8 oz. hank)

Colour A: Lycan (dark grey), 1 (1, 1, 2, 2, 2, 2, 2, 3, 3) hank(s)

Colour B: Fleur de Sel (medium grey), 1 (1, 1, 1, 1, 1, 1, 2, 2, 2) hank(s)

Colour C: White Peppercorn (light grey), 1 (1, 1, 2, 2, 2, 2, 2, 3, 3) hank(s)

NEEDLES

- 4.5 mm / US 7, 40 cm / 16 in., and 80 cm / 32 in. or 100 cm / 40 in. long circular needle, and set of 4 or 5 double-pointed needles or size needed to obtain correct tension
- 4 mm / US 6, 40 cm / 16 in., 60 cm / 24 in., 80 cm / 32 in. or 100 cm / 40 in. long circular needle or 4 or 5 double-pointed needles

Continued on page 116

NOTIONS

- Stitch markers
- Stitch holders or scrap yarn
- Tapestry needle

TENSIONS

19½ sts and 26 rnds = 10 cm / 4 in. in St st
    with smaller needles
23 sts and 26 rnds = 10 cm / 4 in. in
    chart patt with larger needles
Be sure to check your tensions.

NOTES

- This pullover is worked from the
top down with a circular yoke, then
divided to work the body and sleeves
separately. German short rows (see
p. 204) are used to shape the back
neck and the sleeves.
- A colour-stranded pattern is added
below the yoke. If necessary, use a
needle one size larger for the colour-
stranded parts of the pullover.

YOKE

With shortest cir needle or dpn, and
colour A, CO 70 (74, 78, 82, 86, 90,
94, 98, 102, 106) sts. Pm for beg of
rnd and join to work in rnds, being
careful not to twist sts.
Work in K1, P1 Rib for 4 cm / 1½ in.
Knit 1 rnd.

SHAPE BACK NECK

Short Row 1 (RS): K20 (21, 22, 23, 24, 25,
26, 27, 28, 29), turn.
Short Row 2 (WS): DS, purl to 20
(21, 22, 23, 24, 25, 26, 27, 28, 29) sts
past beg-of-rnd marker, then turn.
Short Row 3: DS, knit to 4 sts before
DS, turn.
Short Row 4: DS, purl to 4 sts before
DS, turn.
Rep Short Rows 3 and 4 twice more.
Knit 1 rnd, making sure to knit both
legs of each DS tog as you come
to them.

SHAPE YOKE

*Change to smaller longer cir needle as
number of sts increases.*
Inc rnd 1: K0 (1, 0, 0, 1, 0, 1, 1, 0, 1), M1,
*k3 (4, 3, 3, 3, 3, 3, 3, 3, 3), M1; rep from
* to last 1 (1, 0, 1, 1, 0, 0, 0, 1, 0) st, k1
(1, 0, 1, 1, 0, 0, 1, 0, 0) – 94 (93, 105,
110, 115, 121, 126, 131, 137, 141) sts.
Knit 1 rnd even.
Inc rnd 2: Knit and inc 6 (7, 15, 10, 25,
19, 34, 29, 43, 39) sts evenly spaced –
100 (100, 120, 120, 140, 140, 160, 160,
180, 180) sts.
Knit 1 rnd even.
Change to shorter larger cir needle.
    Work Rows 1–9 of Body Chart
    (chart 52).
Change to smaller cir needle. Knit 1 rnd.

SIZES XS (S) ONLY

Inc rnd 3: *K2, M1; rep from * to end
of rnd – 150 sts.
Work even until piece measures
14 cm / 5½ in. from CO edge at
centre of front.

Inc rnd 4: *K3, M1; rep from * to end
of rnd – 200 sts.
Work even until piece measures
19 cm / 7½ in. from CO edge at
centre of front.
Inc rnd 5: *K4, M1; rep from * to end
of rnd – 250 sts.
Work even until piece measures
20.5 cm / 8½ in. from CO edge at
centre of front.
Inc rnd 6: *K5, M1; rep from * to end
of rnd – 300 sts.

SIZE S ONLY

Work even until piece measures 23 cm /
9 in. from CO edge at centre of front.
Inc rnd 7: *K15, M1; rep from * to end
of rnd – 320 sts.

SIZES M (L) ONLY

Inc rnd 3: *K2, M1, k3, M1; rep from
* to end of rnd – 168 sts.
Work even until piece measures
14 cm / 5½ in. from CO edge at
centre of front.
Inc rnd 4: *K3, M1, k4, M1; rep from
* to end of rnd – 216 sts.
Work even until piece measures
19 cm / 7½ in. from CO edge at
centre of front.
Inc rnd 5: *K4, M1, k5, M1; rep from
* to end of rnd – 264 sts.
Work even until piece measures 20.5
(22) cm / 8½ (8¾) in. from CO edge
at centre of front.
Inc rnd 6: *K5, M1, k6, M1; rep from
* to end of rnd – 312 sts.
Work even until piece measures 24 (25)
cm / 9½ (9¾) in. from CO edge at
centre of front.
Inc rnd 7: *K5 (6), M1, k6 (7), M1; rep
from * to last 4 (0) sts, k4 (0) –
340 (360) sts.

SIZES 1XL (2XL) ONLY

Inc rnd 3: *K3, M1; rep from * to last
2 sts, k2 – 186 sts.
Work even until piece measures
14 cm / 5½ in. from CO edge at
centre of front.

Behind the Magic

A large body of developmental artwork was created for the Hippogriff. Those concept sketches, mostly created mostly by veteran Harry Potter artist Dermot Power, were turned into 3D computer models, which were used to develop and test Buckbeak's movements and personality.

TOP: Concept art of Buckbeak by Dermot Power for *Harry Potter and the Prisoner of Azkaban*. ABOVE: Harry meets Buckbeak in Hagrid's first Care of Magical Creatures class in *Harry Potter and the Prisoner of Azkaban*.

Inc rnd 4: *K4, M1; rep from * to last 2 sts, k2 – 232 sts.

Work even until piece measures 19 cm / 7½ in. from CO edge at centre of front.

Inc rnd 5: *K5, M1; rep from * to last 2 sts, k2 – 278 sts.

Work even until piece measures 23 cm / 9 in. from CO edge at centre of front.

Inc rnd 6: *K6, M1; rep from * to last 2 sts, k2 – 324 sts.

Work even until piece measures 25.5 cm / 10 in. from CO edge at centre of front.

Inc rnd 7: *K7, M1; rep from * to last 2 sts, k2 – 370 sts.

Work even until piece measures 27.5 cm / 10¾ in. from CO edge at centre of front.

Inc rnd 8: *K37 (12), M1; rep from * to last 0 (10) sts, k0 (10) – 380 (400) sts.

SIZES 3XL (4XL) ONLY

Inc rnd 3: K0 (2), *[k3, M1] 2 (1) time(s), [k4, M1] 1 (0) time(s); rep from * to last 0 (2) sts, k0 (2) – 208 (212) sts.

Work even until piece measures 14 cm / 5½ in. from CO edge at centre of front.

Inc rnd 4: K0 (2), *[k4, M1] 2 (1) time(s), [k5, M1] 1 (0) time(s); rep from * to last 0 (2) sts, k0 (2) – 256 (264) sts.

Work even until piece measures 20.5 cm / 8 in. from CO edge at centre of front.

Inc rnd 5: K0 (2), *[k5, M1] 2 (1) time(s), [k6, M1] 1 (0) time(s); rep from * to last 0 (2) sts, k0 (2) – 304 (316) sts.

Work even until piece measures 23 (25.5) cm / 9 (10) in. from CO edge at centre of front.

Inc rnd 6: K0 (2), *[k6, M1] 2 (1) time(s), [k7, M1] 1 (0) time(s); rep from * to last 0 (2) sts, k0 (2) – 352 (368) sts.

Work even until piece measures 26.5 (29) cm / 10½ (11½) in. from CO edge at centre of front.

Inc rnd 7: K0 (2), *[k7, M1] 2 (1) time(s), [k8, M1] 1 (0) time(s); rep from * to last 0 (2) sts, k0 (2) – 400 (420) sts.

Work even until piece measures 28.5 (31) cm / 11¼ (12¼) in. from CO edge at centre of front.

Inc rnd 8: *K8, M1, [k7, M1] 0 (1) time(s); rep from * to end of rnd – 450 (476) sts.

SIZE 5XL ONLY

Inc rnd 3: K1, M1, *k4, M1, [k3, M1] twice; rep from * to last 9 sts, [k4, M1] twice, k1 – 233 sts.

Work even until piece measures 14 cm / 5½ in. from CO edge at centre of front.

Inc rnd 4: K1, M1, *k5, M1, [k4, M1] twice; rep from * to last 11 sts, [k5, M1] twice, k1 – 286 sts.

Work even until piece measures 20.5 cm / 8 in. from CO edge at centre of front.

Inc rnd 5: K1, M1, *k6, M1, [k5, M1] twice; rep from * to last 13 sts, [k6, M1] twice, k1 – 339 sts.

Work even until piece measures 25.5 cm / 10 in. from CO edge at centre of front.

Inc rnd 6: K1, M1, *k7, M1, [k6, M1] twice; rep from * to last 15 sts, [k7, M1] twice, k1 – 392 sts.

Work even until piece measures 29 cm / 11½ in. from CO edge at centre of front.

Inc rnd 7: K1, M1, *k8, M1, [k7, M1] twice; rep from * to last 17 sts, [k8, M1] twice, k1 – 345 sts.

Work even until piece measures 31.5 cm / 12½ in. from CO edge at centre of front.

Inc rnd 8: K3, *M1, k8; rep from * to last 2 sts, k2 – 500 sts.

SIZE 6XL ONLY

Inc rnd 3: *[K3, M1] 5 times, k4, M1; rep from * to last 9 sts, [k3, M1] 3 times – 237 sts.

Work even until piece measures 14 cm / 5½ in. from CO edge at centre of front.

Inc rnd 4: *[K4, M1] 5 times, k5, M1; rep from * to last 12 sts, [k4, M1] 3 times – 294 sts.

Work even until piece measures 20.5 cm / 8 in. from CO edge at centre of front.

Inc rnd 5: *[K5, M1] 5 times, k6, M1; rep from * to last 15 sts, [k5, M1] 3 times – 351 sts.

Work even until piece measures 25.5 cm / 10 in. from CO edge at centre of front.

Inc rnd 6: *[K6, M1] 5 times, k7, M1; rep from * to last 18 sts, [k6, M1] 3 times – 408 sts.

Work even until piece measures 29 cm / 11½ in. from CO edge at centre of front.

Inc rnd 7: *[K7, M1] 5 times, k8, M1; rep from * to last 21 sts, [k7, M1] 3 times – 465 sts.

Work even until piece measures 33.5 cm / 12¾ in. from CO edge at centre of front.

Inc rnd 8: *[K8, M1] 5 times, k9, M1; rep from * to last 24 sts, [k8, M1] 3 times – 522 sts.

ALL SIZES

Work even until piece measures 24 (25.5, 26.5, 28, 29, 30.5, 34.5, 35.5) cm / 9½ (10, 10½, 11, 11½, 12, 12½, 13, 13½, 14) in. from CO edge at centre of front, and inc 0 (0, 0, 0, 0, 0, 2, 0, 0, 0) sts evenly spaced across last rnd – 300 (320, 340, 360, 380, 400, 452, 476, 500, 522) sts.

DIVIDE BODY AND SLEEVES

Next rnd: K40 (44, 48, 52, 56, 60, 69, 73, 77, 81) sts for right back, place next 70 (72, 74, 76, 78, 80, 88, 92, 96, 98) sts on waste yarn for sleeve, CO 10 (12, 14, 16, 18, 20, 22, 24, 26, 27) sts using Backward Loop method, k80 (88, 96, 104, 112, 120, 138, 146, 154, 163) sts for front, place next 70 (72, 74, 76, 78, 80, 88, 92, 96, 98) sts on waste yarn for sleeve, CO 10 (12, 14, 16, 18, 20, 22, 24, 26, 27) sts, then knit rem 40 (44, 48, 52, 56, 60, 69, 73, 77, 82) sts for left back – 180 (200, 220, 240, 260, 280, 320, 340, 360, 380) sts rem.

BODY

Knit 3 rnds even.

Change to longer larger cir needle. Join colour B.

Work Rows 1–35 of Body Chart (chart 52).

Cut colours A and B. Change to longer smaller cir needle Cont with colour C only, knit 5 rnds even.

Pm 45 (50, 55, 60, 65, 70, 80, 85, 90, 95) sts from beg and end of rnd, with 90 (100, 110, 120, 130, 140, 160, 170, 180, 190) sts between markers for front.

Inc rnd: *Knit to 1 st before marker, M1R, k1, sm, k1, M1L; rep from * once more – 4 sts inc'd.

Rep Inc rnd every 11 (13, 15, 17, 19, 21, 21, 21, 21, 21) rnds twice more – 192 (212, 232, 252, 272, 292, 332, 352, 372, 392) sts.

Cont even until piece measures 33 (34.5, 35.5, 37, 38, 39.5, 39.5, 39.5, 39.5, 39.5) cm / 13 (13½, 14, 14½, 15, 15½, 15½, 15½, 15½, 15½) in. from underarm.

Cast off using I-Cord Cast Off.

SLEEVES

With shortest smallest cir needle or dpn, colour A and RS facing, beg at centre of underarm, pick up and knit 5 (6, 7, 8, 9, 10, 11, 12, 13, 13) sts along CO edge, knit 70 (72, 74, 76, 78, 80, 88, 92, 96, 98) held sleeve sts, pick up and knit 0 (0, 0, 0, 0, 0, 0, 0, 0, 1) st in gap, then pick up and knit 5 (6, 7, 8, 9, 10, 11, 12, 13, 14) sts along rem CO edge – 80 (84, 88, 92, 96, 100, 110, 116, 122, 126) sts. Pm and join to work in rnds.

Knit 2 rnds even.

Change to shortest larger cir needle or dpn. Join colour B.

Next rnd: Working Rnd 1 of Sleeve Chart (chart 53), work 0 (2, 4, 6, 8, 10, 5, 8, 1, 6) st(s) before rep, work 20-st rep 4 (4, 4, 4, 4, 4, 5, 5, 6, 6) times, then work 0 (2, 4, 6, 8, 10, 5, 8, 1, 6) st(s) after rep.

Work Rnds 2–35 of chart as established.

Cut colours A and B. Change to shortest smaller cir needle or dpn. Cont with colour C only, knit 2 rnds even.

Inc rnd: *K1, M1L, knit to last st, M1R, k1 – 2 sts inc'd.

Rep Inc rnd every 6 rnds 3 more times – 88 (92, 96, 100, 104, 108, 118, 124, 130, 134) sts. Change to longer smaller cir needle as number of sts increases.

Cont even until sleeve measure 28 cm / 11 in. from underarm.

SHAPE CUFF

Short Row 1 (RS): Knit to 4 (4, 4, 5, 5, 5, 6, 6, 7, 7) sts before marker, turn.

Short Row 2 (WS): DS, purl to 4 (4, 4, 5, 5, 5, 6, 6, 7, 7) sts before marker, turn.

Short Row 3: DS, knit to 4 (4, 4, 5, 5, 5, 6, 6, 6, 6) sts before DS, turn.

Short Row 4: DS, purl to 4 (4, 4, 5, 5, 5, 6, 6, 6, 6) sts before DS, turn.

Rep Short Rows 3 and 4 six more times.

Knit 2 rnds, knitting both legs of each DS tog as you come to them.

Knit 3 rnds even.

Cast off using I-Cord Cast Off.

FINISHING

Weave in ends. Block to finished measurements.

TOP: Buckbeak concept art by Dermot Power.

CHARTS

KEY

- ■ A
- ▨ B
- □ C
- ☐ repeat

BODY

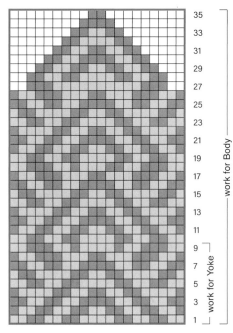

work for Body

work for Yoke

CHART 52

SLEEVE

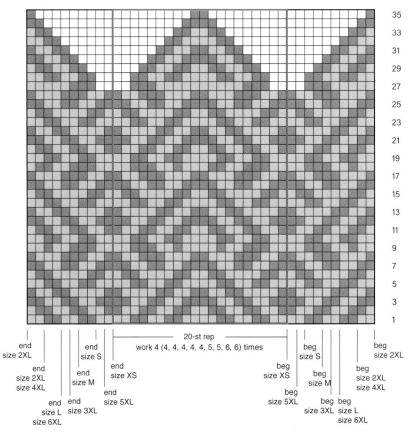

20-st rep
work 4 (4, 4, 4, 4, 5, 5, 6, 6) times

end size 2XL

end size 2XL size 4XL

end size L size 6XL

end size S

end size 3XL

end size M

end size 5XL

end size XS

beg size XS

beg size 5XL

beg size 3XL

beg size M

beg size S

beg size L size 6XL

beg size 2XL size 4XL

beg size 2XL

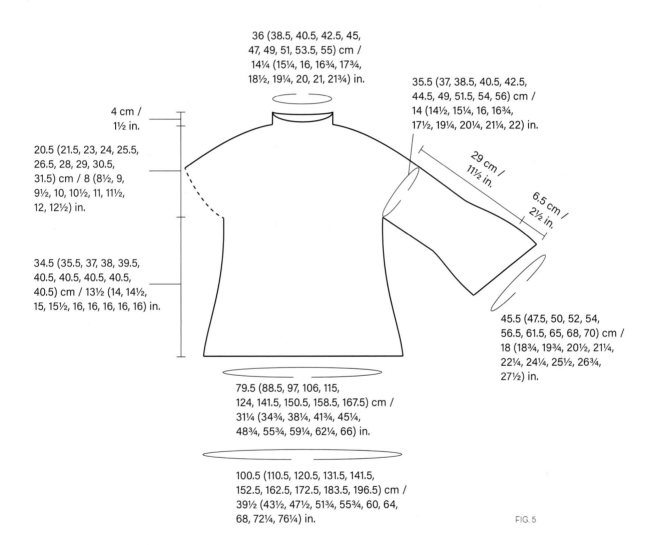

36 (38.5, 40.5, 42.5, 45,
47, 49, 51, 53.5, 55) cm /
14¼ (15¼, 16, 16¾, 17¾,
18½, 19¼, 20, 21, 21¾) in.

35.5 (37, 38.5, 40.5, 42.5,
44.5, 49, 51.5, 54, 56) cm /
14 (14½, 15¼, 16, 16¾,
17½, 19¼, 20¼, 21¼, 22) in.

4 cm /
1½ in.

29 cm /
11½ in.

6.5 cm /
2½ in.

20.5 (21.5, 23, 24, 25.5,
26.5, 28, 29, 30.5,
31.5) cm / 8 (8½, 9,
9½, 10, 10½, 11, 11½,
12, 12½) in.

34.5 (35.5, 37, 38, 39.5,
40.5, 40.5, 40.5, 40.5,
40.5) cm / 13½ (14, 14½,
15, 15½, 16, 16, 16, 16, 16) in.

45.5 (47.5, 50, 52, 54,
56.5, 61.5, 65, 68, 70) cm /
18 (18¾, 19¾, 20½, 21¼,
22¼, 24¼, 25½, 26¾,
27½) in.

79.5 (88.5, 97, 106, 115,
124, 141.5, 150.5, 158.5, 167.5) cm /
31¼ (34¾, 38¼, 41¾, 45¼,
48¾, 55¾, 59¼, 62¼, 66) in.

100.5 (110.5, 120.5, 131.5, 141.5,
152.5, 162.5, 172.5, 183.5, 196.5) cm /
39½ (43½, 47½, 51¾, 55¾, 60, 64,
68, 72¼, 76¼) in.

FIG. 5

Beauxbatons Academy of Magic Capelet

Designed by **DANA WILLIAMS-JOHNSON**

SKILL LEVEL ⚡

I n *Harry Potter and the Goblet of Fire*, two other wizarding schools, Beauxbatons and Durmstrang, arrive at Hogwarts to participate in the Triwizard Tournament. Hailing from France, the Beauxbatons students make a glamorous entrance in their matching French blue silk uniforms. Designed by costume designer Jany Temime, who herself attended French boarding school as a child, the Beauxbatons costume features French blue silk capelets, heels and perky trilby-esque hats, none of which are ideal for the cold Scottish weather at Hogwarts. But they certainly stand out against the sea of Hogwarts blacks, greys and browns.

Make your own (warmer!) version of the Beauxbatons capelet with this lovely pattern. Beginning with a provisional cast on and knit from the top down, the charming capelet grows out with increases placed at intervals and is topped off with an attached I-cord edging (see p. 203) around the bottom edge and sides. The fibre content allows for swing and drape ideal for this breezy accessory. The cast on is removed and the stitches are picked up and worked in a contrasting shade for the double-layered collar, with a simple crochet chain and button fastener to secure it.

SIZES

XS (S, M, L, XL, 2XL, 3XL, 4XL, 5XL, 6XL)
Shown in size XS.
Instructions are written for the
  smallest size, with larger sizes
  given in parentheses; when only one
  number is given, it applies
  to all sizes.

FINISHED MEASUREMENTS

To Fit Bust: 76 (86.5, 96.5, 106.5, 117,
  127, 137, 147.5, 157.5, 167.5) cm / 30 (34,
  38, 42, 46, 50, 54, 58, 62, 66) in.
Length: 34.5 (34.5, 35.5, 35.5, 37, 37, 38,
  38, 39.5, 39.5) cm /13½ (13½, 14, 14,
  14½, 14½, 15, 15, 15½, 15½) in.,
  excluding collar

YARN

Main Colour (MC): DK weight (fine
  #3) yarn, shown in Berroco *Summer
  Silk* (45% silk, 43% cotton, 12%
  nylon); 220 m / 240 yd. per 50 g /
  1¾ oz. ball), in colour #4063 Lake,
  3 (3, 3, 3, 3, 4, 4, 4, 5, 5) balls
Contrast Colour (CC): DK weight (fine
  #3) yarn, shown in Berroco *Remix*
  (30% nylon, 27% cotton, 24% acrylic,
  10% silk, 9% linen; 400 m / 432 yd.
  per 100 g / 3½ oz. skein), in colour
  #6927 Old Jeans, 1 skein

NEEDLES

- 4.5 mm / US 7, 80 cm / 32 in. long
  circular needle or size needed to
  obtain correct tension
- 3.75 mm / US 5, 80 cm / 32 in. long
  circular needle

Continued on page 126

BODY

With larger cir needle and MC, CO 70
(74, 80, 86, 90, 94, 100, 108, 116, 122)
sts using provisional crochet CO.
Do not join.
Beg with a RS row, work 2 rows in St st.
Inc row 1 (RS): *K2, M1; rep from * to
last 2 sts, k2 – 104 (110, 119, 128, 134,
140, 149, 161, 173, 182) sts.
Cont even in St st until piece measures
5 cm / 2 in. from beg, ending with a
WS row.
Inc row 2 (RS): *K2, M1; rep from * to
last 2 (2, 3, 2, 2, 2, 3, 3, 3, 2) sts, k2 (2,
3, 2, 2, 2, 3, 3, 3, 2) – 155 (164, 177, 191,
200, 209, 222, 240, 258, 272) sts.
Cont even in St st until piece measures
10 (10, 10, 10, 11, 11, 11, 11, 11.5, 11.5) cm
/ 4 (4, 4, 4, 4¼, 4¼, 4¼, 4¼, 4½, 4½)
in. from beg, ending with a WS row.
Inc row 3 (RS): *K3, M1; rep from * to
last 5 (5, 3, 2, 2, 2, 3, 3, 3, 2) sts, k5 (5,
3, 2, 2, 2, 3, 3, 3, 2) – 205 (217, 235, 254,
266, 278, 295, 319, 343, 362) sts.

Cont even in St st until piece measures
15 (15, 15, 15, 16.5, 16.5, 16.5, 16.5, 18, 18)
cm / 6 (6, 6, 6, 6½, 6½, 6½, 6½, 7, 7)
in. from beg, ending with a WS row.
Inc row 4 (RS): *K4, M1; rep from * to
last 1 (1, 3, 2, 2, 2, 3, 3, 3, 2) st(s), k1 (1,
3, 2, 2, 2, 3, 3, 3, 2) – 256 (271, 293, 317,
332, 347, 368, 398, 428, 452) sts.
Cont even in St st until piece measures
34.5 (34.5, 35.5, 35.5, 37, 37, 38, 38, 39.5,
39.5) cm / 13½ (13½, 14, 14, 14½, 14½,
15, 15, 15½, 15½) in. from beg, ending
with a WS row.
Cast off kwise.

I-CORD EDGES

With larger cir needle, MC and RS
facing, pick up and knit 53 (53, 55, 55,
57, 57, 59, 59, 61, 61) sts evenly along
one front edge, then CO 2 sts using
Cable CO method (see p. 202).
Row 1: *K1, ssk (last st of CO sts and
next picked-up st) – 1 st dec'd.
Row 2: Sl sts from RH needle to LH
needle, k1, ssk – 1 st dec'd.
Rep last row until 2 sts rem. Cut yarn
leaving a 15 cm / 6 in. long tail. Pull
tail through rem sts.
Rep on rem front edge.

RIGHT: Clémence
Poésy as Fleur
Delacour, sporting
the Beauxbatons
Academy uniform, in
*Harry Potter and the
Goblet of Fire.*

'AND NOW PLEASE JOIN ME
IN WELCOMING THE LOVELY
LADIES OF THE BEAUXBATONS
ACADEMY OF MAGIC AND
THEIR HEADMISTRESS,
MADAME MAXIME.'

Professor Dumbledore, *Harry Potter
and the Goblet of Fire*

COLLAR

Remove provisional CO and place 70 (74, 80, 86, 90, 94, 100, 108, 116, 122) sts on smaller cir needle. Do not join.

Join CC to beg with a RS row.

Work 4 rows in Garter st.

Inc row (RS): K1, k1f&b, knit to last 2 sts, k1f&b, k1 – 2 sts inc'd.

Cont in Garter st and rep Inc row every 6 rows 5 more times – 82 (86, 92, 98, 102, 106, 112, 120, 128, 134) sts.

Work even until collar measures 7.5 cm / 3 in. Cast off loosely kwise.

DECORATIVE TRIANGLES

With smaller cir needle, CC and with RS facing, pick up and knit 16 sts along one front edge in first row of collar. Do not join.

Beg with a WS row, work 5 rows in Garter st.

Dec row (RS): K1, ssk, knit to last 3 sts, k2tog, k1 – 2 sts dec'd.

Rep last 6 rows 5 more times – 4 sts rem.

Knit 10 rows even.

Dec row (RS): Ssk, k2tog – 2 sts rem.

Knit 3 rows even.

Dec row: K2tog – 1 st rem. Cut yarn and pull through rem st.

Rep on opposite side of collar.

FINISHING

Weave in ends. Block to finished measurements.

LOOP

With MC and crochet hook, leaving a 20.5 cm / 8 in. long tail, make a chain 15 cm / 6 in. long. Fasten off, leaving a 20.5 cm / 8 in. tail.

Fold chain in half and tie tails tog next to beg/end of chain to create a loop.

Thread tails of loop from RS to WS under triangle approx 2 cm / ¾ in. from left front edge. Secure ends on WS.

Sew button to right front approx 7.5 cm / 3 in. from left front edge under triangle.

ABOVE: Costume sketches of the Beauxbatons Academy school uniform, sketched by Mauricio Carneiro based on designs by Jany Temime.

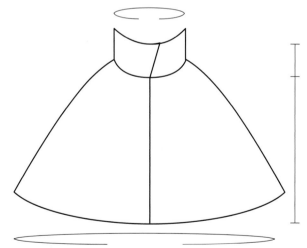

21, 22¼, 24, 25¾, 27)"
39.5 (42, 45, 48.5, 51,
53.5, 56.5, 61, 65.5, 68.5) cm

3"
7.5 cm

13½ (13½, 14, 14, 14½,
14½, 15, 15, 15½, 15½)"
34.5 (34.5, 35.5, 35.5, 37,
37, 38, 38, 39.5, 39.5) cm

57 (60¼, 65, 70½, 73¾,
77, 81¾, 88½, 95, 101¾)"
145 (153, 165, 179, 187.5,
195.5, 207.5, 225, 241, 258.5) cm

FIG. 6

THE CHAMBER OF SECRETS BEANIE

Designed by **TANIS GRAY**

SKILL LEVEL ⚡⚡⚡

After finding the hidden entrance to the chamber in the girls' bathroom in *Harry Potter and the Chamber of Secrets*, Harry, Ron and Professor Lockhart are separated. When Harry finds himself face to face with a large round door adorned with snakes, he uses Parseltongue to open it. The snakes pull back one at a time, and the door swings open. The effect, surprisingly, is not computer generated: Engineers created an actual moving door with seven independently moving snakes.

Designed for a slouchy fit, this hat features a simple off-centre stranded colourwork and duplicate-stitched chart motif inspired by the sinister entrance to the Chamber of Secrets. Beginning with a corrugated rib brim, the hat is worked in the round from the bottom up, with a simple spiral crown decrease to top everything off.

SIZE
One size

FINISHED MEASUREMENTS
Brim Circumference: 51 cm / 20 in.
Length: 20.5 cm / 8 in.

YARN
DK weight (light #3) yarn, shown in Magpie Fibers *Swanky DK* (80% superwash merino, 10% cashmere, 10% nylon; 229 m / 250 yd. per 115 g / 4 oz. hank)
Colour A: Rust in Peace, 1 hank
Colour B: Alloy, 1 hank

NEEDLES
• 3.5 mm / US 4, 40 cm / 16 in. long circular needle and set of 4 or 5 double-pointed needles or size needed to obtain correct tension

NOTIONS
• Stitch markers
• Tapestry needle

TENSION
24 sts and 33 rnds = 10 cm / 4 in. in Fair Isle pattern.
Be sure to check your tension.

Continued on page 132

- Hat is worked in the round from the bottom up.
- When working with one colour, the unused colour may be floated up the back of the work until needed. Rows 1–10 and 24–33 of the chart are worked with colour B only, then the pattern is added using duplicate stitch (see p. 202) when work is finished.

PATTERN STITCHES

Stocking Stitch (any number of sts)
Worked in the round, knit every rnd.

HAT

With cir needle, colour A, CO 126 sts using twisted German CO method (see p. 202). Pm and join to work in the rnd, being careful not to twist sts.
Join colour B.
Rnd 1: *K1 in B, p1 in A; rep from * around.
Rep last rnd 10 more times.
Beg St st and knit 1 rnd with colour A.
With colour B, knit 15 rnds.
Work Rnds 11–23 of Hat Chart (chart 54). Cut colour A.
With colour B, knit 15 rnds.

SHAPE CROWN

Change to dpn when there are too few sts to work comfortably on cir needle.
Rnd 1 (dec): *K7, k2tog; rep from * to end of rnd – 112 sts rem.
Rnd 2 (dec): *K6, k2tog; rep from * to end of rnd – 98 sts rem.
Rnd 3 (dec): *K5, k2tog; rep from * to end of rnd – 84 sts rem.
Rnd 4 (dec): *K4, k2tog; rep from * to end of rnd – 70 sts rem.
Rnd 5 (dec): *K3, k2tog; rep from * to end of rnd – 56 sts rem.
Rnd 6 (dec): *K2, k2tog; rep from * to end of rnd – 42 sts rem.
Rnd 7 (dec): *K1, k2tog; rep from * to end of rnd – 28 sts rem.
Rnd 8 (dec): [K2tog] around – 14 sts rem.
Rnd 9 (dec): [K2tog] around – 7 sts rem.
Cut yarn, leaving a long tail. Thread tail through rem sts and pull tight to close hole. Secure on WS.

FINISHING

Weave in loose ends.
Use duplicate stitch embroidery to add colour A over 38 sts of chart rows 1–10 and 24–33 to hat.
Block lightly.

Behind the Magic

The door to the Chamber of Secrets was designed by special effects supervisor John Richardson and constructed by Mark Bullimore, a special effects supervising engineer who also built the locks on the Gringotts Bank vaults.

TOP: Concept art of the door to the Chamber of Secrets by Andrew Williamson. ABOVE: Harry approaches the door in *Harry Potter and the Chamber of Secrets*.

HAT CHART

KEY

■ A

☐ B

☐ repeat

chart

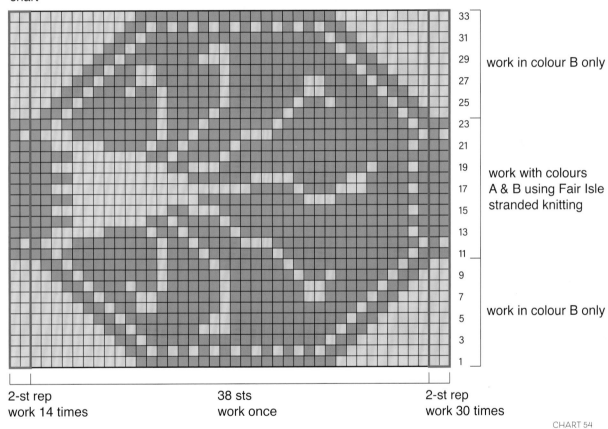

33
31
29 — work in colour B only
27
25
23
21
19 — work with colours
17   A & B using Fair Isle
15   stranded knitting
13
11
9
7
5 — work in colour B only
3
1

2-st rep
work 14 times

38 sts
work once

2-st rep
work 30 times

CHART 54

HERMIONE'S TIME-TURNER SWEATER

Designed by **DIANNA WALLA**

SKILL LEVEL ⚡⚡⚡⚡

H ermione's Time-Turner is one of the most important props in *Harry Potter and the Prisoner of Azkaban*. To create this artifact, graphic artist Miraphora Mina took inspiration from clocks and watches, as well as astrological instruments such as astrolabes. Her final design featured 'a ring within a ring which opened up to allow part of it to spin'. A double catch on the artifact's chain allowed the necklace to be extended around two actors – a necessary feature for the scene when Harry and Hermione go back in time to save Sirius and Buckbeak.

Worked in the round from the top down, this lovely sweater inspired by the Time-Turner uses German short rows (see p. 204) to create extra depth in the back of the yoke for a better fit. The beginning of the round is placed on the left front shoulder, with alternate sizes requiring additional yoke charts. The stranded colourwork motif features the Time-Turner on its chain wrapping around the yoke, with decorative colourwork patterning around the bottom of the torso and sleeves. Easy ribbing is worked around the edges and collar.

SIZES

XS (S, M, L, XL, 2XL, 3XL, 4XL, 5XL, 6XL)
Shown in size S.

Instructions are written for the smallest size, with larger sizes given in parentheses; when only one number is given, it applies to all sizes.

FINISHED MEASUREMENTS

Bust: 75 (84.5, 94, 103, 114.5, 125, 134.5, 143.5, 155, 165) cm / 29½ (33¼, 37, 40½, 45, 49¼, 53, 56½, 61, 65) in.

Back Length: 54.5 (56, 57, 58.5, 59.5, 61.5, 63.5, 66, 68.5, 71) cm / 21½ (22, 22½, 23, 23½, 24¼, 25, 26, 27, 28) in.

YARN

3 ply weight (super fine #1) yarn, shown in Quince & Co. *Finch* (100% American wool; 202 m / 221 yd. per 50 g / 1¾ oz. hank)

Main Colour (MC): Pomegranate, 6 (6, 7, 8, 9, 9, 10, 11, 12, 13) hanks

Contrast Colour (CC): Carrie's Yellow, 1 hank

NEEDLES

- 3.5 mm / US 4 circular needles, 40 cm / 16 in. and 80 cm / 32 in. long and set of 4 or 5 double-pointed needles or size needed to obtain correct tension
- 2.75 mm / US 2 circular needles, 40 cm / 16 in. and 80 cm / 32 in. long and set of 4 or 5 double-pointed needles or two sizes smaller than needle needed for correct tension

Continued on page 138

NOTIONS

- Stitch markers
- Stitch holders or waste yarn
- Tapestry needle

TENSIONS

26 sts and 33 rnds = 10 cm / 4 in. in St st with larger needles

28 sts and 34 rnds = 10 cm / 4 in. in chart patt with larger needles

Be sure to check your tensions.

NOTES

- The pullover is worked in the round from the top down; rounds begin at the front left shoulder.
- For the band of colourwork at the yoke, not all sizes use the same charts; make sure you follow the instructions for your size to ensure that the motifs line up.
- Two sections of short rows are used to shape the back neck for a better fit using the German short row technique (see p. 204). The first set of short rows is worked after the neckband, then the second set of short rows is worked just before dividing the yoke for the body and sleeves.

PATTERN STITCHES

K2, P2 Rib (multiple of 4 sts)

All rnds: *K2, p2; rep from * around.

Stocking Stitch (any number of sts)

All rnds: Knit.

YOKE

With shorter smaller cir needle and MC, CO 124 (124, 132, 144, 152, 152, 152, 156, 160, 160) sts. Pm and join to work in the rnd, being careful not to twist sts.

Work in K2, P2 Rib for 2.5 cm / 1 in. Change to shorter larger cir needle. Knit 1 rnd.

SHORT ROW SECTION

Short Row 1 (RS): K86 (86, 92, 99, 106, 106, 106, 108, 110, 110), pm for right front, k6, turn.

Short Row 2 (WS): DS, [purl to marker, sm] twice, p6, turn.

Short Row 3: DS, [knit to marker, sm] twice, turn.

Short Row 4: DS, [purl to marker, sm] twice, turn.

Short Row 5: DS, knit to marker, sm, knit to 6 sts before marker, turn.

Short Row 6: DS, purl to 6 sts before marker, turn.

Short Row 7: DS, knit to end of rnd. Do not turn.

Knit 1 rnd, removing right front marker.

SHAPE YOKE

Change to longer larger cir needle as the number of sts increases.

SIZES XS (S, M, 6XL) ONLY

Inc rnd 1: *K5 (4, 4, 2), M1; rep from * to last 4 (0, 0, 0) sts, k4 (0, 0, 0) – 148 (155, 165, 240) sts.

SIZE L ONLY

Inc rnd 1: *K4, M1, k3, M1; rep from * to last 4 sts, k4 – 184 sts.

SIZES XL (4XL) ONLY

Inc rnd 1: *[K4 (2), M1] 4 times, k3, M1; rep from * to last 0 (2) sts, k0 (2) – 192 (226) sts.

SIZE 2XL ONLY

Inc rnd 1: *[(K3, M1) twice, k2, M1] 2 times, k3, M1; rep from * to end – 208 sts.

SIZE 3XL ONLY

Inc rnd 1: [K3, M1, k2, M1] 28 times, [k2, M1] 6 times – 214 sts.

SIZE 5XL ONLY

Inc rnd 1: *[K2, M1] 6 times, k3, M1; rep from * to last 10 sts, [k2, M1] 5 times – 235 sts.

ALL SIZES

Knit 3 rnds even.

SIZES XS (S, M) ONLY

Inc rnd 2: K3 (7, 3), M1, *k6 (5, 5), M1; rep from * to last 7 (3, 2) sts, knit to end – 172 (185, 198) sts.

SIZE L ONLY

Inc rnd 2: *K4, M1, k5, M1; rep from * to last 4 sts, knit to end – 224 sts.

SIZE XL ONLY

Inc rnd 2: *[K3, M1] 4 times, k4, M1; rep from * to end – 252 sts.

SIZE 2XL ONLY

Inc rnd 2: K2, M1, *k4, M1; rep from * to last 2 sts, knit to end – 260 sts.

SIZE 3XL ONLY

Inc rnd 2: *[K4, M1] twice, k3, M1; rep from * to last 5 sts, k4, M1, k1 – 272 sts.

SIZE 4XL ONLY

Inc rnd 2: K2, M1, *k4, M1, k3, M1; rep from * to end of rnd – 291 sts.

SIZES 5XL (6XL) ONLY

Inc rnd 2: *K4, M1, [K3, M1] 3 (4) times; rep from * to last 1 (0) st(s), k1 (0) – 307 (315) sts.

ALL SIZES

Knit 3 rnds even.

SIZES XS (S, M, 2XL, 6XL) ONLY

Inc rnd 3: *K7 (6, 6, 5, 4), M1; rep from * to last 4 (5, 0, 0, 3) sts, k4 (5, 0, 0, 3) – 196 (215, 231, 312, 393) sts.

SIZE L ONLY

Inc rnd 3: *K6, M1, k5, M1; rep from * to last 4 sts, knit to end – 264 sts.

SIZE XL ONLY

Inc rnd 3: *[K5, M1] 3 times, k6, M1; rep from * to end – 300 sts.

SIZE 3XL ONLY

Inc rnd 3: *[K5, M1] twice, k4, M1; rep from * to last 6 sts, k5, M1, k1 – 330 sts.

SIZES 4XL (5XL) ONLY

Inc rnd 3: [K2, M1] 1 (0) time(s), *[k4, M1] 3 times, k5, M1; rep from * to last 0 (1) st(s), k0 (1) – 360 (379) sts.

ALL SIZES

Knit 3 (3, 3, 3, 3, 4, 4, 4, 4, 4) rnds even.

SIZES XS (S, M, 2XL) ONLY

Inc rnd 4: K4 (3, 3, 3), M1, *k8 (7, 7, 6), M1; rep from * to last 8 (9, 4, 3) sts, knit to end – 220 (245, 264, 364) sts.

SIZE L ONLY

Inc rnd 4: K3, M1, *k7, M1, k6, M1; rep from * to last 14 sts, k7, M1, knit to end – 304 sts.

SIZES XL (5XL) ONLY

Inc rnd 4: *[K6 (5), M1] 3 (2) times, k7 (6), M1; rep from * to last 0 (11) sts, [(k5, M1) twice, k1] 0 (1) time(s) – 348 (450) sts.

SIZES 3XL (4XL) ONLY

Inc rnd 4: *[K6 (5), M1] 2 (3) times, k5 (6), M1; rep from * to last 7 (3) sts, k6 (3), M1, k1 (0) – 388 (429) sts.

SIZE 6XL ONLY

Inc rnd 4: *K5, M1; rep from * to last 3 sts, k3 – 471 sts.

ALL SIZES

Knit 2 (2, 2, 3, 3, 4, 4, 5, 5, 5) rnds even.

Setup rnd: Knit and inc 4 (inc 0, inc 1, inc 2, dec 1, inc 4, inc 0, inc 0, inc 0, dec 1) st(s) evenly spaced – 224 (245, 265, 306, 347, 368, 388, 429, 450, 470) sts.

SIZES XS (M, L, XL, 3XL, 4XL, 6XL) ONLY

Next rnd: Join CC yarn and working Row 1 of each chart, work Yoke Chart A (chart 56) once, pm, Yoke Chart B (chart 57) once, pm, Yoke Chart C (chart 58) 3 (4, 5, 6, 7, 8, 9) times, pm, then Yoke Chart D (chart 59) once.

SIZES S (2XL, 5XL) ONLY

Next rnd: Join CC yarn and working Row 1 of each chart, work Yoke Chart B once, pm, Yoke Chart C 4 (7, 9) times, pm, then Yoke Chart D once.

ALL SIZES

Work Rows 2–19 of charts as established. Cut CC.

With MC only, knit 1 rnd.

Inc rnd 5: *K12 (13, 12, 16, 15, 16, 15, 16, 14, 13), M1; rep from * to last 8 (11, 1, 2, 17, 0, 13, 13, 2, 2) st(s), knit to end of rnd – 242 (263, 287, 325, 369, 391, 413, 455, 482, 506) sts.

Knit 3 (4, 4, 4, 4, 4, 4, 5, 5) rnds even.

Inc rnd 6: *K13 (14, 13, 17, 17, 17, 16, 17, 15, 14), M1; rep from * to last 8 (11, 1, 2, 12, 0, 13, 13, 2, 2) st(s), knit to end – 260 (281, 309, 344, 390, 414, 438, 481, 514, 542) sts.

Knit 3 (4, 4, 4, 4, 4, 4, 5, 5) rnds even.

Inc rnd 7: *K14 (15, 14, 19, 18, 18, 17, 17, 16, 15), M1; rep from * to last 8 (11, 1, 2, 12, 0, 13, 5, 2, 2) st(s), knit to end – 278 (299, 331, 362, 411, 437, 463, 509, 546, 578) sts.

Knit 3 (4, 4, 4, 4, 4, 5, 5, 5) rnds even.

Inc rnd 8: *K15 (17, 15, 20, 19, 19, 18, 18, 16, 16); rep from * to last 8 (10, 16, 2, 12, 0, 13, 23, 2, 2) sts, knit to end – 296 (316, 352, 380, 432, 460, 488, 536, 580, 614) sts.

Knit 2 (2, 2, 3, 4, 4, 4, 5, 5, 5) rnds even.

Next rnd: K58 (60, 68, 70, 82, 84, 88, 100, 110, 116), pm for left back (A), k90 (98, 108, 120, 134, 146, 156, 168, 180, 191), pm for right back (B), k58 (60, 68, 70, 82, 84, 88, 100, 110, 116), pm for right front (C), k90 (98, 108, 120, 134, 146, 156, 168, 180, 191).

SHORT ROW SECTION 2

Short Row 1 (RS): Knit to marker C, k8, turn.

Short Row 2 (WS): DS, purl to beg-of-rnd marker, p8, turn.

Short Row 3: DS, knit to marker C, turn.

Short Row 4: DS, purl to beg-of-rnd marker, turn.

Short Row 5: DS, knit to 8 sts before marker C, turn.

Short Row 6: DS, purl to 8 sts before beg-of-rnd marker, turn.

Short Row 7: DS, knit to end of rnd.

DIVIDE BODY AND SLEEVES

Next rnd: Removing markers, slip 58 (60, 68, 70, 78, 84, 88, 100, 110, 116) sleeve sts to waste yarn, CO 3 (5, 6, 6, 6, 7, 8, 8, 9, 10) sts, pm for new beg of rnd, CO 3 (5, 6, 6, 6, 7, 8, 8, 9, 10) sts, knit 90 (98, 108, 120, 138, 146, 156, 168, 180, 191) back sts, slip 58 (60, 68, 70, 78, 84, 88, 100, 110, 116) sleeve sts to waste yarn, CO 3 (5, 6, 6, 6, 7, 8, 8, 9, 10) sts, pm for side, CO 3 (5, 6, 6, 6, 7, 8, 8, 9, 10) sts, knit 90 (98, 108, 120, 138, 146, 156, 168, 180, 191) front sts, then knit to beg-of-rnd marker – 192 (216, 240, 264, 292, 320, 344, 368, 396, 422) sts rem.

BODY

Work even in St st for 5 cm / 2 in.

SHAPE WAIST

Dec rnd: *K5, k2tog, knit to 7 sts before marker, ssk, k5, sm; rep from * once more – 4 sts dec'd.

Rep Dec rnd every 7 (8, 8, 9, 9, 10, 10, 10, 11, 11) rnds 3 more times – 176 (200, 224, 248, 276, 304, 328, 352, 380, 406) sts rem.

Work 8 rnds even.

Inc rnd: *K5, M1R, knit to 5 sts before marker, M1L, k5, sm; rep from * once more – 4 sts inc'd.

Rep Inc rnd every 10 rnds 3 more times – 192 (216, 240, 264, 292, 320, 344, 352, 380, 406) sts.

Cont even until body measures approx 26.5 (27.5, 28.5, 29, 30, 31, 33, 35, 37, 39.5) cm / 10½ (10¾, 11¼, 11½, 11¾, 12¼, 13, 13¾, 14½, 15½) in. from underarm, and inc 0 (0, 0, 0, 0, 0, 0, 0, 0, 2) sts on last rnd – 192 (216, 240, 264, 292, 320, 344, 352, 380, 408) sts.

Join CC and work Rnds 1–3 of Border Chart (chart 55). Cut CC.

With MC only, knit 4 rnds.

Change to longer smaller cir needle. Knit 1 rnd.

Work in K2, P2 Rib for 2.5 cm / 1 in. Cast off all sts in patt.

SLEEVES

Place 58 (60, 68, 70, 78, 84, 88, 100, 110, 116) sleeve sts on larger dpn.

With MC, beg at centre of underarm CO edge, pick up and knit 4 (5, 5, 6, 6, 7, 8, 8, 9, 10) along CO edge, knit sleeve sts, pick up and knit 4 (5, 5, 6, 6, 7, 8, 8, 9, 10) along rem CO edge – 66 (70, 78, 82, 90, 98, 104, 116, 128, 136) sts. Divide sts evenly over 4 dpn. Pm and join to work in the rnd.

Work even in St st until sleeve measures approx 12.5 (12.5, 12.5, 12.5, 10, 10, 9, 9, 9, 9) cm / 5 (5, 5, 5, 4, 4, 3½, 3½, 3½, 3½) in. from armhole.

Dec rnd: K2, k2tog, knit to last 4 sts, ssk, k2 – 2 sts dec'd.

Rep Dec rnd every 26 (18, 14, 14, 12, 10, 9, 6, 5, 4) rnds 2 (4, 6, 6, 8, 10, 11, 17, 21, 25) more times – 60 (60, 64, 68, 72, 76, 80, 80, 84, 84) sts rem.

Cont even until sleeve measures approx 37 (38, 39.5, 40.5, 42, 42, 43, 43, 43, 43) cm / 14½ (15, 15½, 16, 16½, 16½, 17, 17, 17, 17) in. from underarm.

Join CC and work Rnds 1–3 of Border Chart (chart 55). Cut CC.

With MC only, knit 4 rnds even.

Change to smaller dpn. Knit 1 rnd.

Work in K2, P2 Rib for 5 cm / 2 in. Cast off all sts in patt.

FINISHING

Weave in ends. Block to measurements.

'IF YOU SUCCEED TONIGHT, MORE THAN
ONE INNOCENT LIFE MAY BE SPARED.
THREE TURNS SHOULD DO IT, I THINK.'

Professor Dumbledore, *Harry Potter
and the Prisoner of Azkaban*

Behind the Magic

The Time-Turner carries two inscriptions on
its rings. The outer ring reads, 'I mark the hours
every one, nor have I yet outrun the sun', while
the inside ring reads, 'My use and value unto
you depends on what you have to do'.

ABOVE: Hermione and Harry prepare to use the Time-Turner to visit the past in *Harry Potter and the Prisoner of Azkaban*.

CHARTS

KEY

■ MC
▢ CC
☐ repeat

BORDER

3
1

└ 4-st ┘
rep

CHART 55

YOKE A

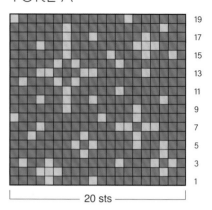

19
17
15
13
11
9
7
5
3
1

├─── 20 sts ───┤

CHART 56

YOKE B

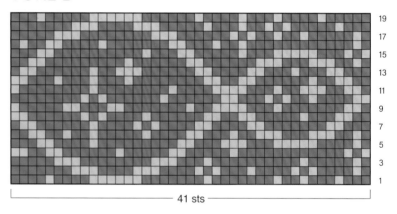

19
17
15
13
11
9
7
5
3
1

├─── 41 sts ───┤

CHART 57

YOKE C

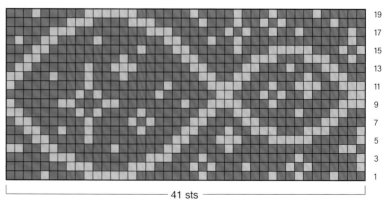

19
17
15
13
11
9
7
5
3
1

├─── 41 sts ───┤

CHART 58

YOKE D

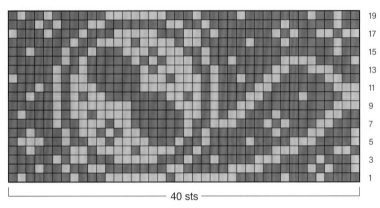

19
17
15
13
11
9
7
5
3
1

|— 40 sts —|

CHART 59

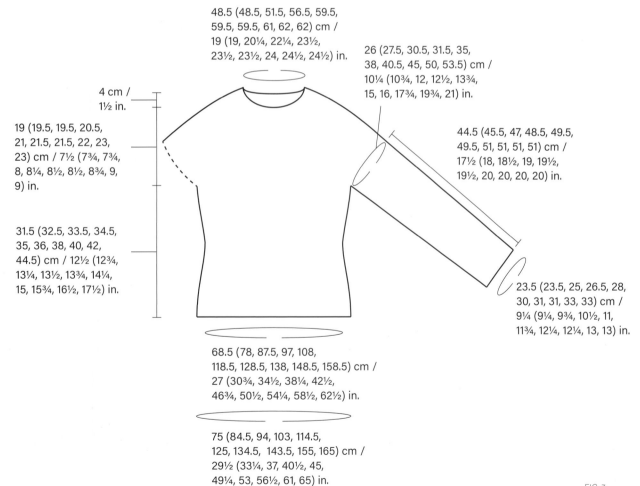

48.5 (48.5, 51.5, 56.5, 59.5,
59.5, 59.5, 61, 62, 62) cm /
19 (19, 20¼, 22¼, 23½,
23½, 23½, 24, 24½, 24½) in.

26 (27.5, 30.5, 31.5, 35,
38, 40.5, 45, 50, 53.5) cm /
10¼ (10¾, 12, 12½, 13¾,
15, 16, 17¾, 19¾, 21) in.

4 cm /
1½ in.

19 (19.5, 19.5, 20.5,
21, 21.5, 21.5, 22, 23,
23) cm / 7½ (7¾, 7¾,
8, 8¼, 8½, 8½, 8¾, 9,
9) in.

44.5 (45.5, 47, 48.5, 49.5,
49.5, 51, 51, 51, 51) cm /
17½ (18, 18½, 19, 19½,
19½, 20, 20, 20, 20) in.

31.5 (32.5, 33.5, 34.5,
35, 36, 38, 40, 42,
44.5) cm / 12½ (12¾,
13¼, 13½, 13¾, 14¼,
15, 15¾, 16½, 17½) in.

23.5 (23.5, 25, 26.5, 28,
30, 31, 31, 33, 33) cm /
9¼ (9¼, 9¾, 10½, 11,
11¾, 12¼, 12¼, 13, 13) in.

68.5 (78, 87.5, 97, 108,
118.5, 128.5, 138, 148.5, 158.5) cm /
27 (30¾, 34½, 38¼, 42½,
46¾, 50½, 54¼, 58½, 62½) in.

75 (84.5, 94, 103, 114.5,
125, 134.5, 143.5, 155, 165) cm /
29½ (33¼, 37, 40½, 45,
49¼, 53, 56½, 61, 65) in.

FIG. 7

Dark Mark Illusion Scarf

Designed by **LINDSAY HENRICKS**

SKILL LEVEL ⚡⚡

T he Dark Mark is Voldemort's symbol. Branded on the inner forearm of each Death Eater, the Mark shows a skull with a snake protruding from its mouth. The Dark Mark can also be conjured by the spell *Morsmordre*, as Harry learns at the Quidditch World Cup in *Harry Potter and the Goblet of Fire*.

Worked back and forth in rows in highly contrasting shades, this garter-based illusion scarf may look like a simple stripe pattern, but it has a hidden Dark Mark motif on one end and its spell, *Morsmordre*, on the other. Breaks in the garter stitch using just knits and purls create these illusions, which are visible only when observed at an angle. Carrying the yarns up the side means minimal finishing. Attach fringe – if you dare!

SIZE
One size

FINISHED MEASUREMENTS
Width: 20.5 cm / 8 in.
Length: 204.5 cm / 80½ in., excluding fringe

YARN
Aran weight (medium #4) yarn, shown in Dragonfly Fibers *Valkyrie* (100% superwash merino; 183 m / 200 yd. per 115 g / 4 oz. hank)
Main Colour (MC): Black is Black, 2 hanks
Contrast Colour (CC): Silver Fox, 2 hanks

NEEDLES
• 4.5 mm / US 7 or size needed to obtain correct tension

NOTIONS
• Tapestry needle
• Crochet hook for attaching fringe

TENSIONS
19½ sts and 31 rows = 10 cm / 4 in. in pattern
Be sure to check your tension.

NOTES
• When changing colours, carry the unused colour loosely up the side of the scarf.
• If you want a shorter scarf, work fewer repeats of the Background Pattern between the two chart motifs. The charts are presented in sections because of the length of each motif.

Continued on page 146

PATTERN STITCH

Background Pattern (any number of sts)

Row 1 (RS): With CC, knit.

Row 2 (WS): With CC, purl.

Row 3: With MC, knit.

Row 4: With MC, knit.

Rep Rows 1–4 for patt.

SCARF

With MC, CO 39 sts.

Knit 2 rows.

Work in Background Patt for 24 rows, ending with Row 4.

DARK MARK PATTERN

Work Rows 1–70 of Dark Mark Chart A (chart 60), then Rows 71–138 of Dark Mark Chart B (chart 61), or as follows:

Row 1 (RS, CC): Knit.

Row 2 (WS, CC): P18, k3, p18.

Row 3 (RS, MC): Knit.

Row 4 (WS, MC): K18, p3, k18.

Row 5 (CC): Knit.

Row 6 (CC): P18, k3, p18.

Row 7 (MC): Knit.

Row 8 (MC): K17, p5, k17.

Row 9 (CC): Knit.

Row 10 (CC): P17, k5, p17.

Row 11 (MC): Knit.

Row 12 (MC): K17, p5, k17.

Row 13 (CC): Knit.

Row 14 (CC): P17, k5, p17.

Row 15 (MC): Knit.

Row 16 (MC): K18, p3, k18.

Row 17 (CC): Knit.

Row 18 (CC): P18, k3, p18.

Row 19 (MC): Knit.

Row 20 (MC): K18, p2, k19.

Row 21 (CC): Knit.

Row 22 (CC): P18, k2, p19.

Row 23 (MC): Knit.

Row 24 (MC): K17, p2, k20.

Row 25 (CC): Knit.

Row 26 (CC): P17, k2, p20.

Row 27 (MC): Knit.

Row 28 (MC): K15, p3, k21.

Row 29 (CC): Knit.

Row 30 (CC): P15, k3, p21.

Row 31 (MC): Knit.

Row 32 (MC): K12, p5, k22.

Row 33 (CC): Knit.

Row 34 (CC): P12, k5, p22.

Row 35 (MC): Knit.

Row 36 (MC): K10, p6, k23.

Row 37 (CC): Knit.

Row 38 (CC): P10, k6, p6, k8, p9.

Row 39 (MC): Knit.

Row 40 (MC): K8, p5, k6, p13, k7.

Row 41 (CC): Knit.

Row 42 (CC): P8, k5, p6, k13, p7.

Row 43 (MC): Knit.

Row 44 (MC): K7, p5, k6, p15, k6.

Row 45 (CC): Knit.

Row 46 (CC): P7, k5, p6, k15, p6.

Row 47 (MC): Knit.

Row 48 (MC): K6, p5, k6, p6, k5, p5, k6.

Row 49 (CC): Knit.

Row 50 (CC): P6, k5, p6, k6, p5, k5, p6.

Row 51 (MC): Knit.

Row 52 (MC): K5, p5, [k7, p5] twice, k5.

Row 53 (CC): Knit.

Row 54 (CC): P5, k5, [p7, k5] twice, p5.

Row 55 (MC): Knit.

Row 56 (MC): K5, p5, k19, p5, k5.

Row 57 (CC): Knit.

Row 58 (CC): P5, k5, p5, k9, p5, k5, p5.

Row 59 (MC): Knit.

Row 60 (MC): K6, p5, k3, p11, k3, p5, k6.

Row 61 (CC): Knit.

Row 62 (CC): P6, k5, p3, k11, p3, k5, p6.

Row 63 (MC): Knit.

Row 64 (MC): K8, p2, k5, p9, k5, p2, k8.

Row 65 (CC): Knit.

Row 66 (CC): P8, k2, p5, k9, p5, k2, p8.

Row 67 (MC): Knit.

Row 68 (MC): K11, p7, k3, p7, k11.

Row 69 (CC): Knit.

Row 70 (CC): P11, k7, p3, k7, p11.

Row 71 (MC): Knit.

Row 72 (MC): K10, p8, k3, p8, k10.

Row 73 (CC): Knit.

Row 74 (CC): P10, k8, p3, k8, p10.

Row 75 (MC): Knit.

Row 76 (MC): K10, p3, k4, p2, k1, p2, k4, p3, k10.

Row 77 (CC): Knit.

Row 78 (CC): P10, k3, p4, k2, p1, k2, p4, k3, p10.

Row 79 (MC): Knit.

Row 80 (MC): K10, p2, k6, p3, k6, p2, k10.

Row 81 (CC): Knit.

Row 82 (CC): P10, k2, p6, k3, p6, k2, p10.

Row 83 (MC): Knit.

Row 84 (MC): K10, p2, k6, p3, k6, p2, k10.

Row 85 (CC): Knit.

Row 86 (CC): P10, k2, p6, k3, p6, k2, p10.

Row 87 (MC): Knit.

Row 88 (MC): K11, p3, k3, p5, k3, p3, k11.

Row 89 (CC): Knit.

Row 90 (CC): P11, k3, p3, k5, p3, k3, p11.

Row 91 (MC): Knit.

Row 92 (MC): K11, p17, k11.

Row 93 (CC): Knit.

Row 94 (CC): P11, k17, p11.

Row 95 (MC): Knit.

Row 96 (MC): K11, p17, k11.

Row 97 (CC): Knit.

Row 98 (CC): P11, k17, p11.

Row 99 (MC): Knit.

Row 100 (MC): K12, p15, k12.

Row 101 (CC): Knit.

Row 102 (CC): P12, k15, p12.

Row 103 (MC): Knit.

Row 104 (MC): K15, p9, k15.

Row 105 (CC): Knit.

Row 106 (CC): P15, k9, p15.

Row 107 (MC): Knit.

Row 108 (MC): Knit.

Row 109 (CC): Knit.

Row 110 (CC): P18, k5, p16.

Row 111 (MC): Knit.

Row 112 (MC): K20, p5, k14.

Row 113 (CC): Knit.

Row 114 (CC): P20, k5, p14.

Row 115 (MC): Knit.

Row 116 (MC): K21, p4, k14.

Row 117 (CC): Knit.

Row 118 (CC): P13, k4, p4, k4, p14.

Row 119 (MC): Knit.

Row 120 (MC): K12, p6, k2, p5, k14.
Row 121 (CC): Knit.
Row 122 (CC): P12, k6, p2, k5, p14.
Row 123 (MC): Knit.
Row 124 (MC): K11, p2, k3, p9, k14.
Row 125 (CC): Knit.
Row 126 (CC): P11, k2, p3, k9, p14.
Row 127 (MC): Knit.
Row 128 (MC): K12, p2, k3, p6, k16.
Row 129 (CC): Knit.
Row 130 (CC): P12, k2, p3, k6, p16.
Row 131 (MC): Knit.
Row 132 (MC): K13, p2, k24.
Row 133 (CC): Knit.
Row 134 (CC): P13, k2, p24.
Row 135 (MC): Knit.
Row 136 (MC): K14, p4, k21.
Row 137 (CC): Knit.
Row 138 (CC): P14, k4, p21.
Next 2 rows (MC): Knit.
Work in Background Patt for 78.5 cm / 31 in., ending with Row 4.

MORSMORDRE PATTERN

Work Rows 1–66 of Morsmordre Chart A (chart 62), Rows 67–132 of Morsmordre Chart B (chart 63), then Rows 133–196 of Morsmordre Chart C (chart 64), or as follows:
Row 1 (CC): Knit.
Row 2 (CC): P13, k2, p4, k6, p14.
Row 3 (MC): Knit.
Row 4 (MC): K13, p2, k4, p2, k2, p2, k14.
Row 5 (CC): Knit.
Row 6 (CC): P12, k2, p4, k3, p2, k4, p12.
Row 7 (MC): Knit.
Row 8 (MC): K12, p2, k4, p3, k2, p4, k12.
Row 9 (CC): Knit.
Row 10 (CC): P13, k12, p14.
Row 11 (MC): Knit.
Row 12 (MC): Knit.
Row 13 (CC): Knit.
Row 14 (CC): P10, k2, p27.
Row 15 (MC): Knit.
Row 16 (MC): K10, p2, k27.
Row 17 (CC): Knit.
Row 18 (CC): P8, k3, p10, k4, p14.
Row 19 (MC): Knit.
Row 20 (MC): K8, p3, k12, p2, k14.

Row 21 (CC): Knit.
Row 22 (CC): P7, k2, p14, k3, p13.
Row 23 (MC): Knit.
Row 24 (MC): K7, p2, k14, p3, k13.
Row 25 (CC): Knit.
Row 26 (CC): P8, k3, p3, k11, p14.
Row 27 (MC): Knit.
Row 28 (MC): K8, p3, k12, p2, k14.
Row 29 (CC): Knit.
Row 30 (CC): P10, k3, p11, k3, p12.
Row 31 (MC): Knit.
Row 32 (MC): K10, p3, k26.
Row 33 (CC): Knit.
Row 34 (CC): P12, k3, p24.
Row 35 (MC): Knit.
Row 36 (MC): K12, p3, k24.
Row 37 (CC): Knit.
Row 38 (CC): P14, k16, p9.
Row 39 (MC): Knit.

Row 40 (MC): K14, p2, k6, p3, k3, p2, k9.
Row 41 (CC): Knit.
Row 42 (CC): P13, k3, p6, k3, p4, k3, p7.
Row 43 (MC): Knit.
Row 44 (MC): K13, p3, k6, p3, k4, p3, k7.
Row 45 (CC): Knit.
Row 46 (CC): P14, k10, p7, k3, p5.
Row 47 (MC): Knit.
Row 48 (MC): K31, p3, k5.
Row 49 (CC): Knit.
Row 50 (CC): P33, k3, p3.
Row 51 (MC): Knit.
Row 52 (MC): K33, p3, k3.
Row 53 (CC): Knit.
Row 54 (CC): P21, k4, p10, k2, p2.
Row 55 (MC): Knit.
Row 56 (MC): K23, p2, k10, p2, k2.
Row 57 (CC): Knit.
Row 58 (CC): P23, k3, p7, k3, p3.

Row 59 (MC): Knit.
Row 60 (MC): K23, p3, k7, p3, k3.
Row 61 (CC): Knit.
Row 62 (CC): P9, k3, p2, k11, p7, k2, p5.
Row 63 (MC): Knit.
Row 64 (MC): K9, p3, k11, p2, k7, p2, k5.
Row 65 (CC): Knit.
Row 66 (CC): P7, k3, p14, k3, p2, k4, p6.
Row 67 (MC): Knit.
Row 68 (MC): K7, p3, k29.
Row 69 (CC): Knit.
Row 70 (CC): P5, k3, p7, k8, p16.
Row 71 (MC): Knit.
Row 72 (MC): K5, p3, k7, p2, k4, p2, k16.
Row 73 (CC): Knit.
Row 74 (CC): P3, k3, p7, k4, p4, k4, p14.
Row 75 (MC): Knit.
Row 76 (MC): K3, p3, k7, p4, k4, p4, k14.
Row 77 (CC): Knit.
Row 78 (CC): P5, k3, p7, k8, p16.
Row 79 (MC): Knit.
Row 80 (MC): K5, p3, k31.
Row 81 (CC): Knit.
Row 82 (CC): P7, k3, p29.
Row 83 (MC): Knit.
Row 84 (MC): K7, p3, k29.
Row 85 (CC): Knit.
Row 86 (CC): P9, k16, p14.
Row 87 (MC): Knit.
Row 88 (MC): K22, p3, k14.
Row 89 (CC): Knit.
Row 90 (CC): P22, k2, p15.
Row 91 (MC): Knit.
Row 92 (MC): K22, p2, k15.
Row 93 (CC): Knit.
Row 94 (CC): P15, k11, p13.
Row 95 (MC): Knit.
Row 96 (MC): K22, p2, k15.
Row 97 (CC): Knit.
Row 98 (CC): P22, k2, p15.
Row 99 (MC): Knit.
Row 100 (MC): K22, p2, k15.
Row 101 (CC): Knit.
Row 102 (CC): P15, k10, p14.
Row 103 (MC): Knit.
Row 104 (MC): K23, p2, k14.
Row 105 (CC): Knit.

Row 106 (CC): P23, k4, p12.
Rows 107–108 (MC): Knit.
Row 109 (CC): Knit.
Row 110 (CC): Purl.
Rows 111–112 (MC): Knit.
Row 113 (CC): Knit.
Row 114 (CC): P12, k8, p4, k4, p11.
Row 115 (MC): Knit.
Row 116 (MC): K18, p2, k6, p2, k11.
Row 117 (CC): Knit.
Row 118 (CC): P11, k3, p4, k4, p4, k3, p10.
Row 119 (MC): Knit.
Row 120 (MC): K11, p3, k4, p4, k4, p3, k10.
Row 121 (CC): Knit.
Row 122 (CC): P12, k4, p4, k8, p11.
Rows 123–124 (MC): Knit.
Row 125 (CC): Knit.
Row 126 (CC): Purl.
Rows 127–128 (MC): Knit.
Row 129 (CC): Knit.
Row 130 (CC): P21, k4, p14.
Row 131 (MC): Knit.
Row 132 (MC): K23, p2, k14.
Row 133 (CC): Knit.
Row 134 (CC): P23, k3, p13.
Row 135 (MC): Knit.
Row 136 (MC): K23, p3, k13.
Row 137 (CC): Knit.
Row 138 (CC): P9, k3, p2, k11, p14.
Row 139 (MC): Knit.
Row 140 (MC): K9, p3, k11, p3, k13.
Row 141 (CC): Knit.
Row 142 (CC): P7, k3, p14, k3, p12.
Row 143 (MC): Knit.
Row 144 (MC): K7, p3, k29.
Row 145 (CC): Knit.
Row 146 (CC): P5, k3, p7, k8, p16.
Row 147 (MC): Knit.
Row 148 (MC): K5, p3, k7, p2, k4, p2, k16.
Row 149 (CC): Knit.
Row 150 (CC): P3, k3, p7, k4, p4, k4, p14.
Row 151 (MC): Knit.
Row 152 (MC): K3, p3, k9, p2, k4, p2, k16.

Row 153 (CC): Knit.
Row 154 (CC): P5, k3, p7, k8, p16.
Row 155 (MC): Knit.
Row 156 (MC): K5, p3, k31.
Row 157 (CC): Knit.
Row 158 (CC): P7, k3, p29.
Row 159 (MC): Knit.
Row 160 (MC): K7, p3, k29.
Row 161 (CC): Knit.
Row 162 (CC): P9, k23, p7.
Row 163 (MC): Knit.
Row 164 (MC): K27, p3, k9.
Row 165 (CC): Knit.
Row 166 (CC): P27, k3, p9.
Row 167 (MC): Knit.
Row 168 (MC): K27, p3, k9.
Row 169 (CC): Knit.
Row 170 (CC): P26, k3, p10.
Row 171 (MC): Knit.
Row 172 (MC): K26, p3, k10.
Row 173 (CC): Knit.
Row 174 (CC): P12, k20, p7.
Row 175 (MC): Knit.
Row 176 (MC): K27, p3, k9.
Row 177 (CC): Knit.
Row 178 (CC): P27, k3, p9.
Row 179 (MC): Knit.
Row 180 (MC): K27, p3, k9.
Row 181 (CC): Knit.
Row 182 (CC): P26, k3, p10.
Row 183 (MC): Knit.
Row 184 (MC): K26, p3, k10.
Row 185 (CC): Knit.
Row 186 (CC): P8, k26, p5.
Row 187 (MC): Knit.
Row 188 (MC): K8, p2, k22, p2, k5.
Row 189 (CC): Knit.
Row 190 (CC): P6, k3, p23, k2, p5.
Row 191 (MC): Knit.
Row 192 (MC): K6, p3, k23, p2, k5.
Row 193 (CC): Knit.
Row 194 (CC): P4, k3, p23, k3, p6.
Rows 195–196 (MC): Knit.
Work in Background Patt for 24 rows, ending with Row 4. Cut CC.
Cast off all sts kwise.

FINISHING

Weave in ends. Pin scarf to finished measurements, and spray with water to saturate. Allow to dry completely.

FRINGE

Cut 72 strands of yarn in each colour, each approx 35.5 cm / 14 in. long. Holding 4 strands of one colour together, use crochet hook to attach to cast-on and cast-off edges. Alternating colours across each edge, attach 18 sets of fringe to each edge. Trim to even length.

ʙEHIND THE ᴍAGIC

Actor Ralph Fiennes transformed into Voldemort through a combination of practical and digital effects. He wore prosthetics to cover his eyebrows, transferable tattoos to create his clammy skin and creepy veins, and false teeth. However his slit-like nose was created digitally, frame by frame.

TOP: Ralph Fiennes as Lord Voldemort in *Harry Potter and the Order of the Phoenix*. ABOVE: Concept art of the Dark Mark at the Quidditch World Cup. Art by Andrew Williamson for *Harry Potter and the Goblet of Fire*.

CHARTS

- ▨ MC
- ☐ CC
- ☐ k on RS; p on WS
- ⊡ p on RS; k on WS

DARK MARK A

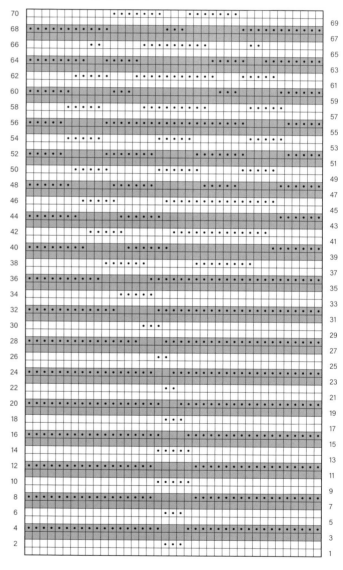

CHART 60

DARK MARK B

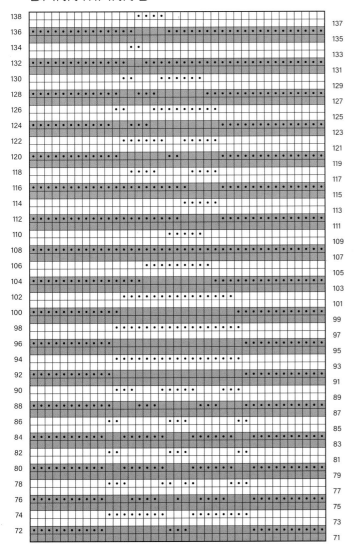

CHART 61

KEY

- ▨ MC
- ☐ CC
- ☐ k on RS; p on WS
- ⊡ p on RS; k on WS

MORSMORDRE A

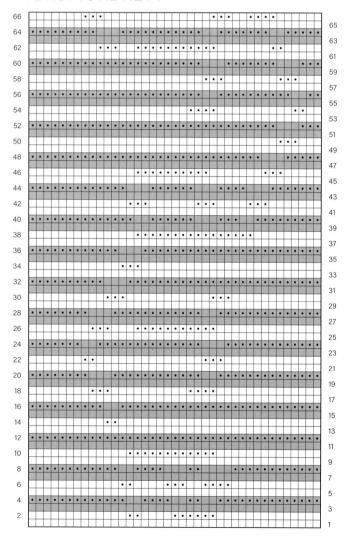

CHART 62

MORSMORDRE B

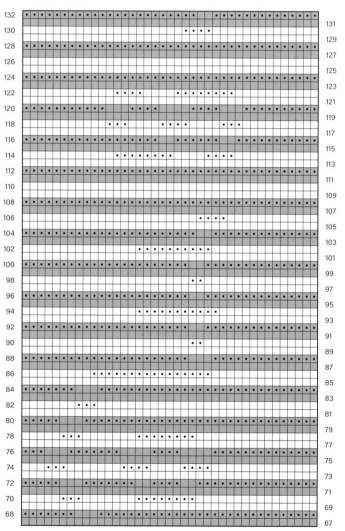

CHART 63

MORSMORDRE C

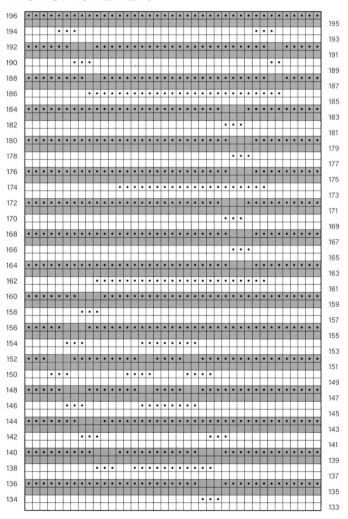

CHART 64

'IT'S THE DARK MARK, HARRY.

IT'S HIS MARK.'

Hermione Granger, *Harry Potter
and the Goblet of Fire*

NAGINI LARIAT

Designed by **TANIS GRAY**

SKILL LEVEL ⚡

Nagini, Voldemort's constant companion and – as Harry eventually learns – a Horcrux, is first introduced in *Harry Potter and the Goblet of Fire*. More than 6 metres (20 feet) long and covered in reflective scales, she protects her master and does his deadly bidding. The design for Nagini evolved through the films, with designers studying and filming real snakes to get this creature just right. Her final design for *Harry Potter and the Deathly Hallows – Parts 1* and *2* combines a python and an anaconda, with cobra and viper elements in her face and movements.

Worked as a four-stitch I-cord (see p. 203) for the desired length, this lariat-style necklace is a quick and straightforward accessory. The head of the snake is knit back and forth in two pieces and joined at the mouth, allowing the I-cord to pass through, wrap around the wearer's neck, and be adjusted for fit. Beaded eyes are sewn on and the muted metallic yarn creates sheen without being scratchy.

SIZE
One size

FINISHED MEASUREMENTS
Circumference: 2.5 cm / 1 in.
Length: 170 cm / 67 in.

YARN
Aran weight (medium #4) yarn, shown in Cascade Yarns *Luminosa* (52% viscose, 44% baby alpaca, 4% merino wool; 220 m / 240 yd. per 100g / 3½ oz. hank) in colour #01 Emerald, 1 hank

NEEDLES
• 4.5 mm / US 7 pair of double-pointed needles or size needed to obtain correct tension

NOTIONS
• Tapestry needle
• Six 5 mm bicone beads, jet black

TENSION
Tension is not important for this project.

NOTES
• Lariat is worked in one piece from the tail to the head, with the top and bottom of the head worked separately like a clamshell and joined at the nose to create an opening. Necklace is adjustable.

LARIAT

CO 4 sts.

Work I-cord (see p. 203) until work measures 165 cm / 65 in. from beg.

SHAPE TOP OF HEAD

Since rows that shape the head are worked on RS only, rows are worked in the same way as the I-cord body. But instead of pulling the yarn tightly across the back of the work, allow the yarn to strand loosely across the back of the work so that the head pieces are flat.

Inc row: KIf&b, k2, kIf&b, slide sts to right end of needle – 6 sts.

Next row: K6, slide sts to right end of needle.

Inc row: KIf&b, k4, kIf&b, slide sts to right end of needle – 8 sts.

Next row: K8, slide sts to right end of needle.

Next row: KIf&b, k6, kIf&b, slide sts to right end of needle – 10 sts.

Next 5 rows: K10, slide sts to right end of needle.

Dec row: Ssk, k6, k2tog, slide sts to right end of needle – 8 sts rem.

Next row: K8, slide sts to right end of needle.

Dec row: Ssk, k4, k2tog, slide sts to right end of dpn – 6 sts rem.

Dec row: Ssk, k2, k2tog, slide sts to right end of needle – 4 sts rem.

Dec row: Ssk, k2tog, slide sts to right end of needle – 2 sts rem.

Dec row: Skp – 1 st rem.

Cut yarn and fasten off rem st.

SHAPE BOTTOM OF HEAD

Turn piece with WS of top of head facing, pick up and knit 4 sts at base of head, slide sts back to right end of needle.

Inc row: KIf&b, k2, kIf&b, slide sts to right end of needle – 6 sts.

Next row: K6, slide sts to right end of needle.

Inc row: KIf&b, k4, kIf&b, slide sts to right end of needle – 8 sts.

Next row: K8, slide sts to right end of needle.

Inc row: KIf&b, k6, kIf&b, slide sts to right end of needle – 10 sts.

Next 5 rows: K10, slide sts to right end of needle.

Dec row: Ssk, k6, k2tog, slide sts to right end of needle – 8 sts rem.

Next row: K8, slide sts to right end of needle.

Dec row: Ssk, k4, k2tog, slide sts to right end of needle – 6 sts rem.

Dec row: Ssk, k2, k2tog, slide sts to right end of needle – 4 sts rem.

Dec row: Ssk, k2tog, slide sts to right end of needle – 2 sts rem.

Dec row: Skp – 1 st rem.

Cut yarn, leaving a 20.5 cm / 8 in. tail and fasten off rem st. Sew tips of heads tog using the long tail.

FINISHING

Sew 3 beads to each side of top of head for eyes.

Weave in ends. Block lightly.

Coil lariat 2 or 3 times, and pull tail through opening in snake head. Adjust as necessary.

TOP LEFT: Concept art of Nagini and Voldemort by Paul Catling for *Harry Potter and the Goblet of Fire*

LUNA LOVEGOOD'S SPECTRESPECS GLOVES

Designed by **STEPHANIE LOTVEN**

SKILL LEVEL ⚡⚡⚡⚡⚡

A close friend of Harry's and a member of Dumbledore's Army, Luna Lovegood is known for her dreamy manner, kind heart and eccentric style. Played by actress Evanna Lynch, who absolutely 'is Luna', according to director David Yates and producer David Heyman, Luna dons her famous Spectrespecs in *Harry Potter and the Half-Blood Prince*. The Spectrespecs have one pink eye and one blue, both set in sparkly winged frames. According to Luna, they allow her to see Wrackspurts, which helps her to find – and rescue – an immobilised Harry when he is hidden by his Invisibility Cloak on the Hogwarts Express.

Show your love for Luna by knitting these colourful gloves inspired by her most famous accessory. Knit in the round from the bottom up, beginning with corrugated ribbing, the palm and thumb gusset of these gloves are on one chart, while all other fingers are individually charted. Colour changes create the illusion of different motifs, designed to mimic the Spectrespecs' unique colour scheme. Cross your hands in front of your eyes and splay your fingers to create your own perfect pair. Don't forget to keep your eye out for Wrackspurts!

SIZE
One size

FINISHED MEASUREMENTS
Hand Circumference: 18 cm / 7 in.
Length: 25.5 cm / 10 in.

YARN
Fingering weight (super fine #1) yarn, shown in Leading Men Fiber Arts *Show Stopper* (75% superwash merino wool, 25% nylon; 423 m / 463 yd. per 100 g / 3½ oz. hank)
Main Colour (MC): Pop the Cork (pale yellow), 1 hank
Contrast Colour 1 (CC1): Perfection (teal), 1 hank
Contrast Colour 2 (CC2): Starlet (hot pink), 1 hank

NEEDLES
- 2.75 mm / US 2 set of 4 or 5 double-pointed needles
- 3.25 mm / US 3 set of 4 or 5 double-pointed needles or size needed to obtain correct tension

NOTIONS
- Stitch markers
- Stitch holders or scrap yarn
- Tapestry needle

TENSION
34 sts and 37 rnds = 10 cm / 4 in. in colourwork patt with larger needles
Be sure to check your tension.

Continued on page 160

- Both gloves are worked using the same charts but reversing contrast colour 1 and contrast colour 2.
- All chart rows are read from right to left, beginning with Row 1. Carry the floats loosely across the wrong side. Thumb gusset increases are worked by picking up the contrast colour bar between stitches and working the make 1 left and make 1 right increases with the contrast colour.
- The cuffs begin with plain K2, P2 Rib with one of the contrasting colours, then the other contrast colour is added and worked as K2, P2 corrugated ribbing; make sure you leave the knit colour at the back of the work when purling stitches, and have both yarns at the back of work before knitting stitches.

STITCH PATTERN

K2, P2 Rib (multiple of 4 sts)

All rnds: *K2, p2; rep from * around.

'DON'T WORRY. YOU'RE JUST
AS SANE AS I AM.'

Luna Lovegood, *Harry Potter
and the Order of the Phoenix*

RIGHT GLOVE
CUFF

With smaller dpn and CC2, CO 60 sts. Distribute sts evenly over 3 or 4 dpn. Pm and join to work in the rnd, being careful not to twist sts.

Work 4 rnds of K2, P2 Rib.

Join CC1.

Next rnd: *K2 CC2, p2 CC1; rep from * to end of rnd.

Rep last rnd until cuff measures 4.5 cm / 1¾ in. from beg.

Knit 1 rnd with CC2.

Cut CC2 and join MC.

PALM AND THUMB GUSSET

Change to larger dpn, and cont with MC and CC1.

Next rnd: Working Rnd 1 of Palm Chart (chart 70), work 30 sts, pm for thumb gusset, k1 st in patt, pm for thumb gusset, then work to end of rnd.

Work Rnds 2–25 of chart as established – 80 sts.

Next rnd: Working Rnd 26, work 30 sts in established patt, remove marker, place 21 thumb sts on waste yarn for thumb, remove marker, CO 1 st using Backward Loop method, then work to end of rnd – 60 sts rem. Rearrange sts if needed over 3 or 4 dpn.

HAND

Work Rnds 27–46 of chart.

Cut MC and CC1.

INDEX FINGER

Place first 21 sts and last 21 sts on waste yarn – 18 sts rem.

Join MC.

Setup rnd: K18, CO 3 sts using Backward Loop method (see p. 202) – 21 sts. Arrange sts evenly over 3 dpn, making sure to beg rnds with sts above back of hand. Pm and join to work in the rnd.

Knit 2 rnds.

Join CC1. Work Rnds 1–15 of Index Finger Chart (chart 65).

Cut CC1.

With MC only, knit 11 rnds, or until finger is 6 mm / ¼ in. short of desired length.

Dec rnd: *K1, k2tog; rep from * to end of rnd – 14 sts rem.

Dec rnd: *K2tog; rep from * to end of rnd – 7 sts rem.

Cut yarn and thread tail through rem sts. Pull tight to close hole, and fasten securely on WS side.

MIDDLE FINGER

Place 7 sts from back of hand on one larger dpn and 7 sts from front of hand on 2nd larger dpn – 14 sts.

Join CC1.

Setup rnd: With thumb at left, k7 sts from back of hand, pick up and knit 3 sts along index finger CO edge, k7 sts from palm, then CO 3 sts – 20 sts. Arrange sts evenly over 3 dpn, making sure to beg rnds with sts above back of hand. Pm and join to work in the rnd.

Knit 2 rnds.

Join CC1. Work Rnds 1–16 of Middle Finger Chart (chart 68).

Cut CC1.

With MC only, knit 11 rnds, or until finger is 6 mm / ¼ in. short of desired length.

Dec rnd: *K1, k2tog; rep from * to last 2 sts, k2 – 14 sts rem.

Dec rnd: *K2tog; rep from * to end of rnd – 7 sts rem.

Cut yarn and thread tail through rem sts. Pull tight to close hole, and fasten securely on WS side.

RING FINGER

Place 7 sts from back of hand on one larger dpn, and 7 sts from front of hand on 2nd larger dpn – 14 sts.

Join CC1.

Setup rnd: With thumb at left, k7 sts from back of hand, pick up and knit 3 sts along middle finger CO edge, k7 sts from palm, then CO 3 sts – 20 sts. Arrange sts evenly over 3 dpn, making sure to beg rnds with sts above back of hand. Pm and join to work in the rnd.

Knit 2 rnds.

ABOVE: Evanna Lynch dons her Spectrespecs as Luna Lovegood in *Harry Potter and the Half-Blood Prince*.

Join CC1. Work Rnds 1–16 of Ring Finger Chart (chart 66).

Cut CC1.

With MC only, knit 9 rnds, or until finger is 6 mm / ¼ in. short of desired length.

Dec rnd: *K1, k2tog; rep from * to last 2 sts, k2 – 14 sts rem.

Dec rnd: *K2tog; rep from * to end of rnd – 7 sts rem.

Cut yarn and thread tail through rem sts. Pull tight to close hole, and fasten securely on WS side.

PINKY FINGER

Place rem 14 sts on larger dpn.

Join C.

Setup rnd: Beg with sts from palm, k14, then pick up and knit 3 sts along ring finger CO edge – 17 sts. Arrange sts evenly over 3 dpn, making sure to beg rnds with sts above palm. Pm and join to work in the rnd.

Knit 2 rnds.

Join CC1.

Work Rnds 1–12 of Pinky Finger Chart (chart 67).

Cut CC1.

With MC only, knit 7 rnds, or until finger is 6 mm / ¼ in. short of desired length.

Dec rnd: *K1, k2tog; rep from * to last 2 sts, k2 – 12 sts rem.

Decr rnd: *K2tog; rep from * to end of rnd – 6 sts rem.

Cut yarn and thread tail through rem sts. Pull tight to close hole, and fasten securely on WS side.

THUMB

Place 21 held sts for thumb on larger dpn.

Join CC1.

Setup rnd: K21, then pick up and knit 5 sts around gap above thumb opening – 26 sts. Pm and join to work in the rnd.

Dec rnd: K21, ssk, k1, k2tog – 24 sts rem.

Join CC1.

Work Rnds 1–11 of Thumb Chart (chart 69).

Cut CC1.

With MC only, knit 7 rnds, or until thumb is 6 mm / ¼ in. short of desired length.

Dec rnd: *K1, k2tog; rep from * to end of rnd – 16 sts rem.

Dec rnd: *k2tog; rep from * to end of rnd – 8 sts rem.

Cut yarn and thread tail through rem sts. Pull tight to close hole, and fasten securely on WS side.

LEFT GLOVE
CUFF

With smaller dpn and CC1, CO 60 sts. Distribute sts evenly over 3 or 4 dpn. Pm and join to work in the rnd, being careful not to twist sts.

Work 4 rnds of K2, P2 Rib.

Join CC2.

Next rnd: *K2 CC1, p2 CC2; rep from * to end of rnd.

Rep last rnd until cuff measures 4.5 cm / 1¾ in. from beg.

Knit 1 rnd with CC1.

Cut CC1 and join MC.

Cont same as for right glove, substituting CC2 for CC1 throughout, and beg rnds for fingers with sts above palm.

FINISHING

Weave in ends. Block to finished measurements.

CHARTS

KEY

☐	MC
■	CC for Right Glove; CC2 for Left Glove
▨	no stitch
☐	knit
◹	M1L
◸	M1R
⓪	CO 1 using Backward Loop method

INDEX FINGER

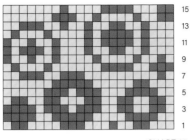

CHART 65

RING FINGER

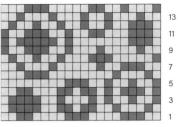

CHART 66

MIDDLE FINGER

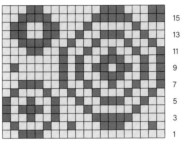

CHART 68

THUMB

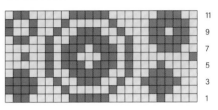

CHART 69

PINKY FINGER

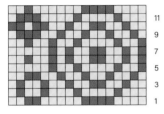

CHART 67

PALM

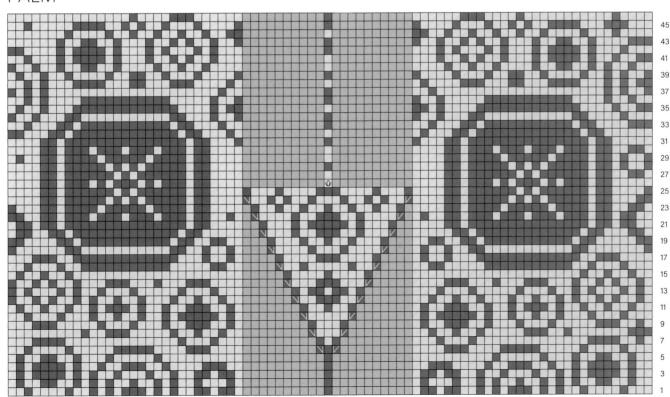

CHART 70

The Deathly Hallows Lace-Knit Beaded Shawl

Designed by **SUSANNA IC**

SKILL LEVEL ⚡⚡⚡

The Deathly Hallows are three magical objects that, according to legend, grant the holder mastery over death. The Hallows are made up of the Elder Wand, the Resurrection Stone and the Cloak of Invisibility. They are represented by a triangular symbol, first seen as a necklace worn by Xenophilius Lovegood in *Harry Potter and the Deathly Hallows – Part 1*. The graphics department on the film, led by Miraphora Mina and Eduardo Lima, was responsible for developing the art for that symbol, as well as every other crest, sigil, logo and insignia shown in the films.

A repeating pattern of Deathly Hallows symbols forms the heart of this beautiful shawl. Beginning with a centre provisional cast on (see p. 202), the shawl is worked in two halves down to the ends to create a mirror image of the pattern. The Deathly Hallows triangular symbol is formed using yarn overs in the lace motif. Beading as you go creates the circle at the centre representing the cloak and adds sparkle, and the wand is made with double decreases sandwiched between twisted stitches, making this the perfect accessory for any magical event.

SIZE
One size

FINISHED MEASUREMENTS
Width: 53.5 cm / 21 in.
Length: 188 cm / 74 in.

YARN
4 ply weight (super fine #1) yarn, shown in Hazel Knits *Artisan Sock* (90% superwash merino wool, 10% nylon; 366 m / 400 yd. per 120 g / 4¼ oz. hank) in colour Queen of the Night, 3 hanks

NEEDLES
- 4 mm / US 6 needles or size needed to obtain correct tension
- 4.5 mm / US 7 needles or one size larger than needle for correct tension

NOTIONS
- Beads: 1000 4 mm (size 6/0) Miyuki beads in Silverlined Crystal
- 0.75 mm crochet hook
- Waste yarn
- Stitch markers (optional)
- Tapestry needle
- Blocking wires (optional)

TENSION
20 sts and 25 rows = 10 cm / 4 in. in patt, blocked
Tension is not critical for this pattern, but the yarn weight and needle size used will affect the finished measurements.

Continued on page 166

SHAWL
FIRST HALF

With waste yarn and smaller needles, CO 105 sts using a provisional method.

Change to main yarn.

Knit 2 rows, ending with a WS row.

Work Chart A (chart 71) Rows 1–48 four times, then work Rows 1–24 once more.

Work Chart B (chart 72) Rows 1–28 once.

With larger needle, cast off as follows: K2, *return sts to LH needle, k2tog, k1; rep from * to end of row. Fasten off rem st.

SECOND HALF

Carefully remove provisional CO and place 105 sts on smaller needles.

With WS facing, join main yarn and knit 1 row.

Work Chart C (chart 73) Rows 1 and 2.

Work Chart A Rows 3–48 once. Work Chart A Rows 1–48 three times, then work Rows 1–24 once more.

Work Chart B Rows 1–28 once.

Cast off same as first half.

FINISHING

Weave in ends but do not trim until after shawl has been blocked.

Soak shawl in cool water until thoroughly wet. Remove from water and squeeze out most of the water, being careful not to wring or twist the piece. Lay shawl between two towels, and roll towels to blot out most of the remaining water.

Pin shawl to measurements; for easier blocking, blocking wires can be threaded through the yarn overs along all straight edges. Allow to dry completely, then trim yarn ends.

BEHIND THE MAGIC

Harry's Invisibility Cloak, later revealed to be the Hallows' Cloak of Invisibility, was designed by Judianna Makovsky for the first film. The Cloak was lined with green screen material so when Daniel Radcliffe flipped it as he put it on, the green screen material would be on the outside, enabling his entire body to be erased in postproduction.

ABOVE LEFT: Rhys Ifans as Xenophilius Lovegood explains the significance of the Deathly Hallows symbol in *Harry Potter and the Deathly Hallows – Part 1*. ABOVE RIGHT: Daniel Radcliffe shoots a scene for *Harry Potter and the Philosopher's Stone* wearing the green-screen Invisibility Cloak.

CHARTS

KEY

☐	k on RS; p on WS
⊡	p on RS; k on WS
⊙	yo
◿	k2tog
◺	ssk
⋀	s2kp
ⱴ	M2
ℒ	k1 tbl
B	place bead
☐	repeat

CHART A

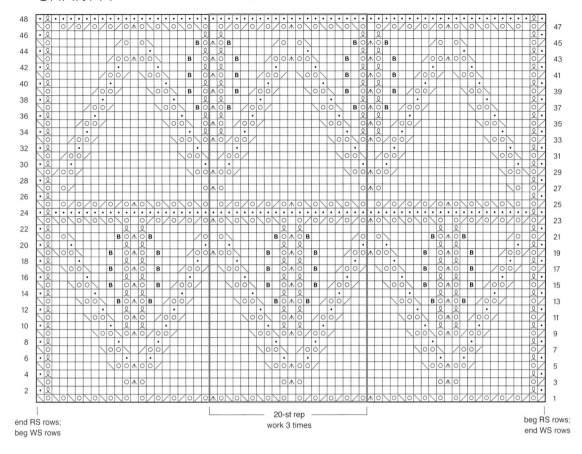

end RS rows;
beg WS rows

20-st rep
work 3 times

beg RS rows;
end WS rows

CHART 71

CHART B

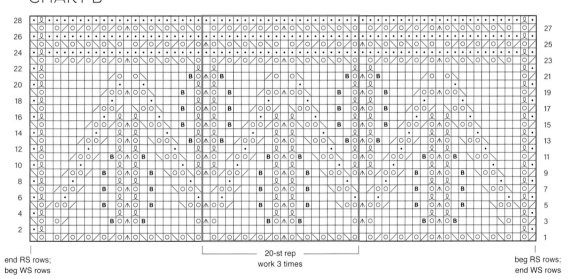

end RS rows;
beg WS rows

20-st rep
work 3 times

beg RS rows;
end WS rows

CHART 72

CHART C

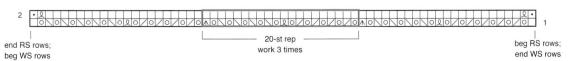

end RS rows;
beg WS rows

20-st rep
work 3 times

beg RS rows;
end WS rows

CHART 73

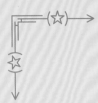
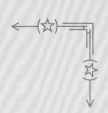

Delightful
Decor

Ron Weasley: 'It's not much but it's home.'

Harry Potter: 'I think it's Brilliant.'

Harry Potter and the Chamber of Secrets

Hogwarts House Mug Cosies

Designed by **TANIS GRAY**

SKILL LEVEL ⚡

A nother great way for fans to show their house pride, this is a simple project incorporating the house colours, perfect for beginner knitters or someone looking to make a quick gift for the Potter fan in their life.

Worked in the round in one piece, each cosy is worked up the same way in the individual house colours. The jogless stripe technique (see p. 203) ensures no jagged stripes, and knitting with washable yarn makes the cosy easy to clean.

The jogless stripe technique (see p. 203)

SIZE
One size

FINISHED MEASUREMENTS
Circumference: 20.5 cm / 8 in.
Length: 9 cm / 3½ in.

YARN
DK weight (Fine #3) yarn, shown in
  Berroco *Comfort DK* (50% super fine
  nylon, 50% super fine acrylic;
  165 m / 178 yd. per 50 g / 1¾ oz.
  hank), 1 skein each
Colour A: #2763 Navy Blue
Colour B: #2762 Spruce
Colour C: #2760 Beet Root
Colour D: #2719 Sunshine
Colour E: #2770 Ash Grey
Colour F: #2734 Liquorice
*You will be able to make six to eight cup
cosies from each skein of the house
MC (see Notes). Only a small amount
of contrast colour is needed for each
cup cosy, and one skein is more than
enough to make a set of all four cosies.*

NEEDLES
• 3.5 mm / US 4 set of 4 or 5 double-
  pointed needles or size needed to
  obtain correct tension

NOTIONS
• Stitch markers
• Tapestry needle

TENSION
26 sts and 39 rnds = 10 cm / 4 in. in St st
Be sure to check your tension.

Continued on page 174

NOTES

- These cosies are worked in the round using double-pointed needles. You can also use two short circular needles or one long circular needle to knit using the Magic Loop method.

- All the cosies are worked in the same way, with only the House colours changing. For Ravenclaw, use colours A (main colour) and E (contrast colour); for Slytherin, use colours B (main colour) and E (contrast colour); for Gryffindor, use colours C (main colour) and D (contrast colour); and for Hufflepuff, use colours D (main colour) and F (contrast colour).

- When changing colours for the stripes, leave the colour being dropped at the back of the work, and carry it loosely up the back until needed again.

- To make sure the stripes line up where rounds begin and end, use the Jogless Join technique (see p. 203).

CUP COSIES

With MC (colour A, B, C or D) for your House, CO 52 sts. Pm and join to work in the rnd, being careful not to twist sts.

Knit 1 rnd.

Purl 1 rnd.

Knit 1 rnd.

Join CC (colour E, E, D or F) for your House, and knit 3 rnds.

Knit 3 rnds with MC.

Knit 3 rnds with CC.

Knit 9 rnds with MC.

Knit 3 rnds with CC.

Knit 3 rnds with MC.

Knit 3 rnds with CC. Cut CC.

Knit 2 rnds with MC.

Purl 1 rnd.

Cast off pwise.

FINISHING

Weave in ends. Block to finished measurements.

ʙᴇʜɪɴᴅ ᴛʜᴇ ᴍᴀɢɪᴄ

House points at Hogwarts are tracked by four hourglass-shaped cylinders mounted to the wall of the Great Hall. Production designer Stuart Craig filled the cylinders with tens of thousands of coloured glass beads, which ended up causing a national shortage across England.

THE SORTING HAT HANGING DISPLAY

Designed by **TINY OWL KNITS**

SKILL LEVEL ⚡⚡⚡⚡

A perfect way to use up leftover yarn bits, this decorative display celebrates the Sorting Hat and each of the four houses, represented by their respective crest animals.

Knit in the round from the centre out, the Sorting Hat is worked in stocking stitch with simple increases and decreases. The face is worked post knit by cinching and stitching, allowing the maker to create the desired expression. Stuffing as you go allows the creatures to take shape and come to life quickly.

Gryffindor's proud lion is worked flat in stocking stitch with simple wrap-and-turn short-row shaping in the body section, with the head worked in the round and attached. Once the pieces are together, a shaggy mane is worked around the face in a manner similar to making a pom-pom.

Hufflepuff's industrious badger is worked in the round beginning at the nose. The body is increased out while the face is duplicate stitched on (see p. 202).

Ravenclaw's wise eagle is knit in the round, starting with the head. The beak and wings are made by picking up and knitting stitches from the body.

Slytherin's sly snake is worked in the round, beginning at the nose. Worked as a simple tube with increases and tuck stitches, it knits up quickly.

Once finished, the creatures are attached to string and fixed to a hanging structure to create a magical decorative piece.

SIZE
One size

FINISHED MEASUREMENTS
SORTING HAT
Height: 18 cm / 7 in.
Width: 10 cm / 4 in.
LION
Height: 11 cm / 4¼ in.,
    excluding mane
Length: 11 cm / 4¼ in.
BADGER
Length: 10 cm / 4 in.
Width: 6.5 cm /2½ in.
EAGLE
Length: 12 cm / 4¾ in.
Width: 14 cm / 5½ in.
SNAKE
Height: 4 cm / 1¾ in.
Diameter: 8.5 cm / 3¼ in., coiled
FINISHED MOBILE
Height: 34.5 cm / 13½ in.
Width: 38 cm / 15 in.

YARN
Aran weight (medium #4) yarn, shown
    in Cascade Yarns *220 Superwash*
    (100% Peruvian Highland wool;
    200 m / 220 yd. per 100 g / 3½ oz.
    hank), 1 hank each colour
Colour A: #8505 White
Colour B: #2414 Ginger
Colour C: #2415 Sunflower
Colour D: #2429 Irelande
Colour E: #2431 Chocolate Heather
Colour F: #8400 Charcoal Grey
Colour G: #8555 Black (only about
    13.5 m / 15 yd. needed)

Continued on page 178

NEEDLES

- 5 mm / US 8 set of 5 double-pointed needles or size needed to obtain correct tension

NOTIONS

- Stitch markers
- Removable stitch markers
- 1 m / 1 yd. of pink embroidery thread, for lion's nose
- Polyester or wool stuffing
- 2 straight branches or dowels, each approx. 38 cm / 15 in. long and 1 cm to 1.3 cm / 3/8 in. to 1/2 in. in diameter
- Twine, thread or string, for hanging
- 1 brown pipe cleaner
- A few small stones or washers, to add weight to the snake
- Floral wire or glue gun and a few pieces of artificial greenery, dried moss and pine cones, to create the top decoration (optional)
- Tapestry needle

TENSION

20 sts and 24 rows/rnds = 10 cm / 4 in. in St st

Be sure to check your tension.

NOTES

- All the creatures are worked flat or in the round, then stuffed with polyester or wool stuffing before seaming. Be sure not to overstuff your creatures or the stuffing will show through. If this happens, run some matching yarn just under the surface to hide white spots.

- Double-pointed needles are used to work all parts of each piece of the display, both for sections worked in the round and those worked back and forth. When the number of stitches decreases to the point where working with three needles is awkward, shift stitches to two needles, or to one needle, and work the round as you would for an I-cord.

- Some sections are begun by casting stitches onto two double-pointed needles or by picking up stitches on two double-pointed needles and working in the round. Working rounds with stitches on just two double-pointed needles may feel awkward at first, but it is similar to making socks from the toe up. If desired, you can place the stitches onto three or four double-pointed needles instead.

SPECIAL TERMS

Overhand knot: Holding both ends parallel, loop one end behind and under the other end.

Double (triple, quadruple) overhand knot: Make an overhand knot but pass the yarn back up, around, and through hole 2 (3, 4) times depending on instructions.

PATTERN STITCH

Stocking Stitch (any number of sts)
Worked back and forth, knit RS rows, purl WS rows.
Worked in the round, knit every rnd.

SORTING HAT

With colour E, CO 8 sts. Divide sts evenly onto 4 dpn. Pm and join to work in the rnd, being careful not to twist sts.

Rnd 1 and all other odd-numbered rnds to Rnd 33: Knit.

Rnd 2 (inc): [K1, M1, k2, M1, k1] twice – 12 sts.

Rnd 4 (inc): [K1, M1, (k2, M1) 2 times, k1] twice – 18 sts.

Rnd 6 (inc): [(K2, M1) 4 times, k1] twice – 26 sts.

Rnd 8 (inc): [(K3, M1) 4 times, k1] twice – 34 sts.

Rnd 10 (inc): [K1, M1, (k4, M1) 4 times] twice – 44 sts.

Rnd 12 (inc): [K2, M1, (k5, M1) 4 times] twice – 54 sts.

Rnd 14 (turning rnd): Purl.

Rnd 16 (dec): [(K4, k2tog) 4 times, k1, k2tog] twice 44 sts rem.

Rnd 18 (dec): [K2tog, (k3, k2tog) 4 times] twice – 34 sts rem.

Rnd 20 (dec): [(K2, k2tog) 4 times, k1] twice – 26 sts rem.

Rnds 21–34: Knit.

Rnd 35: Knit k2tog once randomly placed across rnd – 1 st dec'd.

Rep last rnd 23 more times, redistributing rem sts over fewer dpn as number of sts dec, ending with last 2 sts on one dpn – 2 sts rem. *At the same time*, before the hole gets too small, stuff hat very lightly with polyester stuffing; do not stuff the brim.

Next row: K2, then slide sts back to right end of dpn.

Rep last row once more.

Next row: K2tog – 1 st rem. Fasten off rem st.

FINISHING

Weave in ends.

If you are using 100% wool, now is the time to roll the hat between your hands vigorously for about 5 minutes to dry felt the piece. This makes the

stitches tight and smooth. Thread a tapestry needle with a long piece of colour E. When making stitches to create eye and mouth indents, remember to leave a lot of room as each cinch takes up a lot of length. If your piece isn't looking right, move your cinching stitches higher. Don't be afraid to try again!

Brim: Using your fingers to work the stuffing, move as much stuffing out of the brim section as you can. Work a line of straight stitches around the brim to flatten it.

Mouth: Run a long piece of yarn up through the bottom of the hat, and come out on one side of the hat a little less than a third of the way up. Make a horizontal stitch about 3 sts wide, and run the yarn back down through the bottom of the hat, then pull the ends tight to create the mouth indent. For the corners of the mouth, bring the yarn back up through the bottom, pinch the edges above and below the mouth together and stitch through both layers, then repeat on the other side. Pinch the lower fold to form the bottom lip and work a few stitches in and out of the mouth and outer hat brim.

Eyes: Thread a long piece of yarn up through the bottom of the hat and out to RS about halfway up the hat face above the mouth, where an eye would be. Work 1 duplicate st, then thread the yarn back down through the hat and out the bottom again, then pull the ends tight. Repeat for the other eye.

Folds: Make a fold or two in the back to even out the hat, and stitch them closed by running the yarn in and out of the bottom of the hat each time. Shape the top of the hat by curling it over your fingers.

GRYFFINDOR LION
BODY

With colour C, CO 26 sts. Do not join. Beg with a WS row, work 9 rows in St st.

Next row (RS): Cast off 6 sts, knit to last 6 sts, cast off 6 sts – 14 sts rem. Cut yarn. Join yarn to rem sts.

Short Row 1 (RS): K3, w&t.

Short Row 2 (WS): P3.

Short Row 3: K3, knit next st and wrap together, knit to end of row.

Short Row 4: P3, w&t.

Short Row 5: K3.

Short Row 6: P3, purl next st and wrap together, purl to end of row.

Short Row 7: K4, w&t.

Short Row 8: P4.

Short Row 9: K4, knit next st and wrap together, knit to end of row.

Short Row 10: P4, w&t.

Short Row 11: K4.

Short Row 12: P4, purl next st and wrap together, purl to end of row, CO 6 sts using Backward Loop method – 20 sts.

Next row: Knit to end of row, then CO 6 sts – 26 sts.

Work 8 rows in St st.

Cast off all sts. Weave in ends.

HEAD

With colour C, CO 16 sts. Divide sts evenly over 2 dpn as follows: Hold needle with sts in left hand, and 2 empty dpn in right hand, *sl 1 st pwise to front needle, sl 1 st pwise to back needle; rep from * to end of row. Pm for beg of rnd.

Knit 8 rnds.

Next rnd: Remove beg-of-rnd marker, k4, then pm for new beg of rnd. Weave in ends.

Rearrange sts with first 8 sts on one dpn, and rem 8 sts on second dpn.

Stuff head lightly, then use Kitchener st to join sts for bottom of head. If necessary, shift half of the sts from one dpn to a third dpn in order to stuff the head, then return the shifted sts to the original needle.

FINISHING

Legs: With RS facing, fold CO edge so it meets first cast-off edges. Sew CO edge to cast-off edge to form front legs using mattress st. Rep for back legs. Stuff legs with polyester.

Body: Fold body in half so legs meet. Sew body together along rear and belly. Stuff body lightly with polyester, then sew together along chest.

Weave yarn through sts at bottom of each leg, then pull tight to close. Weave in ends.

If you are using 100% wool, roll lion between your hands vigorously for about 5 minutes to dry felt the piece. This makes the stitches tight and smooth.

Head: Sew head securely to body with whipstitch.

Tail: Join yarn to tail end of body and work a very tight 1-st I-cord for about 4 cm / 1½ in. Fasten off.

Cut 5 pieces of colour B, each about 6.5 cm / 2½ in. long. Attach strands to end of tail as for fringe. Separate the plies to fluff up the tail.

Eyes: Cut a strand of colour G 30.5 cm / 12 in. long. Holding strand doubled, make a double overhand knot in centre of strands. Thread ends through head 2 to 2½ sts from side of head and about 4 rows from CO edge. Pull ends gently to seat the eye. Secure ends. Rep for second eye on other side of face.

Nose: Thread tapestry needle with pink embroidery thread. Holding thread doubled, make 4 horizontal sts on lower face to create nose.

Mane: Thread tapestry needle with 2 long strands of colour B held together. Working on back of head, insert needle through a stitch and pull through, leaving a loop about 2.5 cm / 1 in. tall. Cont stitching all over back of head and under chin until back of head is completely covered. Cut open loops, then trim evenly.

HUFFLEPUFF BADGER

With colour A, CO 8 sts. Divide sts evenly onto 4 dpn. Pm and join to work in the rnd, being careful not to twist sts.

Rnd 1: Knit.

Rnd 2 (inc): K1, M1, k2, M1, k5 – 10 sts.

Rnd 3: Knit.

Rnd 4 (inc): [K1, M1] twice, k2, M1, k1, M1, k5 – 14 sts.

Rnd 5: Remove marker, k2, replace marker for new beg of rnd.

Rnd 6: Knit.

Rnd 7 (inc): [K2, M1] twice, k10 – 16 sts.

Rnd 8: Knit.

Rnd 9 (inc): K3, M1, k2, M1, k11 – 18 sts. Change to colour F.

Rnd 10: Knit.

Rnd 11 (inc): K3, M1, k4, M1, k11 – 20 sts.

Rnd 12: Knit.

Rnd 13 (inc): K3, M1, [k2, M1] 3 times, k11 – 24 sts.

Rnd 14: Remove marker, k2, replace marker for new beg of rnd.

Rnd 15: Knit.

Rnd 16 (inc): K2, M1, k8, M1, k14 – 26 sts.

Rnd 17: Knit.

Rnd 18: K2, M1, k3, M1, k4, M1, k3, M1, k14 – 30 sts.

Rnds 19–22: Knit.

Rnd 23 (dec): *K3, k2tog; rep from * to end of rnd – 24 sts rem.

Rnd 24: Knit.

Rnd 25 (dec): *K2, k2tog; rep from * to end of rnd – 18 sts rem.

Weave in ends, except CO tail. Stuff badger lightly with polyester stuffing.

Rnd 26: Knit.

Rnd 27 (dec): *K1, k2tog; rep from * to end of rnd – 12 sts rem.

Rnd 28 (dec): *K2tog; rep from * to end of rnd – 6 sts rem.

Cut yarn and thread tail through rem sts, pull tight to close.

FINISHING

Thread CO tail through sts of CO edge and pull tight to close hole.

If you are using 100% wool, roll badger between your hands vigorously for about 5 minutes to dry felt the piece. This makes the stitches tight and smooth.

Eye stripes: Thread long strand of colour D in tapestry needle. Holding yarn doubled, work 2 rows of duplicate stitch from snout to end of face. Fasten off and pull yarn to inside.

Nose: With a strand of colour D held doubled, make a single horizontal straight st at tip of snout. Fasten off and pull yarn to inside.

Ears: Cut 3 strands of colour F, each about 10 cm / 4 in. long. Thread strands through head next to eye stripes. Make a quadruple overhand knot, then pull ends tight. Pull ends to inside. Roll ear between fingers to smooth. Rep for rem ear.

RAVENCLAW EAGLE

With colour E, CO 8 sts. Divide sts evenly onto 4 dpn. Pm and join to work in the rnd, being careful not to twist sts.

Rnd 1: Knit.

Rnd 2 (inc): K1, M1, k2, M1, k5 – 10 sts.

Rnds 3–6: Knit.

Rnd 7: Knit, remove marker, k1, then replace marker for new beg of rnd.

Rnd 8 (inc): K1, M1, k2, M1, [k3 and place removable marker on last st worked for start of wing] twice, k1 – 12 sts.

Rnds 9–16: Knit.

Rnd 17 (dec): K1, [k2tog] twice, k7 – 10 sts rem.

Rnd 18 (dec): [K2tog] twice, k6 – 8 sts rem.

Rnd 19: Knit.

Stuff body lightly with polyester stuffing.

Rnds 20–23: Knit.

Cast off all sts loosely. Thread CO tail through sts of CO edge and pull to close hole. Weave in ends.

If you are using 100% wool, roll the body between your hands vigorously for about 5 minutes to dry felt the piece. This makes the stitches tight and smooth.

With a piece of contrasting colour yarn, run a line of tacking along each side of the 2 sts at the centre of the back to mark placement for wings; these 2 marked sts should be between the wings.

LEFT WING

With one dpn and colour E, beg at marker, pick up and knit 9 sts evenly along side of body in first leg of column of sts to left of marked sts, and ending about 3 cm / 1¼ in. from end of tail, turn and with second dpn pick up and knit 9 sts in second leg of same column of sts – 18 sts. Pm and join to work in the rnd. Rnds beg with top of wing.

Rnds 1–8: Knit.

Rnds 9–12: Ssk, k6, [k1f&b] twice, k6, k2tog.

Holding both dpn together, cast off 4 sts using Three-Needle Cast Off, then working rem sts on each dpn separately, knit to last st of front needle, k1f&b, then on second dpn, k1f&b, k3 – 10 sts rem.

Cast off rem of sts using Three-Needle Cast Off. Weave in ends.

RIGHT WING

With one dpn and colour E, beg about 3 cm / 1¼ in. from end of tail, pick up and knit 9 sts evenly along side of body in second leg of column of sts to right of marked sts, and ending at marker, turn and with second dpn pick up and knit 9 sts in first leg of same column of sts – 18 sts. Pm and join to work in the rnd. Rnds beg at underside of wing.

Rnds 1–8: Knit.

Rnds 9–12: Ssk, k6, [k1f&b] twice, k6, k2tog.

Holding both dpn together, cast off 4 sts using Three-Needle Cast Off, then working rem sts on each dpn separately, knit to last st of front needle, k1f&b, then on second dpn, k1f&b, k3 m– 10 sts rem.

Cast off rem of sts using Three-Needle Cast Off. Weave in ends.

BEAK

With colour C, pick up and knit 6 sts in the CO edge. Divide sts evenly over 2 dpn. Pm and join to work in the rnd.

Rnd 1 (dec): K1, [k2tog] twice, k1 – 4 sts rem.

Rnd 2 (dec): [K2tog] twice – 2 sts rem. Shift rem sts to one dpn.

Rnd 3: K2tog – 1 st rem. Fasten off rem st. Weave in ends. Shape beak by curving it over your fingers.

FINISHING

Sew tail closed, making sure tail is parallel to the wings.

Eyes: Cut a strand of colour G 30.5 cm / 12 in. long. Holding strand doubled, make a double overhand knot in centre of strands. Thread ends through side of head and about 3 rows from CO edge. Pull ends gently to seat the eye. Secure ends. Rep for second eye on other side of head.

SLYTHERIN SNAKE

With colour D, cast on 8 sts. Divide sts evenly onto 4 dpn. Pm and join to work in the rnd, being careful not to twist sts. Stuff the snake as you work, ending stuffing before beginning to shape the tail.

Rnd 1: Knit.

Rnd 2 (inc): [K1, M1, k2, M1, k1] twice – 12 sts.

Rnd 3: Knit.

Rnd 4 (inc): [K1, M1, k4, M1, k1] twice – 16 sts.

Rnds 5–6: Knit.

Rnd 7 (dec): [Ssk, k4, k2tog] twice – 12 sts rem.

Rnds 8–9: Knit.

Rnd 10 (dec): [Ssk, k2, k2tog] twice – 8 sts rem.

Rnd 11: Knit.

Rnd 12: K3, [k1-b] twice, k3.

Rnd 13: Knit.

Rnd 14: K3, [k1-b] twice, k3.

Rnd 15 (inc): K1, M1, k6, M1, k1 – 10 sts.

Rnds 16–17: Knit.

Rnd 18 (inc): K1, M1, k8, M1, k1 – 12 sts.

Rnds 19–20: Knit.

Rnd 21: K5, [k1-b] twice, k5.

Cont even until piece measures 12.5 cm / 5 in. from CO edge.

SHAPE TAIL

Next rnd: K5, [k1-b] twice, k5.

Dec rnd: K2tog, knit to end – 11 sts rem.

Knit 4 rnds even.

Rep last 5 rnds 9 more times, shift sts to fewer dpn as number of sts dec – 2 sts rem. Shift rem sts to one dpn.

Dec rnd: K2tog – 1 st rem.

Knit 2 rnds even. Fasten off rem st. Weave in ends.

FINISHING

If you are using 100% wool, roll snake between your hands vigorously for about 5 minutes to dry felt the piece. This makes the stitches tight and smooth.

Shape snake into a coil, and use tapestry needle threaded with straight sts in colour D to secure the snake into shape, allowing the tip of the tail to curl up a bit.

Eyes: Cut 4 strands of colour G each about 7.5 cm / 3 in. long. Holding strands together, make a single overhand knot in the centre of the strands. Thread ends through side of head. Pull ends gently to seat the eye. Secure ends. Rep for second eye on other side of head.

ASSEMBLY

Branches: Arrange branches or dowels in an *X* shape. Slip pipe cleaner under centre of the X, then wrap up and over the top. Give ends of pipe cleaner two tight twists. Wrap ends of pipe cleaner down between other sides of branches so they form an X over the top of the branches and meet at bottom. Make two more tight twists. Finally, wrap ends of pipe cleaner up again, twist them at the top, and shape leftovers into a ring, twisting them together to secure. Thread a long piece of string through the ring for hanging.

Creatures: Run twine or thread through top of each creature, experimenting to find the balancing point. Double the twine, then trim to desired length (display is about 34.5 cm / 13½ in. cm tall). Tie an overhand knot near the creature. Tie ends of doubled twine. Place the creatures on the ends of the branches or dowels. Hang the Sorting Hat at the centre.

Balancing: The lion is the heaviest, so you may have to slip a few small stones, washers or weights between the sts of the snake to get them to balance out. Bend the pipe cleaner loop to further refine the balancing.

Greenery (optional): Attach a few bits of greenery and pine cones with floral wire or glue gun.

'HMM, DIFFICULT, VERY DIFFICULT. PLENTY OF COURAGE, I SEE, AND NOT A BAD MIND EITHER. THERE'S TALENT, OH YES, AND A THIRST TO PROVE YOURSELF, BUT WHERE TO PUT YOU?'

Sorting Hat, *Harry Potter and the Philosopher's Stone*

BEHIND THE MAGIC

The Sorting Hat was designed by costume designer Judianna Makovsky for *Harry Potter and the Philosopher's Stone*. Seven physical versions of the hat were made for the eight films, and a digital version was used when the hat had to speak.

ABOVE: Harry Potter is sorted into Gryffindor house during his first night at Hogwarts.

THE SEVEN HORCRUXES WASHCLOTHS

Designed by **TANIS GRAY**

SKILL LEVEL ⚡

In *Harry Potter and the Half-Blood Prince*, Harry witnesses a memory of a young Tom Riddle asking Professor Slughorn about Horcruxes: enchanted objects in which a magical person conceals a portion of their soul, rendering themselves immortal. Despite his teacher's strong advice against it, Riddle – the future Lord Voldemort – eventually creates seven Horcruxes: Marvolo Gaunt's ring, Salazar Slytherin's locket, Helga Hufflepuff's cup, Rowena Ravenclaw's diadem, his own diary, Harry Potter and Nagini the snake. The only way to truly destroy Voldemort is to destroy the Horcruxes.

These seven Horcrux-themed washcloths may not make you immortal, but they will help keep you clean! Knit back and forth in rows with knits and purls creating a relief texture – using cotton for durability and ease of care – these washcloths are the perfect accessory for the bathroom. Each completely reversible washcloth represents a different Horcrux.

SIZE
One size

FINISHED MEASUREMENTS
Width: 26.5 cm / 10½ in.
Length: 26.5 cm / 10½ in.

YARN
Worsted weight (medium #4) yarn, shown in Blue Sky Fibers *Organic Cotton Worsted* (100% certified organic cotton); 137 m / 150 yd. per 100 g / 3½ oz. hank), 1 hank each washcloth

Colour A: #633 Pickle (Nagini and locket)
Colour B: #625 Graphite (ring and locket)
Colour C: #619 Tomato (Harry)
Colour D: #638 Dandelion (cup)
Colour E: #632 Mediterranean (diadem)

NEEDLES
- 5 mm / US 8 needles or size needed to obtain correct tension

NOTIONS
- Tapestry needle

TENSION
15 sts and 23 rows = 10 cm / 4 in. in St st
Be sure to check your tension.

NOTES
- Each washcloth uses about half a hank. If you're making all the washcloths in the colours listed above, you may need a second hank of colours A and B.
- Because of the nature of stocking stitch, finished washcloths are completely reversible.

Continued on page 186

WASHCLOTHS

With colour for desired washcloth, CO 40 sts.

Work from appropriate chart, or as follows for each washcloth:

NAGINI

Rows 1–5: Knit.
Rows 6, 8 and 10 (WS): K3, p34, k3.
Rows 7 and 9 (RS): Knit.
Row 11: K17, p6, k17.
Row 12: K3, p12, k10, p12, k3.
Row 13: K13, p13, k14.
Row 14: K3, p9, k16, p9, k3.
Row 15: K11, p18, k11.
Row 16: K3, p7, k20, p7, k3.
Row 17: K9, p6, k7, p9, k9.
Row 18: K3, p6, k8, p10, k5, p5, k3.
Row 19: K7, p5, k12, p8, k8.
Row 20: K3, p5, k7, p14, k4, p4, k3.
Row 21: K6, p4, k15, p8, k7.
Row 22: K3, p4, k7, p16, k4, p3, k3.
Row 23: K6, p4, k16, p7, k7.
Row 24: K3, p4, k6, p17, k4, p3, k3.
Row 25: K6, p4, k17, p6, k7.
Row 26: K3, p4, k6, p17, k4, p3, k3.
Row 27: K6, p4, k4, p5, k8, p6, k7.
Row 28: K3, p4, k6, p7, k7, p2, k4, p4, k3.
Row 29: K7, p14, k6, p6, k7.
Row 30: K3, p5, k5, p6, k3, p3, k8, p4, k3.
Row 31: K8, p6, k3, p4, k6, p5, k8.
Row 32: K3, p6, k5, p5, k12, p6, k3.
Row 33: K9, p11, k5, p6, k9.
Row 34: K3, p7, k5, p6, k11, p5, k3.
Row 35: K8, p4, k12, p5, k11.
Row 36: K3, p9, k5, p12, k3, p5, k3.
Row 37: K8, p3, k11, p5, k13.
Row 38: K3, p11, k5, p10, k3, p5, k3.
Row 39: K8, p3, k8, p5, k6, p1, k1, p1, k7.
Row 40: K3, p5, k1, p8, k5, p7, k2, p6, k3.
Row 41: K10, p1, k6, p5, k9, p1, k8.
Row 42: K3, p5, k1, p10, k5, p4, k1, p8, k3.
Row 43: K15, p5, k11, p1, k8.
Row 44: K3, p4, k4, p10, k5, p11, k3.
Row 45: K13, p5, k10, p5, k7.
Row 46: K3, p4, k6, p10, k5, p9, k3.
Row 47: K11, p5, k10, p3, k1, p3, k7.
Row 48: K3, p5, k6, p10, k5, p8, k3.
Row 49: K10, p6, k10, p5, k9.

Row 50: K3, p7, k5, p9, k6, p7, k3.
Row 51: K10, p6, k8, p5, k11.
Row 52: K3, p11, k3, p6, k6, p8, k3.
Row 53: K11, p7, k4, p3, k15.
Row 54: K3, p13, k12, p9, k3.
Row 55: K13, p10, k17.
Row 56: K3, p15, k8, p11, k3.
Row 57: k16, p4, k20.
Rows 58 and 60: K3, p34, k3.
Rows 59 and 61–64: Knit.
Cast off kwise.

LOCKET

Rows 1–5: Knit.
Rows 6 and 8 (WS): K3, p34, k3.
Row 7 (RS): Knit.
Row 9: K17, p5, k18.
Row 10: K3, p14, k7, p13, k3.
Row 11: K15, p9, k16.
Row 12: K3, p12, k3, p5, k3, p11, k3.
Rows 13, 15, 17, 19, 21, and 23: K14, p2, k7, p2, k15.
Rows 14, 16, 18, 20, 22, and 24: K3, p12, k2, p7, k2, p11, k3.
Row 25: K14, p3, k5, p3, k15.
Row 26: K3, p13, k9, p12, k3.
Row 27: K16, p7, k17.
Row 28: K3, p15, k5, p14, k3.
Row 29: K19, p1, k20.
Row 30: K3, p17, k1, p16, k3.
Row 31: K18, p1, k1, p1, k19.
Row 32: K3, p16, k1, p1, k1, p15, k3.
Row 33: K13, p4, k2, p1, k20.
Row 34: K3, p15, k10, p9, k3.
Row 35: K12, p2, k3, p6, k17.
Row 36: K3, p7, k9, p7, k2, p9, k3.
Row 37: K11, p3, k8, p9, k9.
Row 38: K3, p5, k2, p17, k3, p7, k3.
Row 39: K9, p3, k19, p2, k7.
Row 40: K3, p3, k2, p21, k3, p5, k3.
Row 41: K7, p3, k22, p2, k6.
Rows 42, 44, 46 and 48: K3, p3, k2, p23, k2, p4, k3.
Rows 43, 45 and 47: K7, p2, k23, p2, k6.
Row 49: K7, p3, k21, p3, k6.
Row 50: K3, p4, k3, p19, k3, p5, k3.
Row 51: K9, p3, k17, p3, k8.
Row 52: K3, p6, k3, p15, k3, p7, k3.
Row 53: K11, p3, k13, p3, k10.

Row 54: K3, p8, k3, p11, k3, p9, k3.
Row 55: K13, p6, k6, p3, k12.
Row 56: K3, p10, k12, p12, k3.
Row 57: K17, p9, k14.
Rows 58 and 60: K3, p34, k3.
Rows 59 and 61–64: Knit.
Cast off kwise.

DIARY

Rows 1–5: Knit.
Rows 6 and 8 (WS): K3, p34, k3.
Row 7 (RS): Knit.
Row 9: K23, p6, k11.
Row 10: K3, p8, k11, p15, k3.
Row 11: K14, p15, k11.
Row 12: K3, p8, k19, p7, k3.
Row 13: K8, p22, k10.
Rows 14 and 16: K3, p7, k23, p4, k3.
Rows 15 and 17: K7, p23, k10.
Rows 18, 20 and 22: K3, p7, k22, p1, k1, p3, k3.
Rows 19 and 21: K6, p1, k1, p22, k10.
Row 23: K6, p1, k1, p23, k9.
Row 24: K3, p6, k23, p1, k1, p3, k3.
Rows 25, 27, 29 and 31: K7, p1, k1, p22, k9.
Rows 26, 28 and 30: K3, p6, k22, p1, k1, p4, k3.
Row 32: K3, p5, k23, p1, k1, p4, k3.
Rows 33, 35 and 37: K8, p1, k1, p22, k8.
Rows 34 and 36: K3, p5, k22, p1, k1, p5, k3.
Row 38: K3, p5, k21, p1, k1, p6, k3.
Rows 39, 41, 43 and 45: K9, p1, k1, p22, k7.
Rows 40, 42, 44 and 46: K3, p4, k22, p1, k1, p6, k3.
Row 47: K10, p1, k1, p21, k7.
Rows 48 and 50: K3, p3, k22, p1, k1, p7, k3.
Row 49: K10, p1, k1, p22, k6.
Row 51: K11, p1, k1, p21, k6.
Row 52: K3, p3, k21, p1, k1, p8, k3.
Row 53: K12, p16, k4, p1, k7.
Row 54: K3, p5, k4, p4, k10, p1, k1, p9, k3.
Row 55: K12, p1, k1, p5, k5, p5, k11.
Row 56: K3, p13, k5, p5, k1, p10, k3.
Row 57: K13, p7, k20.
Rows 58 and 60: K3, p34, k3.
Rows 59 and 61–64: Knit.
Cast off kwise.

HARRY POTTER: 'BUT IF YOU COULD FIND THEM ALL, IF YOU COULD DESTROY EVERY HORCRUX.'

PROFESSOR DUMBLEDORE: 'ONE DESTROYS VOLDEMORT.'

Harry Potter and the Half-Blood Prince

TOP RIGHT: Concept art of Marvolo Gaunt's ring by Adam Brockbank.

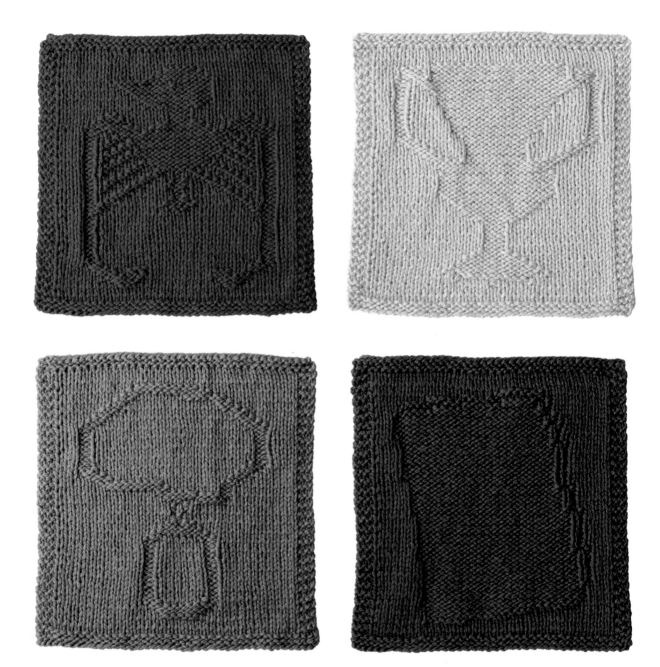

RING

Rows 1–5: Knit.
Rows 6, 8 and 10 (WS): K3, p34, k3.
Rows 7 and 9 (RS): Knit.
Row 11: K15, p9, k16.
Row 12: K3, p12, k11, p11, k3.
Row 13: K13, p13, k14.
Row 14: K3, p10, k15, p9, k3.
Row 15: K11, p4, k9, p4, k12.
Row 16: K3, p8, k4, p11, k4, p7, k3.
Row 17: K9, p4, k13, p4, k10.
Row 18: K3, p6, k4, p15, k4, p5, k3.
Row 19: K8, p4, k15, p4, k9.
Rows 20: K3, p5, k4, p17, k4, p4, k3.
Rows 21: K7, p4, k17, p4, k8.
Rows 22–35: Rep Rows 20 and 21 seven times.
Rows 36–37: Rep Rows 18 and 19.
Row 38: Repeat Row 18.
Row 39: K8, p5, k13, p5, k9.
Row 40: K3, p7, k5, p11, k5, p6, k3.
Row 41: K9, p6, k9, p6, k10.
Row 42: K3, p7, k8, p5, k8, p6, k3.
Row 43: K10, p19, k11.
Row 44: K3, p8, k19, p7, k3.
Row 45: K10, p6, k3, p1, k3, p6, k11.
Row 46: K3, p9, k4, p3, k3, p3, k4, p8, k3.
Row 47: K12, p3, k2. p5, k2, p3, k13.
Row 48: K3, p11, k2, p1, k7, p1, k2, p10, k3.
Row 49: K14, p11, k15.
Row 50: K3, p11, k11, p12, k3.
Row 51: K13, p13, k14.
Row 52: K3, p12, k11, p11, k3.
Row 53: K15, p9, k16.
Row 54: K3, p14, k7, p13, k3.
Row 55: K17, p5, k18.
Row 56: K3, p16, k3, p15, k3.
Row 57: K19, p1, k20.
Rows 58 and 60: K3, p34, k3.
Rows 59, and 61–64: Knit.
Cast off kwise.

HARRY

Rows 1–5: Knit.
Rows 6, 8, 10, 12, 14 and 16 (WS): K3, p34, k3.
Rows 7, 9, 11, 13 and 15 (RS): Knit.
Row 17: K9, p5, k12, p5, k9.

Row 18: K3, p5, k7, p10, k7, p5, k3.
Row 19: K7, p9, k8, p9, k7.
Row 20: K3, p3, k4, p3, k4, p6, k4, p3, k4, p3, k3.
Row 21: [K6, p3, k5, p3] twice, k6.
Rows 22 and 24: K3, p3, k2, p7, k2, p6, k2, p7, k2, p3, k3.
Rows 23 and 25: [K6, p2, k7, p2] twice, k6.
Row 26: K3, p1, k4, p7, k4, p2, k4, p7, k4, p1, k3.
Row 27: K4, p4, k7, p10, k7, p4, k4.
Row 28: K3, p1, k4, p7, k10, p7, k4, p1, k3.
Row 29: K6, p2, k7, [p2, k2] twice, p2, k7, p2, k6.
Rows 30–31: Rep Rows 22 and 23.
Row 32: K3, p3, k3, p5, k3, p6, k3, p5, k3, p3, k3.
Row 33: [K6, p4, k3, p4] twice, k6.
Row 34: K3, p4, k9, p8, k9, p4, k3.
Row 35: K8, p7, k10, p7, k8.
Row 36: K3, p6, k5, p12, k5, p6, k3.
Row 37: Knit.
Row 38: K3, p2, k1, p31, k3.
Row 39: K32, p2, k6.
Row 40: K3, p4, k2, p28, k3.
Row 41: K30, p2, k8.
Row 42: K3, p6, k3, p25, k3.
Row 43: K27, p3, k10.
Row 44: K3, p8, k3, p23, k3.
Row 45: K24, p4, k12.
Row 46: K3, p10, k4, p20, k3.
Row 47: K22, p4, k14.
Row 48: K3, p7, k9, p18, k3.
Row 49: K20, p9, k11.
Row 50: K3, p9, k9, p16, k3.
Row 51: K18, p8, k14.
Row 52: K3, p12, k3, p19, k3.
Row 53: K21, p3, k16.
Row 54: K3, p15, k2, p17, k3.
Row 55: K19, p2, k19.
Row 56: K3, p17, k2, p15, k3.
Row 57: K17, p1, k22.
Rows 58 and 60: K3, p34, k3.
Rows 59 and 61–64: Knit.
Cast off kwise.

RIGHT: The prop of the fake locket, left in the Crystal Cave by Regulus Black, that is rediscovered by Harry Potter and Professor Dumbledore in *Harry Potter and the Half-Blood Prince*.

BEHIND THE MAGIC

According to graphic artist Miraphora Mina, the locket was one of the more challenging Horcruxes to design because it had to seem 'full of evil, but also needed to have a beauty to it – to be something appealing and historical'. Its final design was inspired by a piece of Spanish jewellery from the eighteenth century that Mina saw in a museum.

Behind the Magic

In the films, three of the Horcruxes – the ring, the locket and Nagini – are ultimately destroyed by the Sword of Gryffindor. To create this hero prop, the prop makers researched medieval swords and even purchased a real one at auction for reference.

TOP RIGHT: The prop of Ravenclaw's diadem used in *Harry Potter and the Deathly Hallows – Part 2*. ABOVE: Ron Weasley (Rupert Grint) destroys Slytherin's locket with the Sword of Gryffindor in *Harry Potter and the Deathly Hallows – Part 1*.

CUP

Rows 1–5: Knit.
Rows 6 and 8 (WS): K3, p34, k3.
Row 7 (RS): Knit.
Row 9: K19, p1, k20.
Row 10: K3, p12, [k1, p4] twice, k1, p11, k3.
Row 11: K15, p9, k16.
Row 12: K3, p10, k1, p1, k11, p1, k1, p9, k3.
Row 13: K13, p13, k14.
Row 14: K3, p12, k11, p11, k3.
Row 15: K15, p9, k16.
Row 16: K3, p14, k7, p13, k3.
Row 17: K17, p5, k18.
Rows 18, 20 and 22: K3, p16, k3, p15, k3.
Rows 19, 21 and 23: K18, p3, k19.
Row 24: K3, p14, k7, p13, k3.
Row 25: K15, p9, k16.
Row 26: K3, p12, k11, p11, k3.
Row 27: K13, p13, k14.
Row 28: K3, p10, k15, p9, k3.
Rows 29, 31 and 33: K11, p17, k12.
Rows 30 and 32: K3, p9, k17, p8, k3.
Row 34: K3, p10, k15, p9, k3.
Row 35: Rep Row 29.
Row 36: K3, p8, k19, p7, k3.
Row 37: K9, p3, k3, p9, k3, p3, k10.
Row 38: K3, p6, k3, p4, k9, p4, k3, p5, k3.
Row 39: K7, p3, k5, p9, k5, p3, k8.
Row 40: K3, p4, k3, p6, k9, p6, k3, p3, k3.
Row 41: K5, p3, k7, p9, k7, p3, k6.
Row 42: K3, p3, k2, p7, k11, p7, k2, p2, k3.
Rows 43 and 45: K5, p2, k6, p13, k6, p2, k6.
Row 44: K3, p3, k2, p6, k13, p6, k2, p2, k3.
Rows 46 and 48: K3, p3, k2, p5, k15, p5, k2, p2, k3.
Row 47: K5, p2, k5, p15, k5, p2, k6.
Row 49: K5, p2, k4, p17, k4, p2, k6.
Row 50: K3, p3, k2, p4, k17, p4, k2, p2, k3.
Row 51: K5, p2, k3, p19, k3, p2, k6.
Row 52: K3, p3, k2, p2, k21, p2, k2, p2, k3.
Row 53: K5, p2, k1, p23, k1, p2, k6.
Row 54: K3, p3, k29, p2, k3.
Row 55: K6, p3, k1, p19, k1, p3, k7.
Row 56: K3, p4, k3, p1, k19, p1, k3, p3, k3.
Row 57: K10, p19, k11.
Rows 58 and 60: K3, p34, k3.
Rows 59 and 61–64: Knit.
Cast off kwise.

DIADEM

Rows 1–5: Knit.
Rows 6 and 8 (WS): K3, p34, k3.
Row 7 (RS): Knit.
Row 9: K11, p2, k13, p2, k12.
Row 10: K3, p8, k4, p11, k4, p7, k3.
Row 11: [K9, p6] twice, k10.
Row 12: K3, p6, k3, p1, k3, p9, k3, p1, k3, p5, k3.
Row 13: K7, p3, k19, p3, k8.
Row 14: K3, p4, k3, p21, k3, p3, k3.
Rows 15, 17, 19, 21 and 23: K6, p2, k23, p2, k7.
Rows 16, 18, 20, 22 and 24: K3, p4, k2, p23, k2, p3, k3.
Row 25: K6, p3, k10, p1, k10, p3, k7.
Row 26: K3, p4, k4, p8, k3, p8, k4, p3, k3.
Row 27: K6, p2, k1, p2, k6, p5, k6, p2, k1, p2, k7.
Row 28: K3, p4, k2, p2, k2, p6, k3, p6, k2, p2, k2, p3, k3.
Row 29: K6, p2, k3, p2, k6, p1, k6, p2, k3, p2, k7.
Row 30: K3, p4, k2, p1, k1, p2, k2, p5, k1, p5, k2, p2, k1, p1, k2, p3, k3.
Row 31: K6, p2, k1, p2, k2, p2, k3, p3, k3, p2, k2, p2, k1, p2, k7.
Row 32: K3, p4, [k2, p2] 3 times, k3, [p2, k2] 3 times, p3, k3.
Row 33: K6, p2, k3, [p2, k2] twice, p1, [k2, p2] twice, k3, p2, k7.
Row 34: K3, p4, k2, p1, k1, [p2, k2] twice, p1, k1, p1, [k2, p2] twice, k1, p1, k2, p3, k3.
Row 35: K6, p2, k1, [p2, k2] twice, p5, [k2, p2] twice, k1, p2, k7.
Row 36: K3, p4, [k2, p2] twice, k11, [p2, k2] twice, p3, k3.
Row 37: K6, p2, k1, p1, k1, p2, k2, p9, k2, p2, k1, p1, k1, p2, k7.
Row 38: K3, p4, [k2, p1] twice, k15, [p1, k2] twice, p3, k3.
Row 39: K6, p2, k2, p2, k1, p13, k1, p2, k2, p2, k7.
Row 40: K3, p4, k2, p1, k1, p1, k2, p1, k11, p1, k2, p1, k1, p1, k2, p3, k3.
Row 41: K6, [p2, k1] twice, p15, [k1, p2] twice, k7.
Row 42: K3, p4, k2, p2, k2, p1, k13, p1, k2, p2, k2, p3, k3.

Row 43: K6, p3, k2, p17, k2, p3, k7.
Row 44: K3, p4, k8, p1, k9, p1, k8, p3, k3.
Row 45: K7, p6, k3, p7, k3, p6, k8.
Row 46: K3, p6, k4, p6, k3, p6, k4, p5, k3.
Row 47: K9, p2, k7, p3, k7, p2, k10.
Row 48: K3, p16, k3, p15, k3.
Row 49: K16, p8, k16.
Row 50: K3, p12, k10, p12, k3.
Row 51: K15, p11, k14.
Row 52: K3, p10, k12, p12, k3.
Row 53: K15, p13, k12.
Row 54: K3, p8, k8, p1, k5, p12, k3.
Row 55: K15, p9, k16.
Row 56: K3, p14, k7, p13, k3.
Row 57: K17, p5, k18.
Rows 58 and 60: K3, p34, k3.
Rows 59 and 61–64: Knit.
Cast off kwise.

FINISHING

Weave in ends. Block to finished measurements.

CUP

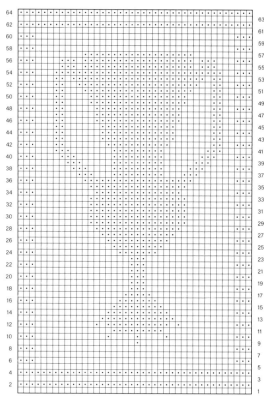

CHART 74

CHARTS

KEY

☐ k on RS; p on WS

· p on RS; k on WS

RING

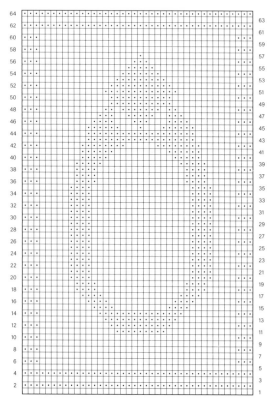

CHART 77

HARRY

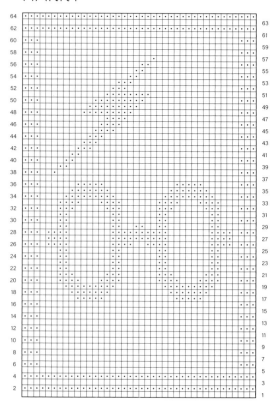

CHART 78

DIADEM

CHART 75

DIARY

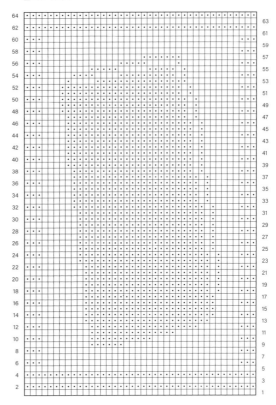

CHART 76

LOCKET

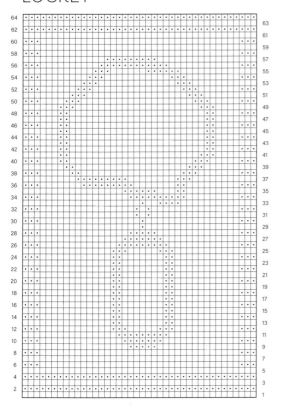

CHART 79

NAGINI

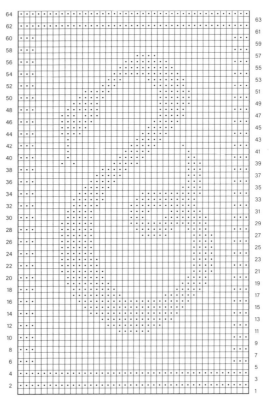

CHART 80

Order of the Phoenix Lace-Knit Throw Blanket

Designed by **JENNIFER LORI**

SKILL LEVEL ⚡⚡⚡

Introduced in the fifth film, the Order of the Phoenix is a group of skilled witches and wizards dedicated to fighting Lord Voldemort. The Order is named after the magical bird that bursts into flame at the end of its life and is reborn from the ashes. In the films, phoenixes are commonly associated with Professor Dumbledore, who is the founder of the Order and has a phoenix called Fawkes for a companion.

Knit in fiery orange-red yarn, this blanket celebrates the Order of the Phoenix and its spectacular winged namesake. Worked in the round from the centre out, beginning with a circular cast on, this blanket grows outwards rapidly. The inner medallion motif creates small flames, followed by 'The Order of the Phoenix' spelled out in lace letters. Gorgeous phoenix feathers fan out in multiple tiers, and the cast off creates a scalloped edge. Want a bigger or smaller blanket? A heavier or lighter weight of yarn and corresponding needles make the size easy to adjust.

SIZE
One size

FINISHED MEASUREMENTS
Diameter: 139.5 cm / 55 in.

YARN
DK weight (light #3) yarn, shown in Neighborhood Fiber Co. *Studio DK* (100% superwash merino wool; 251 m / 275 yd. per 113 g / 4 oz. hank) in colour Bolton Hill, 7 hanks

NEEDLES
- 4 mm / US 6 circular needles, 60 cm / 24 in. , 80 cm / 32 in. and 120 cm / 47 in. long, and set of 5 double-pointed needles or size needed to obtain correct tension

NOTIONS
- Stitch markers (with one in a distinct colour for beg of rnd)
- Blocking pins
- Tapestry needle

TENSION
21 sts and 29 rnds = 10 cm / 4 in. in St st, blocked
Tension is not critical for this pattern, but the yarn weight and needle size used will affect the finished measurements.

Continued on page 196

- Markers are used to indicate the beginning of the round and the chart sections for the text. Slip all markers as you come to them unless instructed otherwise.
- Even-numbered rounds of charts B, C, D, E and F (charts 82–85 and 87) and the Feather Chart (chart 86) are not shown; these rounds should be knit.

SPECIAL TECHNIQUE

Circular Cast On: Make a clockwise loop with yarn around last 3 fingers of your left hand, with the tail *over* the strand coming from the ball at the outside of your hand. Hold the tail end with your left thumb, leaving tail approximately 30.5 cm / 12 in. long. Holding the double-pointed needle in your right hand and using the end of the yarn coming from the ball, *yarn over, insert double-pointed needle into loop on your left hand, yarn over, and draw yarn through a loop (2 stitches cast on); repeat from * until required number of stitches have been cast on. After a few rounds have been worked, you can pull on the tail to close the loop into a tight circle.

SPECIAL TERM

M2 (make 2): [K1, yo, k1] in the same st – 2 sts inc'd.

BLANKET

With dpn, CO 8 sts using Circular CO. Divide sts evenly over 4 dpn. Pm and join to work in the rnd, being careful not to twist sts.

Change to circular needle as the number of stitches increases, then to longer circular needle when needed.

Setup rnd: [K1, k1 tbl] 4 times.

Work Chart A (chart 81), or as follows:

Rnd 1 (inc): [K1f&b] 8 times – 16 sts.
Rnd 2: Knit.
Rnd 3 (inc): [K1, yo, k1] 8 times – 24 sts.
Rnd 4: [K1, k1 tbl, k1] 8 times.
Rnd 5 (inc): [K2, yo, k1] 8 times – 32 sts.
Rnd 6: [K2, k1 tbl, k1] 8 times.
Rnd 7 (inc): [K1, yo, k3] 8 times – 40 sts.
Rnd 8: [K1, k1 tbl, k3] 8 times.
Rnd 9 (inc): [K4, yo, k1] 8 times – 48 sts.
Rnd 10: [K4, k1 tbl, k1] 8 times.
Rnd 11 (inc): [K1, yo, k5] 8 times – 56 sts.
Rnd 12: [K1, k1 tbl, k5] 8 times.
Rnd 13 (inc): [K6, yo, k1] 8 times – 64 sts.
Rnd 14: [K6, k1 tbl, k1] 8 times.
Rnd 15 (inc): [K1, yo, k2tog, yo, M2, yo, ssk, k2] 8 times – 88 sts.
Rnd 16: [K1, k1 tbl, k9] 8 times.
Rnd 17 (inc): [K2, k2tog, yo, k1, M2, k1, yo, ssk, k1, yo, k1] 8 times – 112 sts.
Rnd 18: [K12, k1 tbl, k1] 8 times.
Rnd 19 (inc): [K1, yo, k1, k2tog, yo, k2, M2, k2, yo, ssk, k3] 8 times – 136 sts.
Rnd 20: [K1, k1 tbl, k15] 8 times.
Rnd 21 (inc): [K3, k2tog, yo, k3, M2, k3, yo, ssk, k2, yo, k1] 8 times – 160 sts.
Rnd 22: [K18, k1 tbl, k1] 8 times.
Rnd 23 (inc): [K1, yo, k2, k2tog, yo, k4, M2, k4, yo, ssk, k4] 8 times – 184 sts.
Rnd 24: [K1, k1 tbl, k21] 8 times.
Rnd 25 (dec): [K4, k2tog, yo, k4, s2kp, k4, yo, ssk, k3, yo, k1] 8 times – 176 sts rem.
Rnd 26: [K20, k1 tbl, k1] 8 times.
Rnd 27 (dec): [K1, yo, k3, k2tog, yo, k3, s2kp, k3, yo, ssk, k5] 8 times – 168 sts rem.
Rnd 28: [K1, k1 tbl, k19] 8 times.

Rnd 29 (dec): [K5, k2tog, yo, k2, s2kp, k2, yo, ssk, k4, yo, k1] 8 times – 160 sts rem.
Rnd 30: [K18, k1 tbl, k1] 8 times.
Rnd 31 (dec): [K1, yo, k4, k2tog, yo, k1, s2kp, k1, yo, ssk, k6] 8 times – 152 sts rem.
Rnd 32: [K1, k1 tbl, k17] 8 times.
Rnd 33 (dec): [K6, k2tog, yo, s2kp, yo, ssk, k5, yo, k1] 8 times – 144 sts rem.
Rnd 34: [K16, k1 tbl, k1] 8 times.

Knit 4 rnds even.

Work Chart B (chart 82), or as follows:

Rnd 1: [K6, k2tog, yo, k1, yo, ssk, k7] 8 times.
Rnds 2, 4, 6 and 8: Knit.
Rnd 3: [K5, k2tog, yo, k3, yo, ssk, k6] 8 times.
Rnd 5: [K4, k2tog, yo, k5, yo, ssk, k3, k2tog, yo] 8 times.
Rnd 7: [Yo, ssk, k1, k2tog, yo, k7, yo, ssk, k1, k2tog, yo, k1] 8 times.
Rnd 9: [K1, yo, s2kp, yo, k9, yo, s2kp, yo, k2] 8 times.

Knit 3 rnds even.

Inc rnd: [K1, yo] around – 288 sts.

Knit 7 rnds even.

Setup rnd: K108, pm, k38, pm, k24, pm, k80, pm, k38.

Next rnd: Working Rnd 1 each chart, work Chart C (chart 83) over next 108 sts, sm, Chart D (chart 84) over next 38 sts, sm, Chart E (chart 85) over next 24 sts, sm, Chart F (chart 87) over next 80 sts, sm, then Chart D over rem 38 sts.

Work Rnds 2–31 of charts as established.

Knit 9 rnds even, and remove all markers except beg-of-rnd marker.

Inc Rnd: [K1, yo] around – 576 sts.

Knit 1 rnd even.

Work Feather Chart (chart 86), or as follows:

Rnd 1: *K4, yo, s2kp, yo, k5; rep from * to end of rnd.
Rnd 2 and all other even-numbered rnds: Knit.

Rnd 3: *K3, yo, k1, s2kp, k1, yo, k4; rep from * to end of rnd.

Rnd 5: *K2, yo, k2, s2kp, k2, yo, k3; rep from * to end of rnd.

Rnd 7: *K1, yo, k3, s2kp, k3, yo, k2; rep from * to end of rnd.

Rnds 9, 11, 13 and 15: *Yo, k4, s2kp, k4, yo, k1; rep from * to end of rnd.

Rnd 17: Remove marker, sl 1 wyib, replace marker, k5, *k4, yo, s2kp, yo, k5; rep from * to last 7 sts, k4, yo, s2kp, yo.

Rnd 19: Remove marker, sl 1 wyib, replace marker, k4, *k3, yo, k1, s2kp, k1, yo, k4; rep from * to last 8 sts, k3, yo, k1, s2kp, k1, yo.

Rnd 21: Remove marker, sl 1 wyib, replace marker, k3, *k2, yo, k2, s2kp, k2, yo, k3; rep from * to last 9 sts, k2, yo, k2, s2kp, k2, yo.

Rnd 23: Remove marker, sl 1 wyib, replace marker, k2, *k1, yo, k3, s2kp, k3, yo, k2; rep from * to last 10 sts, k1, yo, k3, s2kp, k3, yo.

Rnd 25: Remove marker, sl 1 wyib, replace marker, k1, *yo, k4, s2kp, k4, yo, k1; rep from * to last 11 sts, yo, k4, s2kp, k4, yo.

Rnds 27, 29, 31, 33, and 35: K1, *yo, k4, s2kp, k4, yo, k1; rep from * to last 11 sts, yo, k4, s2kp, k4, yo.

Rnd 37: Remove marker, sl 2 wyib, replace marker, *k9, yo, s2kp, yo; rep from * to end of rnd.

Rnds 39–45: Rep Rnds 19–25.

Rnds 47, 49, 51, 53, 55, 57 and 59: Rep Rnd 27.

Rnd 61: Rep Rnd 37.

Rnds 63–69: Rep Rnds 19–25.

Rnds 71–87: Rep Rnd 27.

Rnd 89: Rep Rnd 37.

Rnd 90: Knit to last st, sl 1, remove beg-of-rnd marker, return sl st to LH needle, replace marker for new beg of rnd.

BORDER

Row 1 (RS): K11, turn – 12 sts on RH needle.

Row 2 (WS): P10, turn.

Row 3: K9, turn.

Row 4: P8, turn.

Row 5: K7, turn.

Row 6: P6, turn.

Row 7: K5, turn.

Row 8: P4, turn.

Row 9: K3, turn.

Row 10: P8, turn.

Row 11: Cast off 12 sts loosely kwise – 1 st rem on RH needle. *Last st on RH needle should be st above s2kp of last rnd.*

Rep Rows 1–11 forty-six more times – 12 sts rem.

Rep Rows 1–10 once more, then cast off rem sts loosely kwise.

FINISHING

Weave in ends but do not cut until after blanket has been blocked.

Soak blanket in cool water until thoroughly wet. Remove from water and squeeze out most of the water, being careful not to wring or twist the piece. Lay blanket between two towels, and roll towels to blot out most of the remaining water. Pin blanket out to 157.5 cm / 62 in. diameter, placing pins in tips of feathers and allowing rem cast-off edge to scallop; piece will relax to finished measurements after removing pins. Allow to dry completely. Trim yarn ends.

BEHIND THE MAGIC

The Order of the Phoenix is headquartered at Number 12 Grimmauld Place – the ancestral home of Sirius Black, invisible to Muggle eyes. The façade of a row of townhouses was built at Pinewood Studios to film the exterior shots, while the sudden appearance of the house was achieved through digital effects.

ABOVE LEFT: The façade of Number 12 Grimmauld Place, headquarters of the Order of the Phoenix. ABOVE RIGHT: Members of the Order of the Phoenix arrive at Number 4 Privet Drive, to rescue Harry in *Harry Potter and the Order of the Phoenix*.

CHARTS

KEY

□	knit	◢	k3tog
⊙	yo	⋀	s2kp
ℓ	k1 tbl	⩔	M2
◿	k2tog	◺	k1f&b
◺	ssk	▢	repeat

A

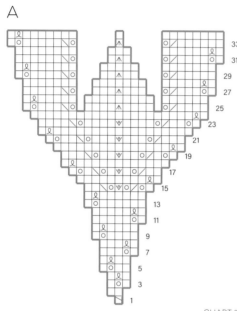

CHART 81

B

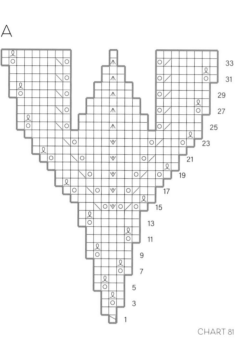

NOTE: Chart shows only odd-numbered rounds. Knit all even-numbered rounds; chart ends with Round 9.

CHART 82

C

NOTE: Chart shows only odd-numbered rounds. Knit all even-numbered rounds; chart ends with Round 31.

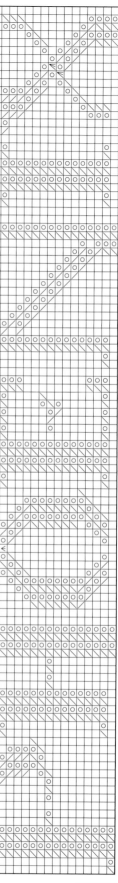

CHART 83

D

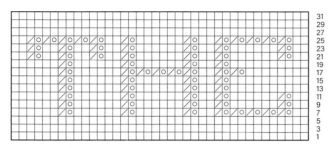

NOTE: Chart shows only odd-numbered rounds. Knit all even-numbered rounds; chart ends with Round 31.

CHART 84

E

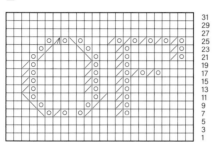

NOTE: Chart shows only odd-numbered rounds. Knit all even-numbered rounds; chart ends with Round 31.

CHART 85

FEATHER

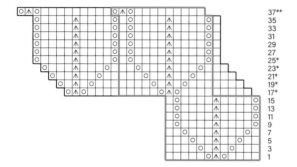

NOTE: Chart shows only odd-numbered rounds. Knit all even-numbered rounds; chart ends with Round 37.
* Shift beg of rnd by removing beg-of-rnd marker, sl 1 wyib, then replace marker.
** Shift beg of rnd by removing beg-of-rnd marker, sl 2 wyib, then replace marker.

F

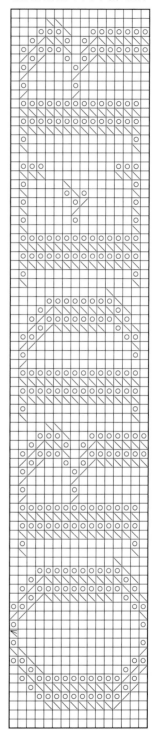

NOTE: Chart shows only odd-numbered rounds. Knit all even-numbered rounds; chart ends with Round 31.

CHART 87

GLOSSARY

CAST ONS

BACKWARD-LOOP CAST ON

*Holding the yarn over your left thumb with the end coming from the ball between your last three fingers and at the outside of the thumb, insert the needle up under the yarn next to the outside of your thumb. Remove your thumb from the loop, and pull the end to tighten the yarn slightly to snug the yarn up on the needle. Repeat from * until the required number of stitches has been cast on.

CABLE CAST ON

Make a slip knot and place it on the needle. Holding the needle with the slip knot in your left hand, insert the right needle into the stitch. Knit but do not slip stitch from the left needle. Place this new stitch on the left needle. *Insert right needle between the first two stitches on the left needle and knit, place the new stitch on the left needle. Repeat from * until the required number of stitches are on the needle.

LONG-TAIL CAST ON

Make a slip knot with the yarn, leaving a tail long enough to cast on the required number of stitches (usually about 2.5 cm / 1 in. per stitch), and place the slip knot onto the needle. Holding the needle in your right hand, clasp both strands in your lower three fingers with the long tail over your thumb and the end coming from the ball over your index finger.

*Spread your thumb and index finger apart to form a V. Insert the needle tip up between the two strands on your thumb. Bring the needle tip over the top of the first strand around your index finger, then down to draw a loop between the strands on your thumb. Remove your thumb and tighten the stitch on the needle – 1 stitch cast on. Place your thumb and index finger between the strands of yarn again. Repeat from * until the required number of stitches has been cast on.

TWISTED GERMAN CAST- ON

Make a slip knot and place it on the needle. *Holding the needle and yarn as for a long tail cast on, bring the needle towards you, under the strands around your thumb. Swing the tip up and towards you again, then down into the loop on your thumb, then up in front of the loop on your thumb. Then swing it over the top of the loops and over the first strand on your index finger, catch that strand, and bring the needle back down through the thumb loop and to the front, turning your thumb as needed to make room for the needle to pass through. Remove your thumb from the loop, then pull the strands to tighten the stitch. Repeat from * until the required number of stitches has been cast on.

PROVISIONAL CAST ONS

CROCHET PROVISIONAL CAST ON

With waste yarn, make a slip knot and place it on the crochet hook. Hold the needle in your left hand, the waste yarn over your left index finger, and the crochet hook in your right hand.

*Hold the needle above the yarn coming from the hook. With the crochet hook, reach over the top of the needle and make a chain, making sure the yarn goes around the needle – 1 stitch cast on. Repeat from * until the required number of stitches has been cast on. Cut the yarn and fasten off the last chain, being careful not to tighten the stitch. Change to the working yarn.

When going to finish the edge or pick up the stitches to continue working in the other direction, pull the waste yarn tail out of the last stitch cast on, and pull carefully to unzip the edge, placing the resulting stitches onto the needle.

CHAINED CAST ON

With a crochet hook and waste yarn, make a chain a few stitches longer than the number needed to begin knitting. Cut the waste yarn and fasten off the remaining stitch, making sure not to tighten the last stitch too much.

With the working yarn, begin a couple of chains from one end, *insert the needle into the back bump of the next chain, wrap the yarn around the needle, and draw through a loop – 1 stitch cast on. Repeat from * until the required number of stitches are on the needle and at least one or two chains remain at the end of the pick-up.

When going to finish the edge or pick up the stitches to continue working in the other direction, pull the waste yarn tail out of the last stitch cast on, and pull carefully to unzip the edge, placing the resulting stitches onto the needle.

DUPLICATE STITCH

Sometimes called Swiss Darning, duplicate stitch is a way of adding sections of colour to a knitted piece without having to work stranded knitting or intarsia. The technique covers each stitch completely. Large areas can become thick and stiff, so it's best used in small areas.

With the colour to be stitched threaded into a tapestry needle, insert the needle from wrong side to right side in the stitch *below* the first stitch to be covered. *Insert the tapestry needle under both legs of the stitch in the row *above* the stitch to be covered, and pull the yarn through, being careful not to pull the yarn too tightly. Insert the needle back into the same spot where you initially brought it to the RS, and pull the yarn through to completely cover the first stitch. Bring the needle up through the stitch below the next stitch to be covered. Repeat from * to continue covering stitches.

I-CORD

An I-cord is a long, narrow knitted tube that can be used as a tie or decorative element sewn to a piece of knitting. It is best worked on double-pointed needles.

Cast on the number of stitches listed in the pattern (usually from 2 to 4 stitches).

Row 1: Knit, then slide stitches back to right end of needle. Do not turn.

Row 2: Pull yarn across back of work, then knit. Slide stitches back to right end of needle. Do not turn.

Repeat Row 2 until the cord is the desired length. Finish off the cord as directed in the pattern.

INCREASES

K1f&b: Knit into the front of the next stitch but do not remove it from the left-hand needle. Bring the right needle to the back of work and knit into the back of the same stitch, then slip the stitch from the left needle – 1 stitch increased.

Make 1 / make 1 left leaning (M1/M1L): Insert left needle under the strand between the stitch just worked and the next stitch, from front to back, then knit through the back loop – 1 stitch increased.

Make 1 right leaning (M1R): Insert left needle under the strand between the stitch just worked and the next stitch, from back to front, then knit through the front loop – 1 stitch increased.

Left lifted increase (LLI): Insert the left needle into the back of the stitch *below* the last stitch worked on the right needle, then knit this stitch – 1 stitch increased.

Right lifted increase (RLI): Insert the right needle into the front of the stitch *below* the next stitch to be worked on the left needle, then knit this stitch – 1 stitch increased.

JOGLESS JOIN

The Jogless Join is a way of knitting stripes in the round so the beginning and end of the round are not noticeable. Knitting in the round creates a spiral so the beginning and end of each round are offset by a half stitch, creating the 'jog' in the knitting. This is most noticeable when working stripes. You will need to be working at least two rounds with the same colour in order to use this technique.

When changing colours, knit the first round with the new colour, slip the beginning-of-round marker, twist the yarns as if getting ready to change colours, but then let the colour not in use fall to the wrong side of the work, slip the first stitch of the next round, then knit to the end of the round. Continue knitting without slipping the first stitch of the round until you need to change colours again.

KITCHENER STITCH

Sometimes also called grafting, Kitchener stitch joins two sets of live stitches without a visible seam. This seaming method is not well suited for joining shoulder seams, which need to support the weight of the body and sleeves of the garment. It should be used for smaller seamed areas or for joining sections of a scarf or shawl that is expected to be stretched.

Work a few stitches at a time, pulling the yarn loosely, then adjust the length of each stitch to match the tension on each side of the join.

Place each set of stitches to be joined on separate needles, making sure the needle tips are at the right-hand edge.

Hold both needles in your left hand with needle tips pointing to the right.

Step 1: Insert tapestry needle purlwise through first stitch on front needle and pull the yarn through, leaving stitch on front needle.

Step 2: Insert tapestry needle knitwise through first stitch on back needle and pull the yarn through, leaving stitch on back needle.

Step 3: Insert tapestry needle knitwise through first stitch on front needle, slip stitch from front needle and pull the yarn through.

Step 4: Insert tapestry needle purlwise through next stitch on front needle and pull the yarn through, leaving stitch on front needle.

Step 5: Insert tapestry needle purlwise through first stitch on back needle, slip stitch from back needle and pull the yarn through.

Step 6: Insert tapestry needle knitwise through next stitch on back needle and pull the yarn through, leaving stitch on back needle.

Repeat Steps 3–6 until the yarn has been threaded through the last stitch of each needle once. Insert tapestry needle knitwise into last stitch on front needle, slip stitch from needle and pull yarn through. Then insert tapestry needle knitwise into last stitch on back needle, slip stitch from needle and pull yarn through. Fasten off on the wrong side.

MATTRESS STITCH

Mattress stitch creates an invisible seam along vertical edges.

Place the pieces being sewn together side by side on a flat surface, with the right sides facing you. Thread a piece of yarn about 3 times longer than the seam to be sewn into a tapestry needle.

Beginning at the bottom edge, insert the tapestry needle under one bar between the edge stitches on one piece, then under the corresponding bar on the other piece. *Insert the tapestry needle under the next two bars of the first piece, then under the next two bars of the other piece. Repeat from *, alternating sides until the seam is complete, ending on the last bar of pairs of bars on the first piece. Fasten off on the wrong side.

ONE-ROW BUTTONHOLE

Work to marked spot to begin buttonhole, bring yarn to front if not already there, slip 1 stitch and bring yarn to back of work. *Slip 1, pass first stitch over and off needle; repeat from * until the required number of stitches have been cast off, and place remaining stitch from right needle back on left needle. Turn work. Bring yarn to back of work, *insert right needle between first 2 stitches on left needle, yarn over and draw through a loop, then place loop on left needle; repeat from * until the same number of stitches have been cast on as were cast off plus one more, and bring yarn to front before placing last stitch on left needle. Turn work. Slip 1, pass last cast-on stitch over and off needle, then return slip stitch to left needle.

SHORT ROWS

WRAP AND TURN (W&T) SHORT ROWS

On knit rows: Knit to the stitch before wrapping with the yarn at the back of the work, slip the next stitch purlwise to the right needle, bring the yarn to the front between needles, slip the stitch back to the left needle, and bring the yarn back between needles to the purl side. Turn work.

On purl rows: Purl to the stitch before wrapping, with the yarn at the front of the work, slip the next stitch purlwise to the right needle, bring the yarn to the back between needles, slip the stitch back to the left needle, and bring the yarn to the front between needles to the purl side. Turn work.

To hide the wrap on a subsequent row: Work to the wrapped stitch, pick up the wrap from front to back for a knit stitch (and from back to front for a purl stitch), and place the wrap on the left needle. Work the wrap together with the stitch.

GERMAN SHORT ROWS

Work to the turning point, and turn work.

Slip the first stitch purlwise with the yarn at the front of the work, from the left needle to the right needle. Pull the yarn tightly up and over the top of the right needle so both legs of the slipped stitch are pullover over the top of the needle, creating a double stitch (DS). If the next stitch is a purl stitch, bring the yarn back to the front between the needles. If the next stitch is a knit stitch, keep the yarn at the back of the work.

To work the DS, on the next knit or purl row, knit or purl *both* legs of the DS together.

STRANDED COLOURWORK

Usually referred to as Fair Isle knitting, stranded colourwork uses two colours per round, with the colour not currently being used stranded loosely across the WS. Both yarns can be held in either the right or left hand, however you prefer to knit, or with one colour in each hand. Whichever method you use, make sure you maintain even tension. When rounds of stranded colourwork are placed between rounds of stocking stitch, make sure you check both tensions before you begin; most knitters will work the stranded colourwork section more tightly than plain stocking stitch. If this describes you, adjust your needle size when switching to the stranded section, and remember to change back to the smaller needle(s) when beginning the next section of plain stocking stitch.

As you work across a round of the pattern, spread the stitches just worked apart slightly before knitting the next stitch with the colour that has been floated across the wrong side. The float across the back should be relaxed, not sagging or pulling.

If floats between colour changes will be more than 1.3–2 cm / ½–¾ in. long, it's a good idea to weave in the unused colour to reduce the risk of snagging the float later. The easiest way to do this is to hold the colour to be woven in your left hand and the working colour in your right hand. Insert the right needle into the next stitch and *under* the floated yarn, then knit as usual, allowing the floated yarn to come back down behind the needles so the working yarn will lie over the top of it on the next stitch. If you weave in the floated colour every other stitch, that uses more yarn than weaving in every few stitches and can create a stiff fabric.

THREE-NEEDLE CAST OFF

The three-needle cast off is a way of joining two sets of live stitches in a bound-off edge, creating a firm seam. This method of seaming is ideal for seams that need the firmness to support the weight of the body and sleeves of a garment.

Place each set of stitches to be joined on separate needles, making sure the needle tips are at the right-hand edge.

Hold both needles in your left hand with the needle tips pointing to the right.

Insert the right needle knitwise into the first stitch on both needles, then knit them together – 1 stitch from each needle has been joined. *Knit the next stitch on both needles together, lift the first stitch worked over the stitch just worked and off the needle – 1 stitch cast off. Repeat from * until all stitches have been worked and 1 stitch remains on the right needle. Cut yarn and fasten off the remaining stitch.

Abbreviations

approx	approximately	**pm**	place marker
beg	begin(ning)(s)	**pwise**	purlwise (as if to purl)
CC	contrast colour	**rem**	remain(s)(ing)
ch	chain	**rep**	repeat(s)
cir	circular	**RH**	right-hand
cm	centimetre(s)	**RLI**	right lifted increase
cn	cable needle	**rnd(s)**	round(s)
CO	cast on	**RS**	right side
cont	continu(e)(ing)	**s2kp**	slip 2 stitches together knitwise, knit 1, then pass slipped stitches over (2 stitches decreased)
dec('d)	decreas(es)(ed)(ing)		
dpn	double-pointed needle(s)	**skp**	slip 1 stitch knitwise, knit 1, pass slipped stitch over (1 stitch decreased)
DS	double stitch		
g	gram(s)	**sl**	slip
in.	inch(es)	**sm**	slip marker
inc('d)	increas(es)(ed)(ing)	**ssk**	slip, slip, knit: slip 2 stitches knitwise, one at a time, insert left needle into front loop of both stitches, and knit them together through the back loops (1 stitch decreased)
k	knit		
k1-b	knit 1 in the row below		
k1f&b	knit into the front and back of the same stitch		
k2tog	knit 2 stitches together (1 stitch decreased)	**St st**	stocking stitch
k3tog	knit 3 stitches together (2 stitches decreased)	**st(s)**	stitch(es)
		tbl	through the back loop(s)
kwise	knitwise (as if to knit)	**tog**	together
LH	left-hand	**w&t**	wrap and turn
LLI	left lifted increase	**WS**	wrong side
m	metre(s)	**wyib**	with yarn in back
M1	make 1 stitch	**yd.**	yard(s)
M1L	make 1 stitch, left leaning	**yo**	yarn over
M1R	make 1 stitch, right leaning	**[ ]**	used to indicate instructions to be repeated
MC	main colour	**( )**	used for instructions for additional sizes
mm	millimetre(s)	**/**	used to separate metric from imperial measurements, with additional sizes in parentheses ( )
oz.	ounce(s)		
p	purl		
p2tog	purl 2 stitches together	*****	used to indicate the beginning and end of a length of instructions to be repeated
p2tog-tbl	purl 2 stitches together through the back loops		
patt	pattern(s)		

Yarn Substitution

All of the patterns in this book list the exact yarns used to create the project. If, however, you are unable to source the yarn listed, it is possible to find substitutions by searching for them online – www.yarbsub.com is a useful resource. Alternatively, you can find substitute yarns yourself. First, you will need to identify the thickness of the original yarn. The best way to ascertain this is to check the tension instruction at the beginning of every pattern. Opposite is a yarn weight conversion table that will help with finding the right weight. Note that the yarns listed in the projects use UK weight terms. Additionally, look for a yarn with a similar fibre content. Then knit a tension swatch with your chosen yarn to make sure you use the right needles. Lastly, to make sure you have the right amount of yarn, multiply the length of original yarn by the amount of balls listed. Then divide this figure by the number of metres/yards stated on the substituted yarn, which will give you the number of balls you need.

HOW TO DO A TENSION SWATCH

Every knitting pattern in this book will give a tension instruction. In this instruction contains the numbers of stitches and rounds/rows that the designer has worked to; if your knitting doesn't match these then your finished project won't knit to the correct measurements. In order to knit to the right size, you need to knit a tension swatch. Using the yarn and needles given in the tension instruction, cast on at least ten more than you need to achieve. Working in the stitch pattern stated, knit at least 15 cm / 6 in.

Do not cast off. Lay the swatch on a flat surface, without stretching it. Place a pin four stitches in from the edge and another 10 cm / 4in. away from the first pin, keeping away from the cast-on and cast-off edges, which may pull the fabric in. Do the same thing vertically. Count the number of rows and stitches between the pins, including a half stitch if there is one.

If you have too few stitches to 10 cm / 4in., then your tension is too loose and you should use a smaller sized needle; if you have too many stitches then your tension is too tight and you should use larger needles. You may need to do a few tension swatches to make sure you are using the right needles

YARN WEIGHT CONVERSION*

UK	US
SUPER CHUNKY	SUPER BULKY
CHUNKY	BULKY
ARAN	WORSTED
DK	DK
4 PLY	SPORT/FINGERING
3 PLY	FINGERING
LACE	LACE

*THESE ARE APPROXIMATE WEIGHTS

Yarn Resource Guide

THE ALPACA YARN COMPANY
WWW.THEALPACAYARNCO.COM

BERROCO
WWW.BERROCO.COM

BLUE SKY FIBERS
WWW.BLUESKYFIBERS.COM

BROWN SHEEP COMPANY
WWW.BROWNSHEEP.COM

CASCADE YARNS
WWW.CASCADEYARNS.COM

DRAGONFLY FIBERS
WWW.DRAGONFLYFIBERS.COM

THE GREEN MOUNTAIN SPINNERY
WWW.SPINNERY.COM

HARRISVILLE DESIGNS
WWW.HARRISVILLE.COM

HAZEL KNITS
WWW.HAZELKNITS.COM

JAMIESON'S OF SHETLAND
WWW.SIMPLYSHETLAND.NET

LANG YARNS
WWW.LANGYARNS.COM

LEADING MEN FIBER ARTS
WWW.LEADINGMENFIBERARTS.COM

THE LEMONADE SHOP
WWW.THELEMONADESHOPYARNS.COM

MAGPIE FIBERS
WWW.MAGPIEFIBERS.COM

MISS BABS
WWW.MISSBABS.COM

NEIGHBORHOOD FIBER CO.
WWW.NEIGHBORHOODFIBERCO.COM

O-WOOL
WWW.O-WOOL.COM

QUINCE & CO.
WWW.QUINCEANDCO.COM

ROWAN
WWW.KNITROWAN.COM

SHIBUI KNITS
WWW.SHIBUIKNITS.COM

TANIS FIBER ARTS
WWW.TANISFIBERARTS.COM

WOOL AND THE GANG
WWW.WOOLANDTHEGANG.COM

FOR ASTRID. EVERY LITTLE THING SHE DOES IS MAGIC.

ACKNOWLEDGEMENTS

Thank you to Hilary VandenBroek, the best Muggle and editor I could have asked for to guide me down this magical path. You are the Dumbledore to my Harry.

High praise to Therese Chynoweth, the best technical editor this side of Diagon Alley.

Infinite gratitude for the talented and clever knitwear designers inside these pages. How wonderful to see your ideas come to life! It's an honour to share your company.

Heaps of thanks for the skilled hands of sample knitters Kathey Harris, Drew Harder, Jane Stanley, Jill Krone and Alyssa Sharar.

As always, I am immensely grateful for my husband Roger, and my children Callum and Astrid. Your patience and willingness to go down the Harry Potter rabbit hole with me helped me along a journey I couldn't have made alone.

Finally, thank you to the brilliant folks at Insight Editions. Butterbeers on me.

First published in the United Kingdom in 2020 by
Pavilion
43 Great Ormond Street
London
WC1N 3HZ

ISBN: 978-1-91164-192-6

A CIP catalogue record for this book is available from the British Library.

10 9 8 7 6 5 4 3 2 1

Publisher: Raoul Goff
President: Kate Jerome
Associate Publisher: Vanessa Lopez
Creative Director: Chrissy Kwasnik
Designer: Judy Wiatrek Trum
Editor Hilary VandenBroek
Editorial Assistant: Gabby Vanacore
Managing Editor: Lauren LePera
Production Editor: Jennifer Bentham
Production Director/Subsidiary Rights: Lina s Palma
Senior Production Manager: Greg Steffen
Production Coordinator: Eden Orlesky

Photography by Laura Flippen
Prop Styling by Mikhael Romain
Hair and Makeup by Chris McDonald
Technical Editor: Therese Chynoweth

Thank you to our models: Binh Au, Amy DeGrote, Megan Sinaed Harris, Beverly
Irwin, Faith Jones, Jeric Llanes, Hanna Rahimi, Nancy Rahimi, Saburi Sai, and
Hilary VandenBroek.

Pavilion, in association with Roots of Peace, will plant two trees for each tree used
in the manufacturing of this book. Roots of Peace is an internationally renowned
humanitarian organization dedicated to eradicating land mines worldwide and
converting war-torn lands into productive farms and wildlife habitats. Roots of
Peace will plant two million fruit and nut trees in Afghanistan and provide farmers
there with the skills and support necessary for sustainable land use.

Printed and bound in China by Insight Editions

www.pavilionbooks.com